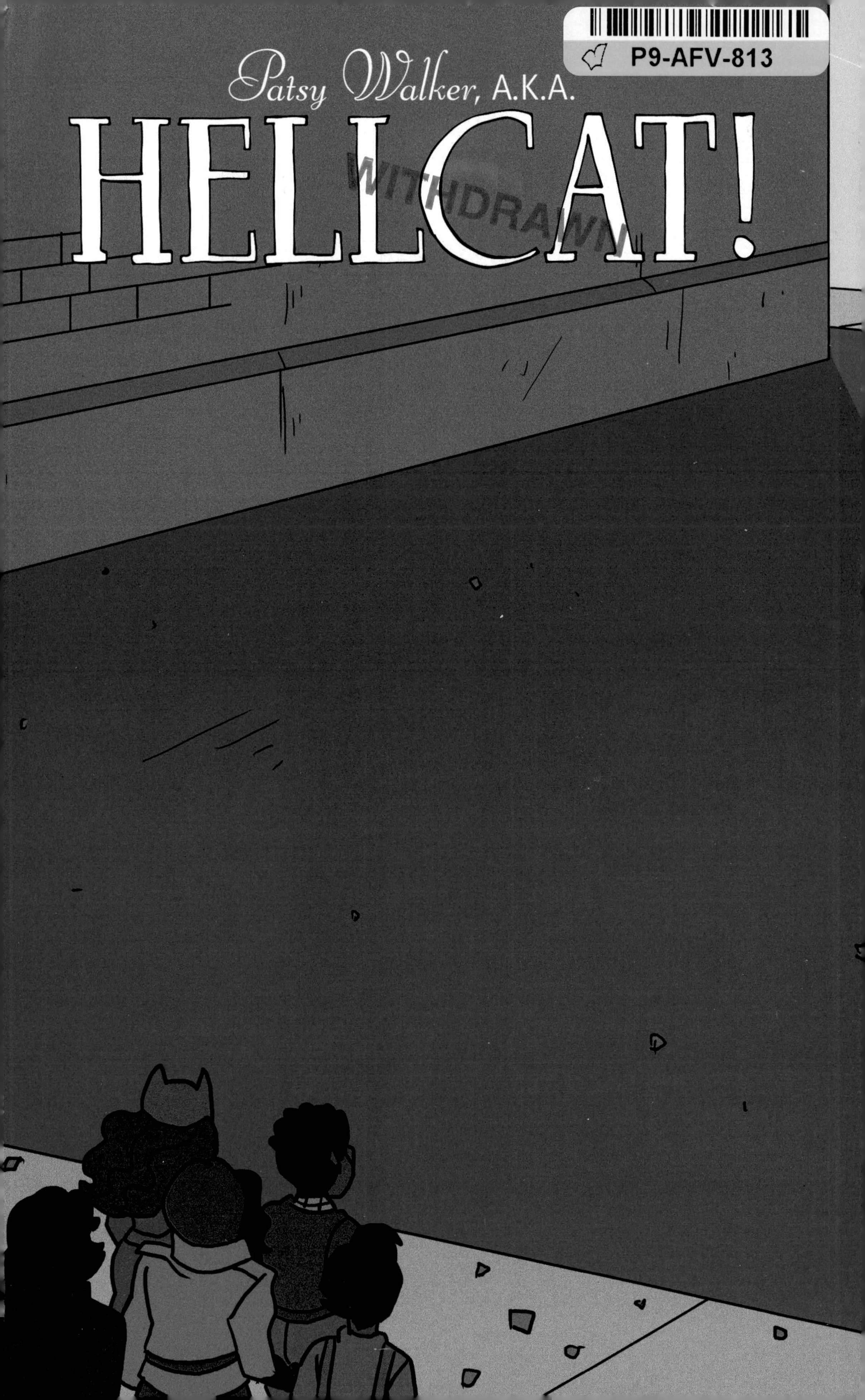
Patsy Walker, A.K.A.
HELLCAT!

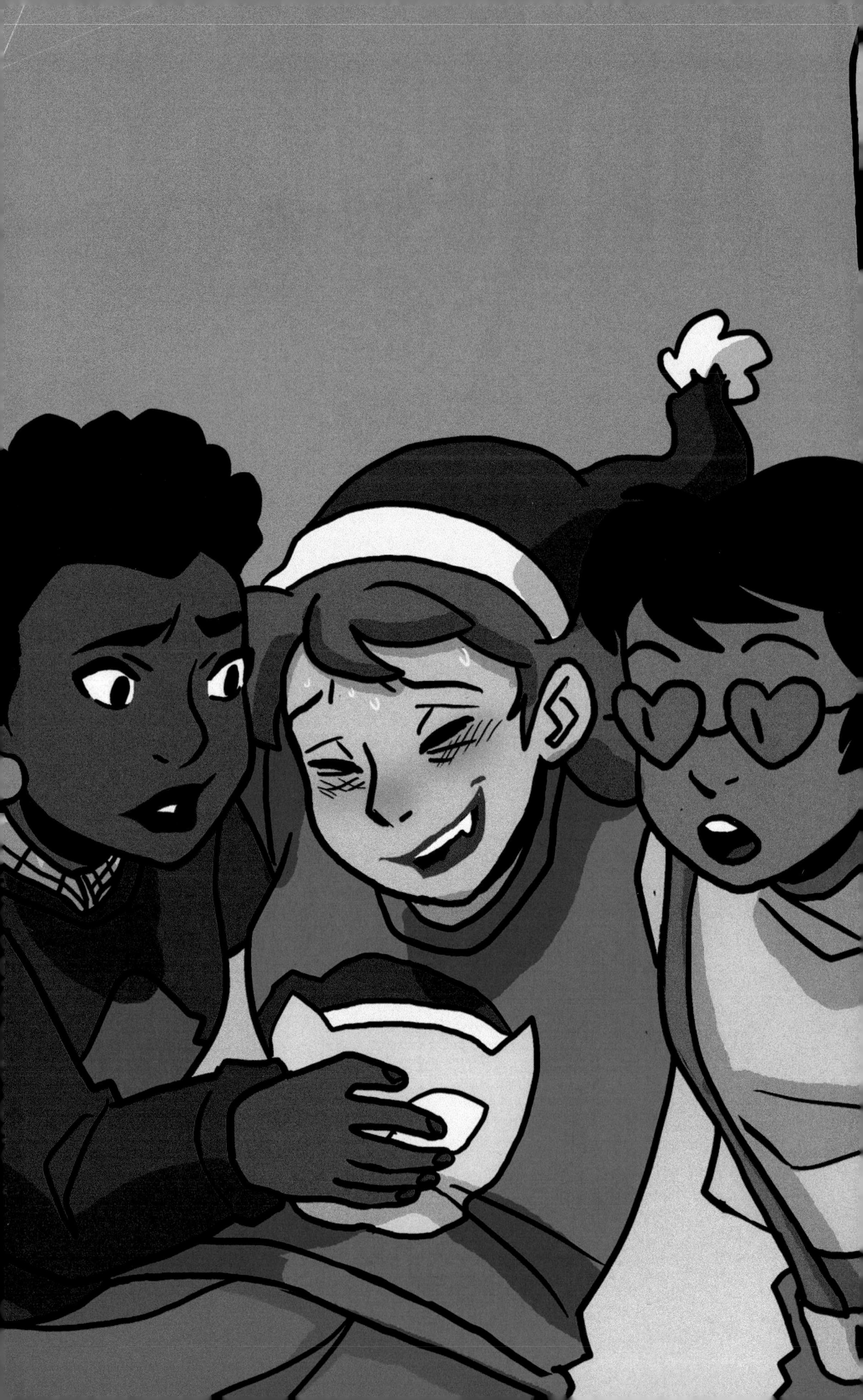

Patsy Walker, A.K.A. HELLCAT!

Careless Whisker(s)

Kate Leth
WRITER

Brittney L. Williams
ARTIST

Rachelle Rosenberg
COLOR ARTIST

VC's Clayton Cowles
LETTERER

Brittney L. Williams (#13-14 & #16-17)
and **Elsa Charretier & Tamra Bonvillain** (#15)
COVER ART

Kathleen Wisneski
ASSISTANT EDITOR

Jake Thomas
EDITOR

Tom Brevoort
EXECUTIVE EDITOR

Jennifer Grünwald
COLLECTION EDITOR

Caitlin O'Connell
ASSISTANT EDITOR

Kateri Woody
ASSOCIATE MANAGING EDITOR

Mark D. Beazley
EDITOR, SPECIAL PROJECTS

Jeff Youngquist
VP PRODUCTION & SPECIAL PROJECTS

David Gabriel
SVP PRINT, SALES & MARKETING

Jay Bowen
BOOK DESIGNER

Axel Alonso
EDITOR IN CHIEF

Joe Quesada
CHIEF CREATIVE OFFICER

Dan Buckley
PRESIDENT

Alan Fine
EXECUTIVE PRODUCER

PATSY WALKER, A.K.A. HELLCAT! VOL. 3: CARELESS WHISKER(S). Contains material originally published in magazine form as PATSY WALKER, A.K.A. HELLCAT! #13-17. First printing 2017. ISBN# 978-1-302-90662-7. Published by MARVEL WORLDWIDE, INC., a subsidiary of MARVEL ENTERTAINMENT, LLC. OFFICE OF PUBLICATION: 135 West 50th Street, New York, NY 10020. Copyright © 2017 MARVEL No similarity between any of the names, characters, persons, and/or institutions in this magazine with those of any living or dead person or institution is intended, and any such similarity which may exist is purely coincidental. **Printed in the U.S.A.** DAN BUCKLEY, President, Marvel Entertainment; JOE QUESADA, Chief Creative Officer; TOM BREVOORT, SVP of Publishing; DAVID BOGART, SVP of Business Affairs & Operations, Publishing & Partnership; C.B. CEBULSKI, VP of Brand Management & Development, Asia; DAVID GABRIEL, SVP of Sales & Marketing, Publishing; JEFF YOUNGQUIST, VP of Production & Special Projects; DAN CARR, Executive Director of Publishing Technology; ALEX MORALES, Director of Publishing Operations; SUSAN CRESPI, Production Manager; STAN LEE, Chairman Emeritus. For information regarding advertising in Marvel Comics or on Marvel.com, please contact Vit DeBellis, Integrated Sales Manager, at vdebellis@marvel.com. For Marvel subscription inquiries, please call 888-511-5480. **Manufactured between 5/26/2017 and 6/27/2017 by QUAD/GRAPHICS WASECA, WASECA, MN, USA.**

10 9 8 7 6 5 4 3 2 1

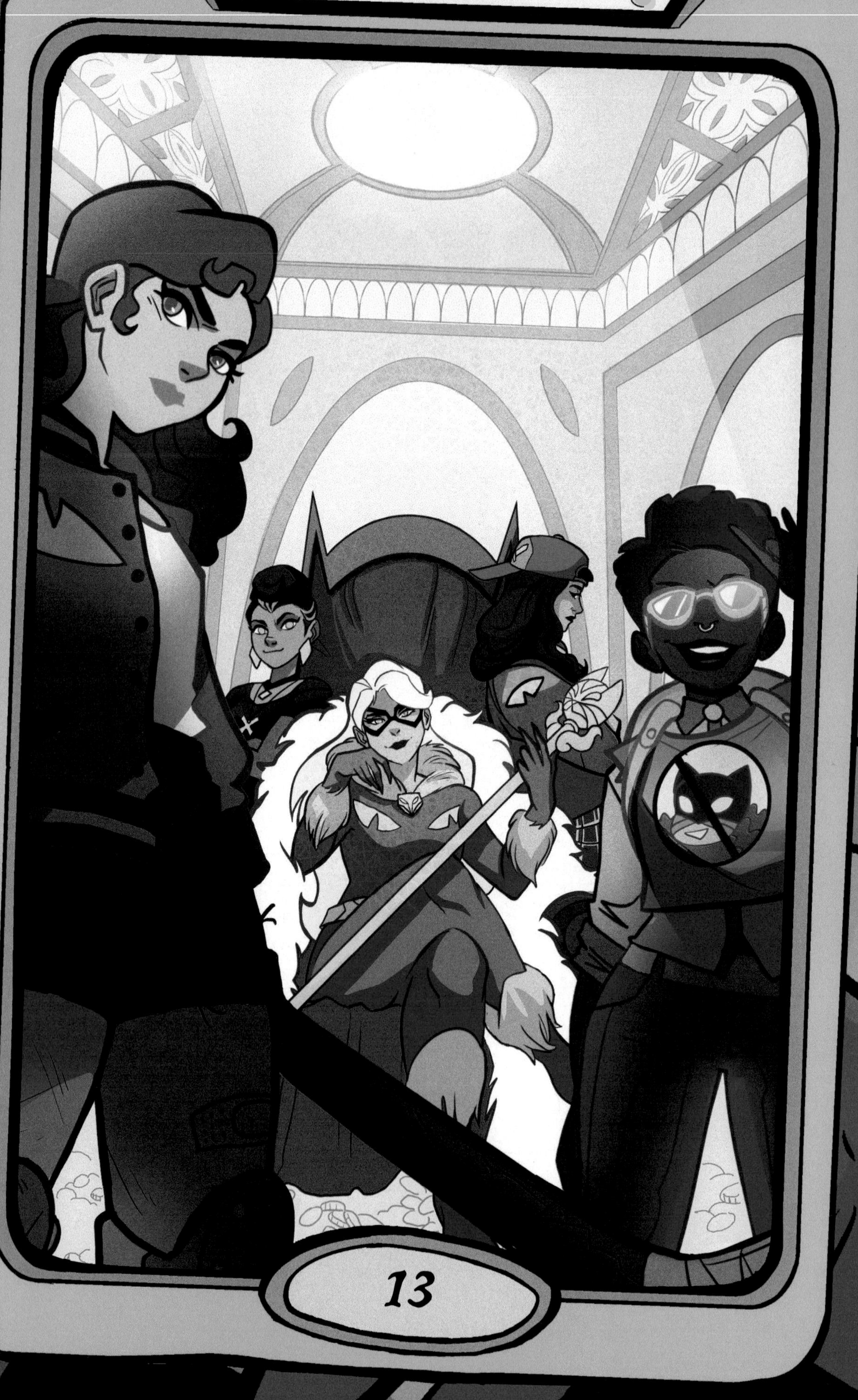
13

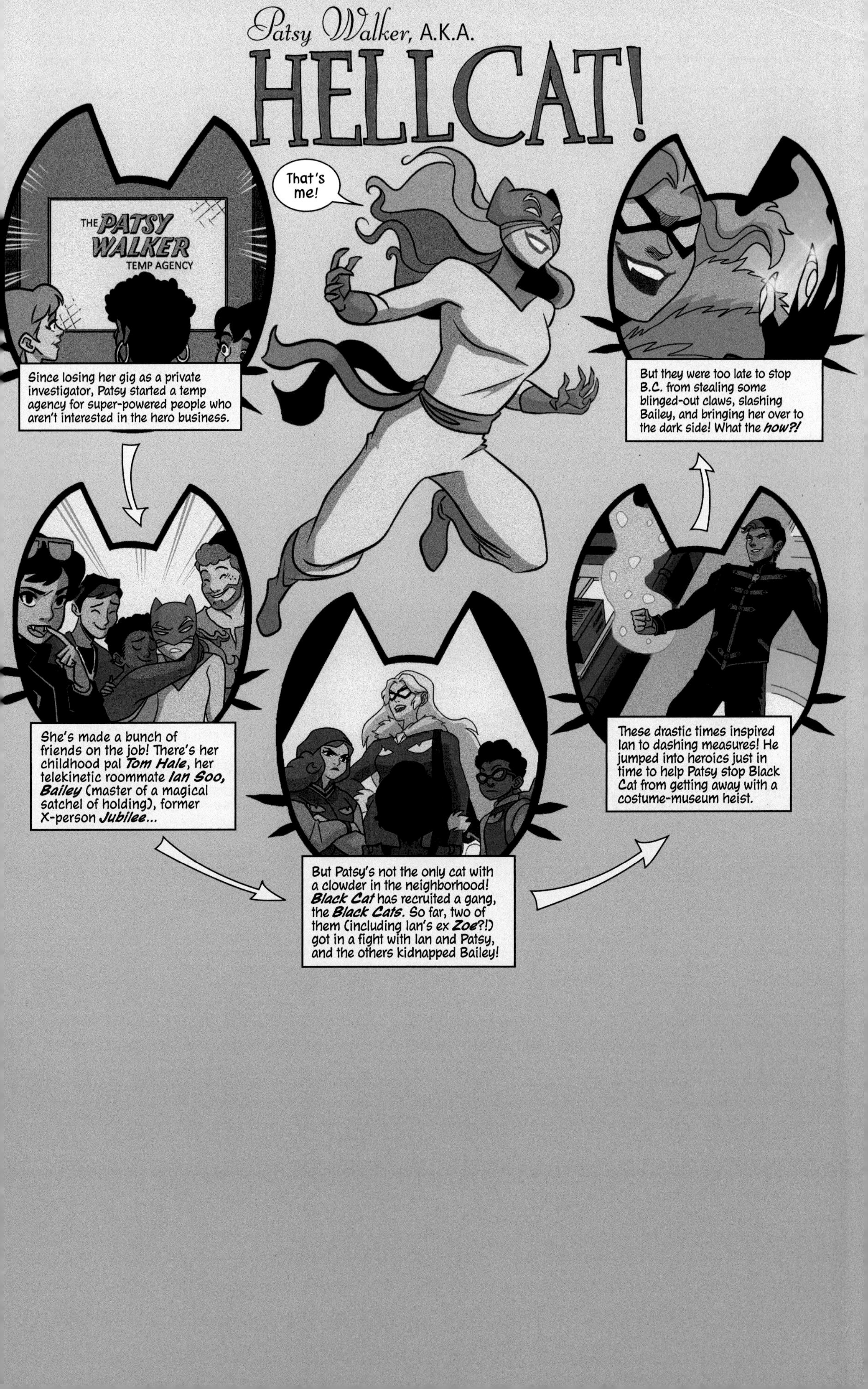
Patsy Walker, A.K.A.
HELLCAT!
That's me!
THE PATSY WALKER TEMP AGENCY
Since losing her gig as a private investigator, Patsy started a temp agency for super-powered people who aren't interested in the hero business.
She's made a bunch of friends on the job! There's her childhood pal Tom Hale, her telekinetic roommate Ian Soo, Bailey (master of a magical satchel of holding), former X-person Jubilee...
But Patsy's not the only cat with a clowder in the neighborhood! Black Cat has recruited a gang, the Black Cats. So far, two of them (including Ian's ex Zoe?!) got in a fight with Ian and Patsy, and the others kidnapped Bailey!
These drastic times inspired Ian to dashing measures! He jumped into heroics just in time to help Patsy stop Black Cat from getting away with a costume-museum heist.
But they were too late to stop B.C. from stealing some blinged-out claws, slashing Bailey, and bringing her over to the dark side! What the how?!

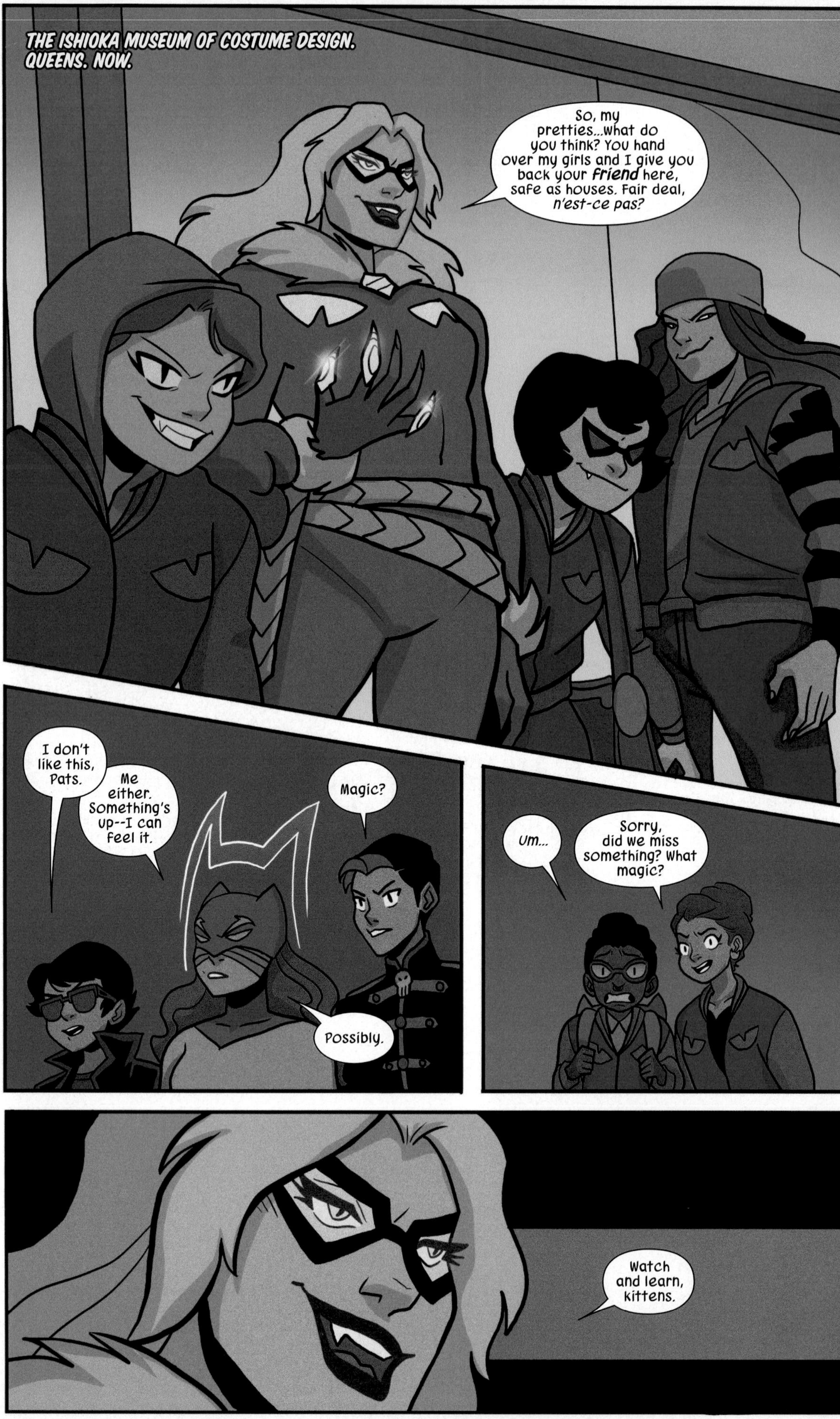
THE ISHIOKA MUSEUM OF COSTUME DESIGN. QUEENS. NOW.
So, my pretties...what do you think? You hand over my girls and I give you back your friend here, safe as houses. Fair deal, n'est-ce pas?
I don't like this, Pats.
Me either. Something's up--I can feel it.
Magic?
Possibly.
Um...
Sorry, did we miss something? What magic?
Watch and learn, kittens.

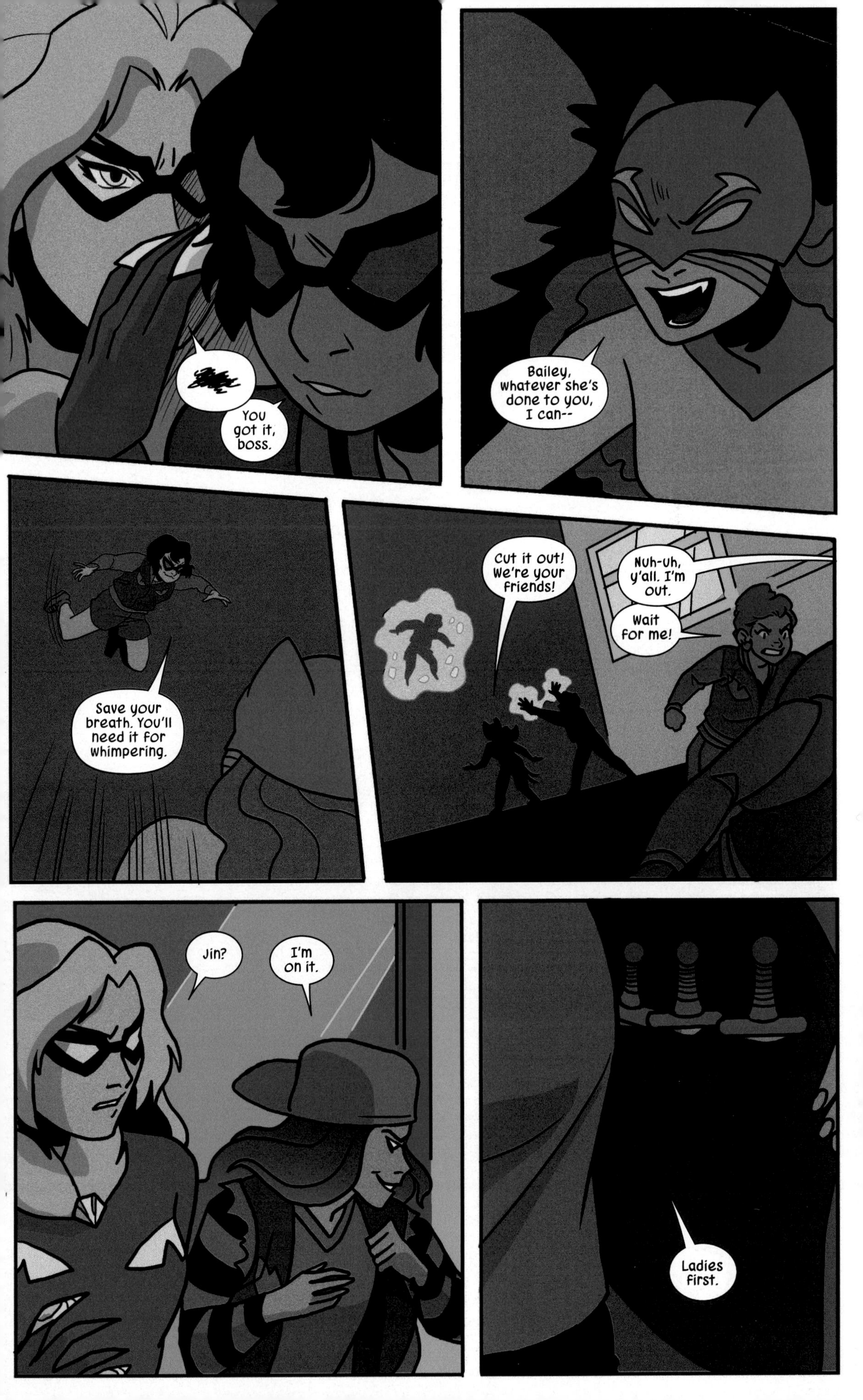
You got it, boss.
Bailey, whatever she's done to you, I can--
Save your breath. You'll need it for whimpering.
Cut it out! We're your friends!
Nuh-uh, y'all. I'm out.
Wait for me!
Jin?
I'm on it.
Ladies first.

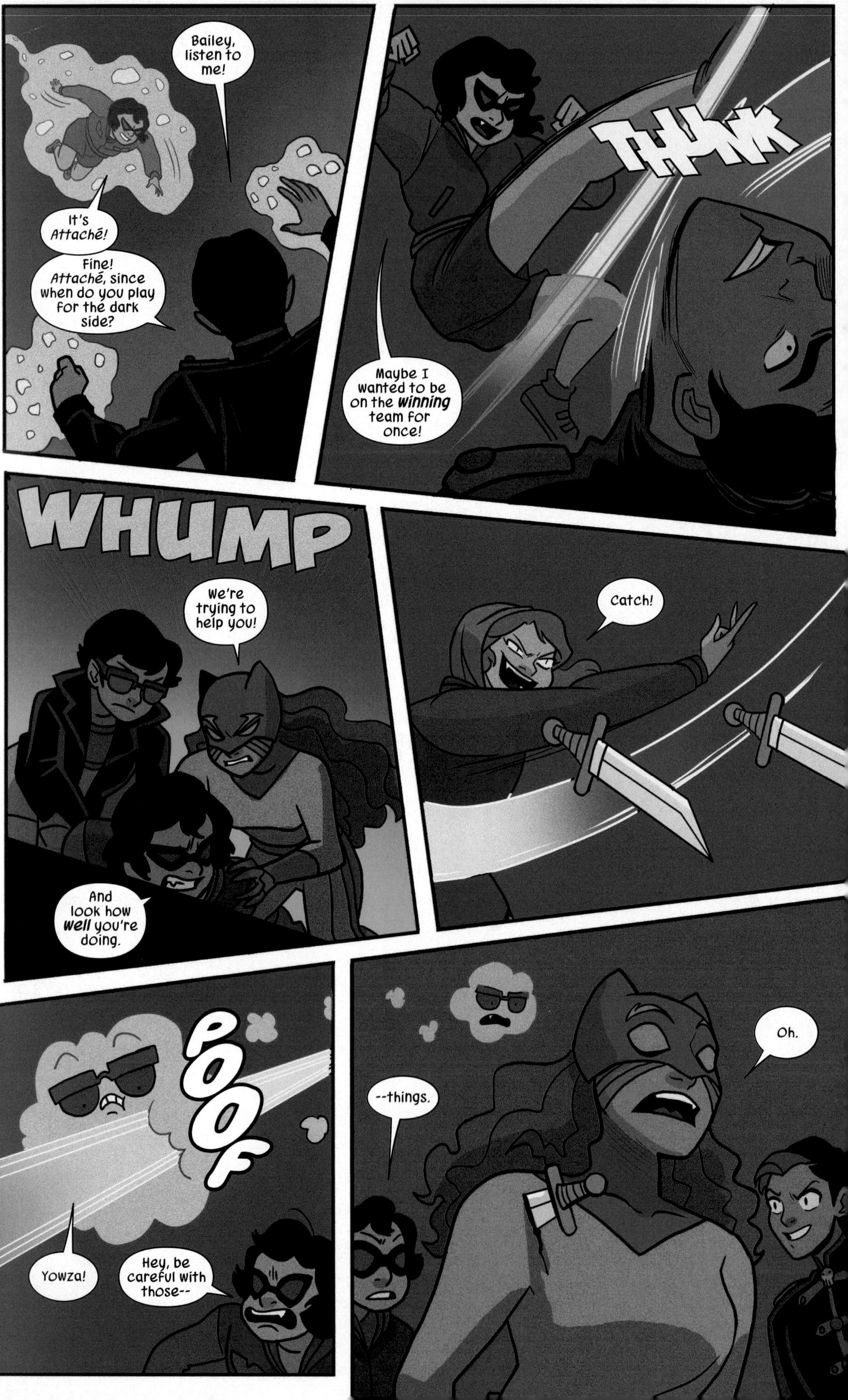
Bailey, listen to me!
It's Attaché!
Fine! Attaché, since when do you play for the dark side?
THUNK
Maybe I wanted to be on the winning team for once!
WHUMP
We're trying to help you!
And look how well you're doing.
Catch!
POOF
Yowza!
Hey, be careful with those--
--things.
Oh.

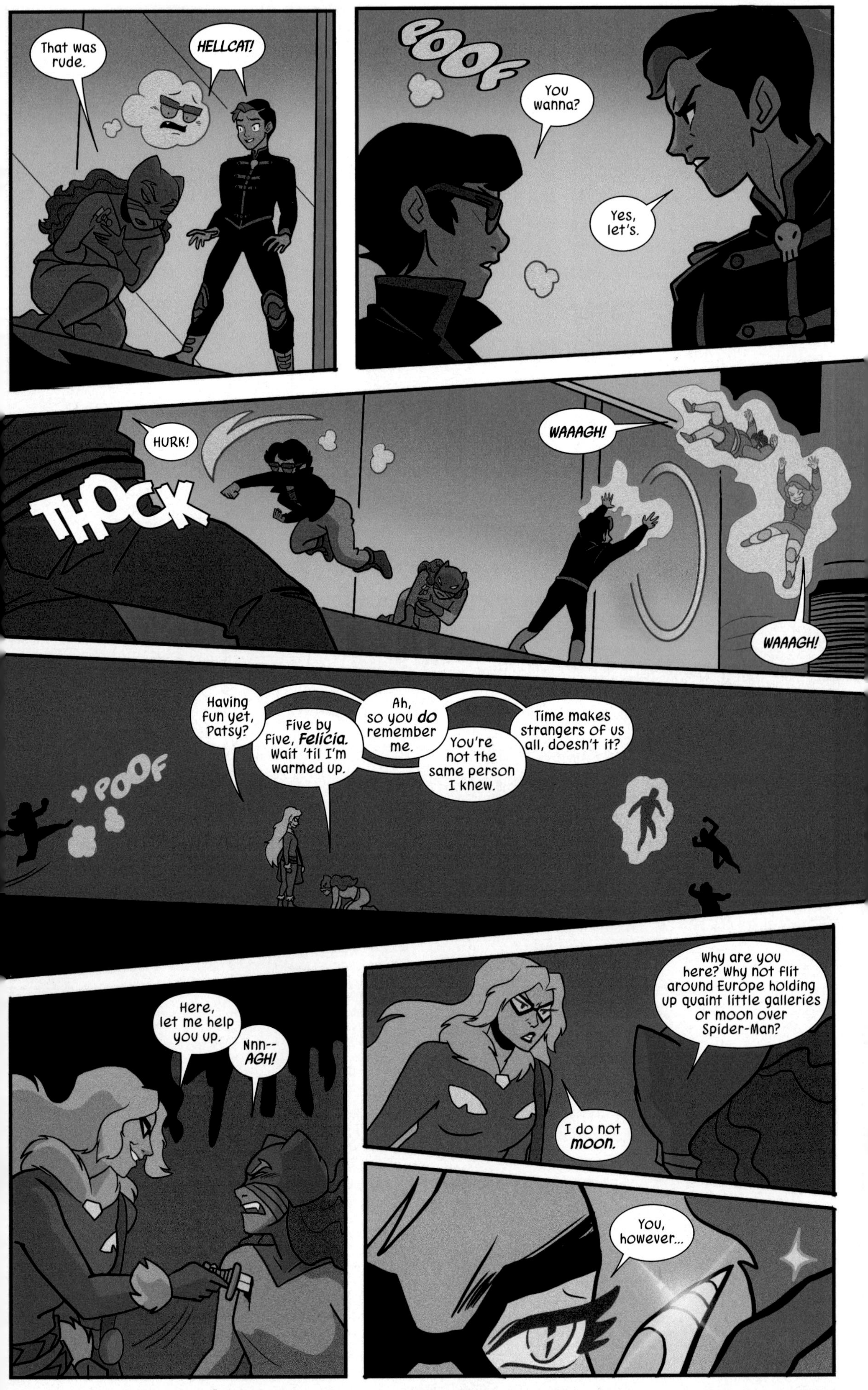

That was rude.
HELLCAT!
POOF
You wanna?
Yes, let's.
HURK!
THOCK
WAAAGH!
WAAAGH!
POOF
Having fun yet, Patsy?
Five by five, Felicia. Wait 'til I'm warmed up.
Ah, so you do remember me.
You're not the same person I knew.
Time makes strangers of us all, doesn't it?
Here, let me help you up.
Nnn-- AGH!
Why are you here? Why not flit around Europe holding up quaint little galleries or moon over Spider-Man?
I do not moon.
You, however...

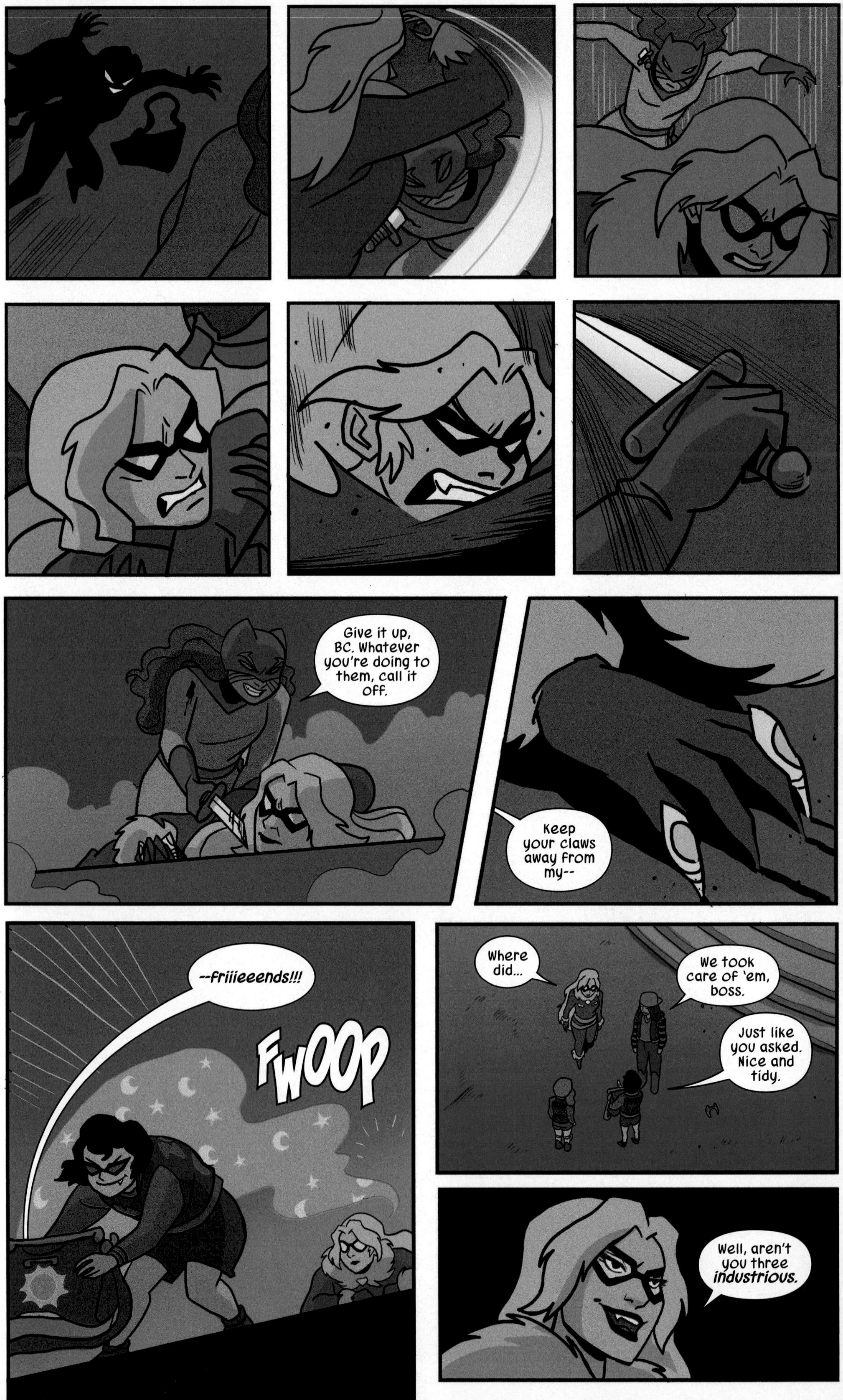
Give it up, BC. Whatever you're doing to them, call it off.
Keep your claws away from my--
--friiieeends!!!
FWOOP
Where did...
We took care of 'em, boss.
Just like you asked. Nice and tidy.
Well, aren't you three *industrious.*

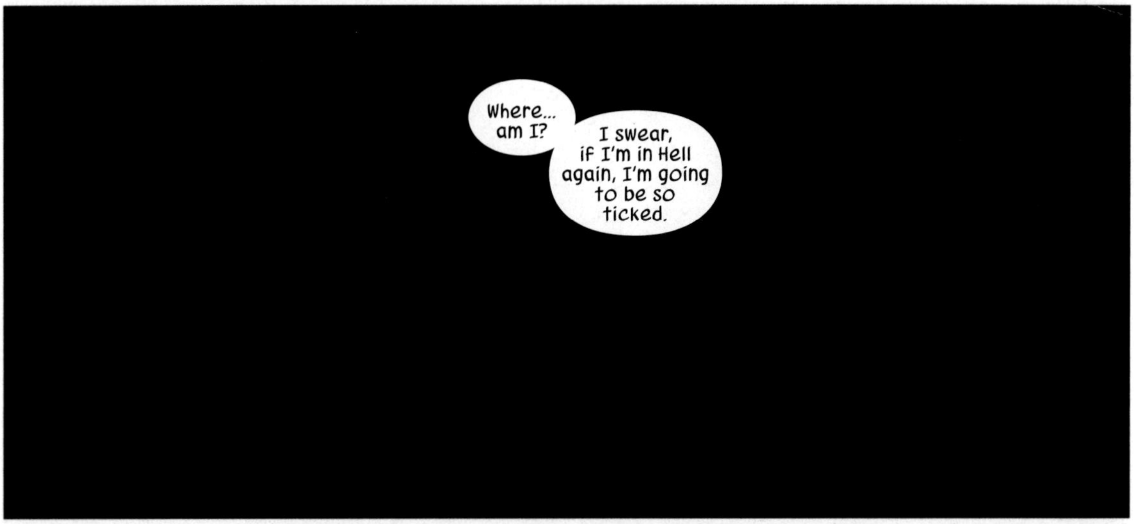
Where... am I?
I swear, if I'm in Hell again, I'm going to be so ticked.

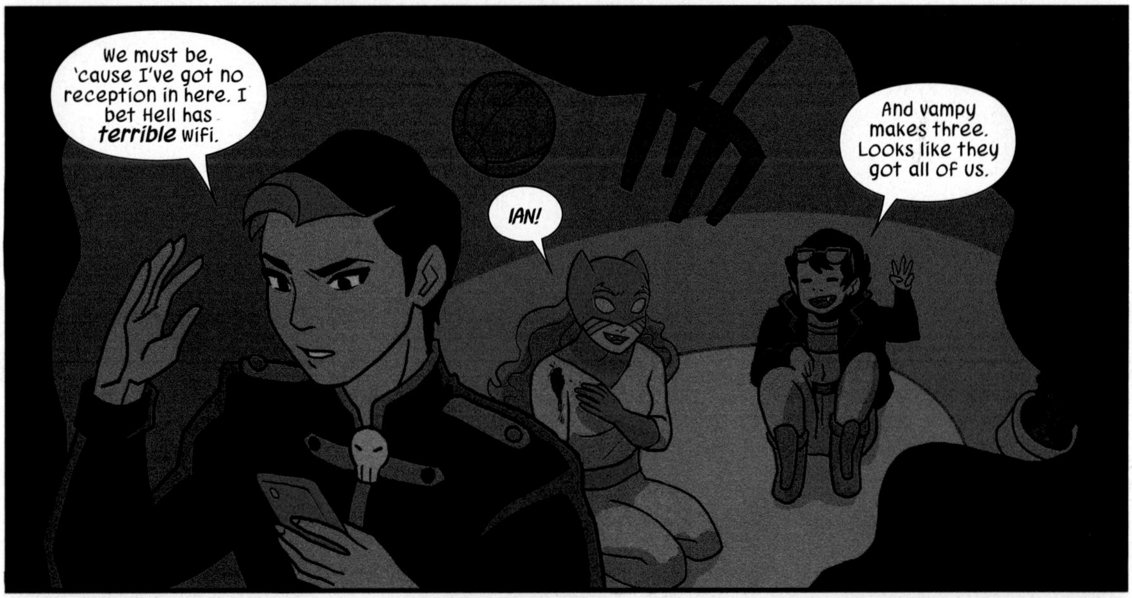
We must be, 'cause I've got no reception in here. I bet Hell has *terrible* wifi.
IAN!
And vampy makes three. Looks like they got all of us.

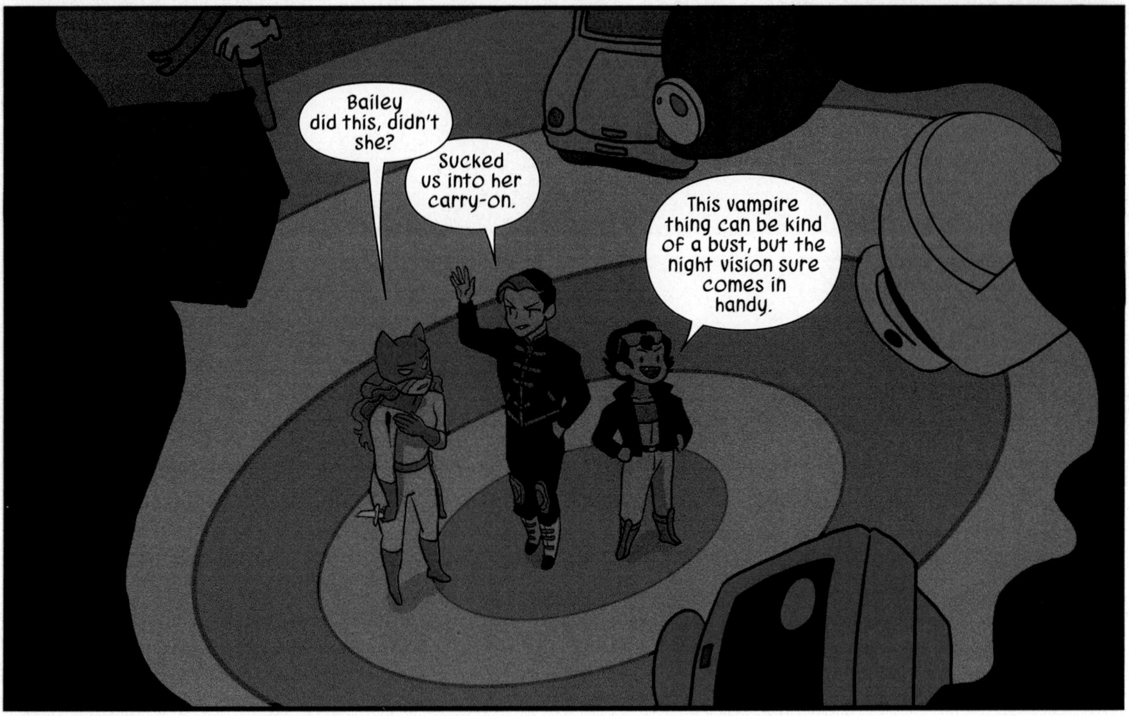
Bailey did this, didn't she?
Sucked us into her carry-on.
This vampire thing can be kind of a bust, but the night vision sure comes in handy.

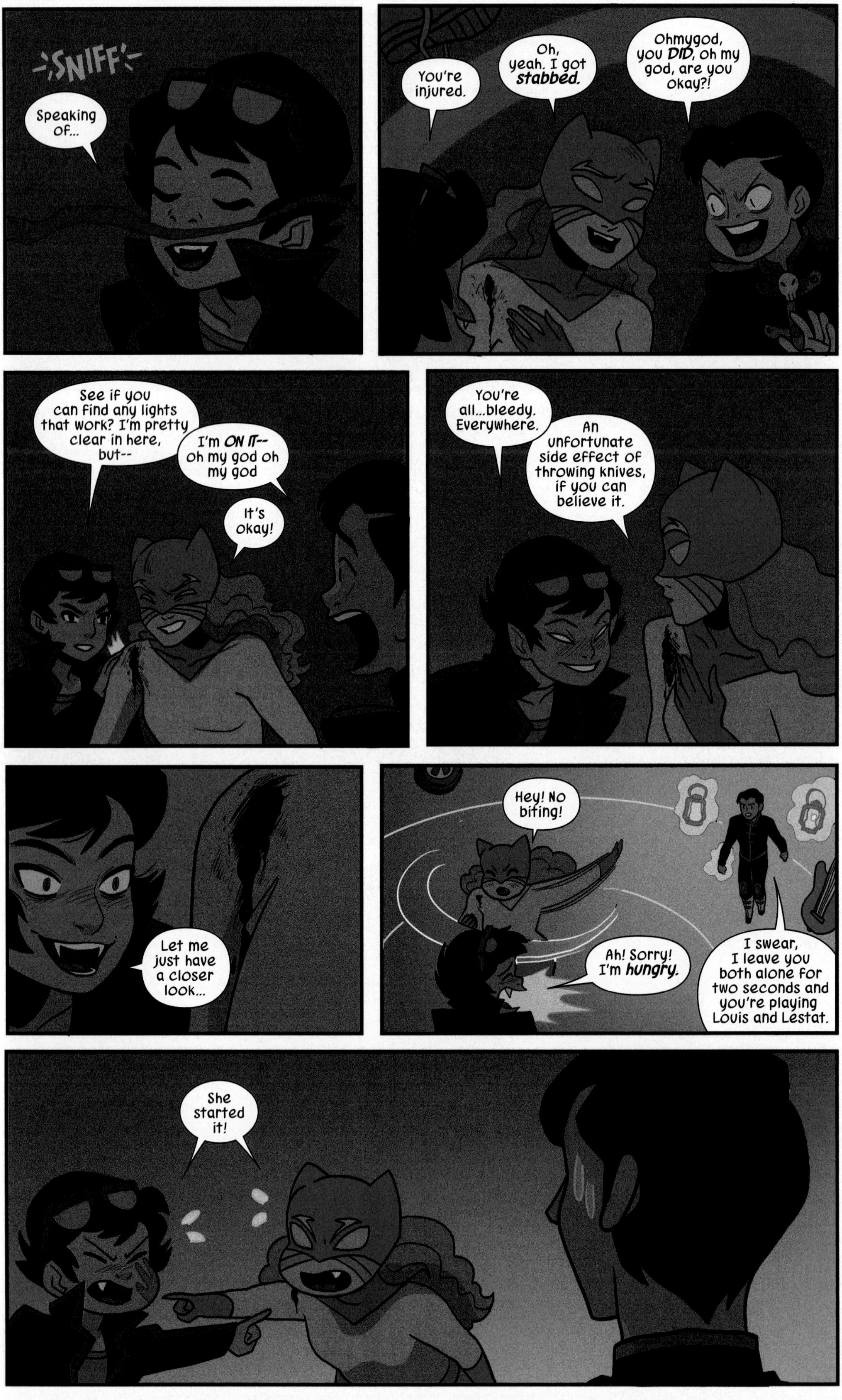

SNIFF
Speaking of...
You're injured.
Oh, yeah. I got stabbed.
Ohmygod, you DID, oh my god, are you okay?!
See if you can find any lights that work? I'm pretty clear in here, but--
I'm ON IT-- oh my god oh my god
It's okay!
You're all...bleedy. Everywhere.
An unfortunate side effect of throwing knives, if you can believe it.
Let me just have a closer look...
Hey! No biting!
Ah! Sorry! I'm hungry.
I swear, I leave you both alone for two seconds and you're playing Louis and Lestat.
She started it!

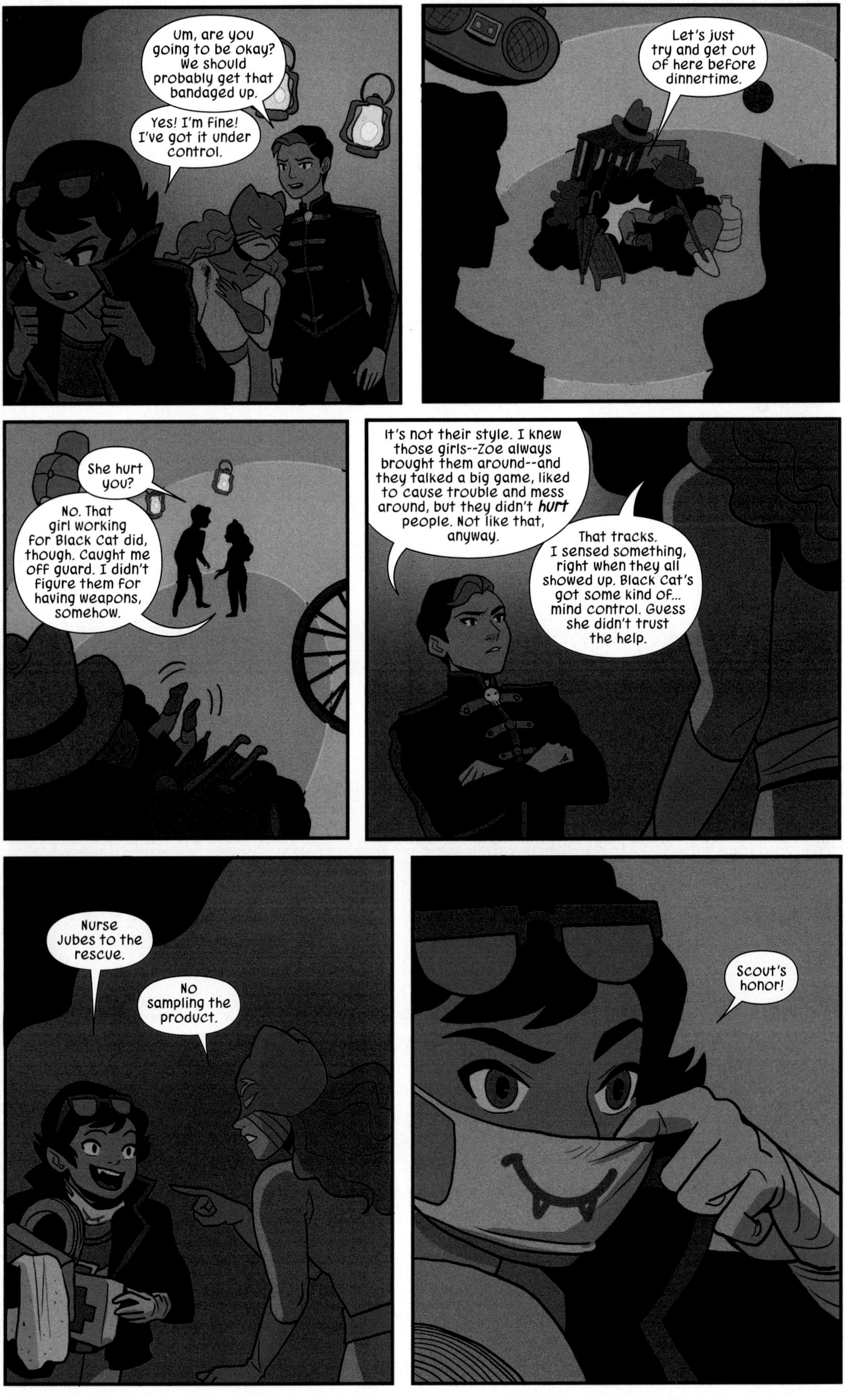
Um, are you going to be okay? We should probably get that bandaged up.
Yes! I'm fine! I've got it under control.
Let's just try and get out of here before dinnertime.
She hurt you?
No. That girl working for Black Cat did, though. Caught me off guard. I didn't figure them for having weapons, somehow.
It's not their style. I knew those girls--Zoe always brought them around--and they talked a big game, liked to cause trouble and mess around, but they didn't *hurt* people. Not like that, anyway.
That tracks. I sensed something, right when they all showed up. Black Cat's got some kind of... mind control. Guess she didn't trust the help.
Nurse Jubes to the rescue.
No sampling the product.
Scout's honor!

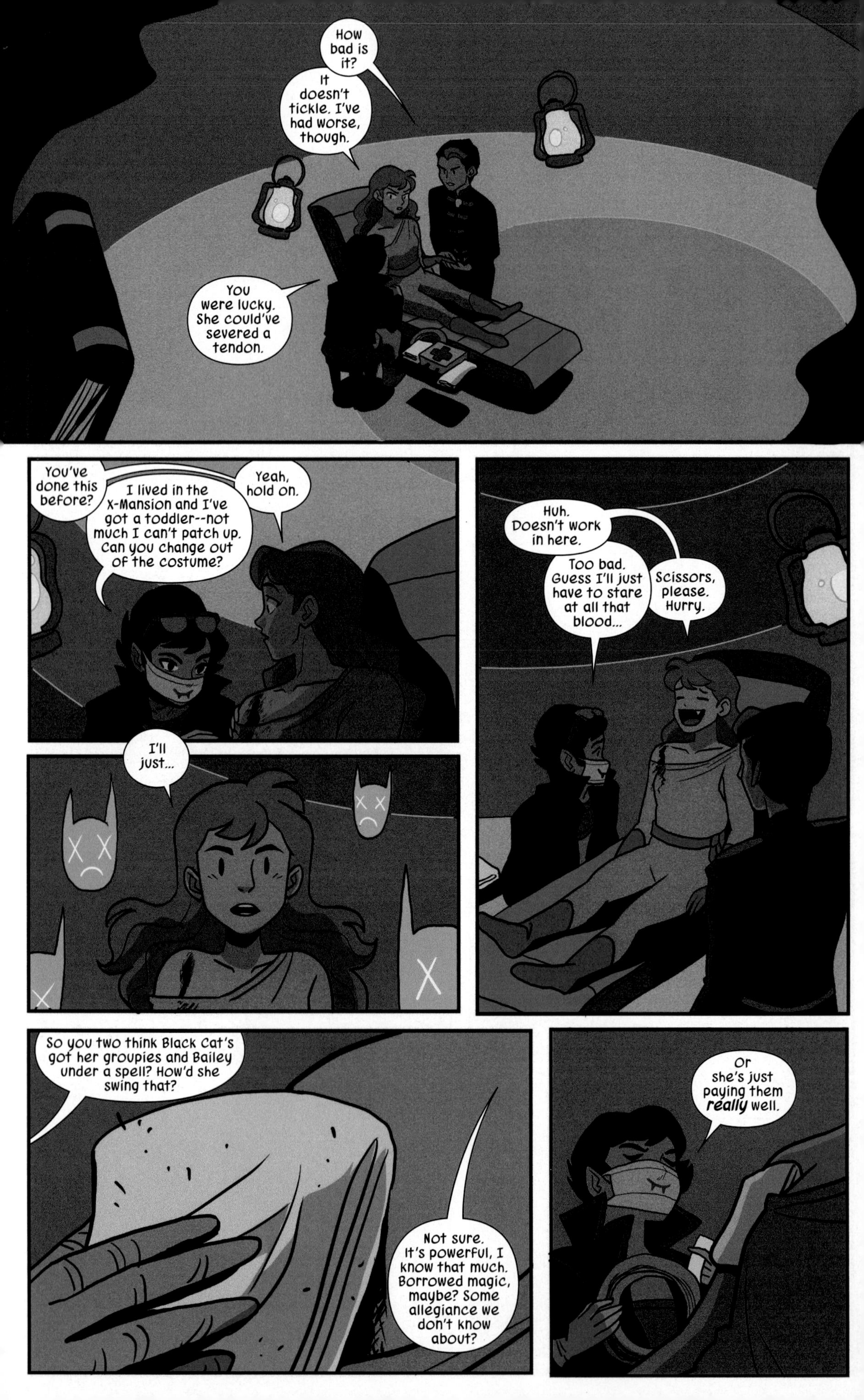
How bad is it?
It doesn't tickle. I've had worse, though.
You were lucky. She could've severed a tendon.
You've done this before?
I lived in the X-Mansion and I've got a toddler--not much I can't patch up. Can you change out of the costume?
Yeah, hold on.
I'll just...
Huh. Doesn't work in here.
Too bad. Guess I'll just have to stare at all that blood...
Scissors, please. Hurry.
So you two think Black Cat's got her groupies and Bailey under a spell? How'd she swing that?
Not sure. It's powerful, I know that much. Borrowed magic, maybe? Some allegiance we don't know about?
Or she's just paying them *really* well.

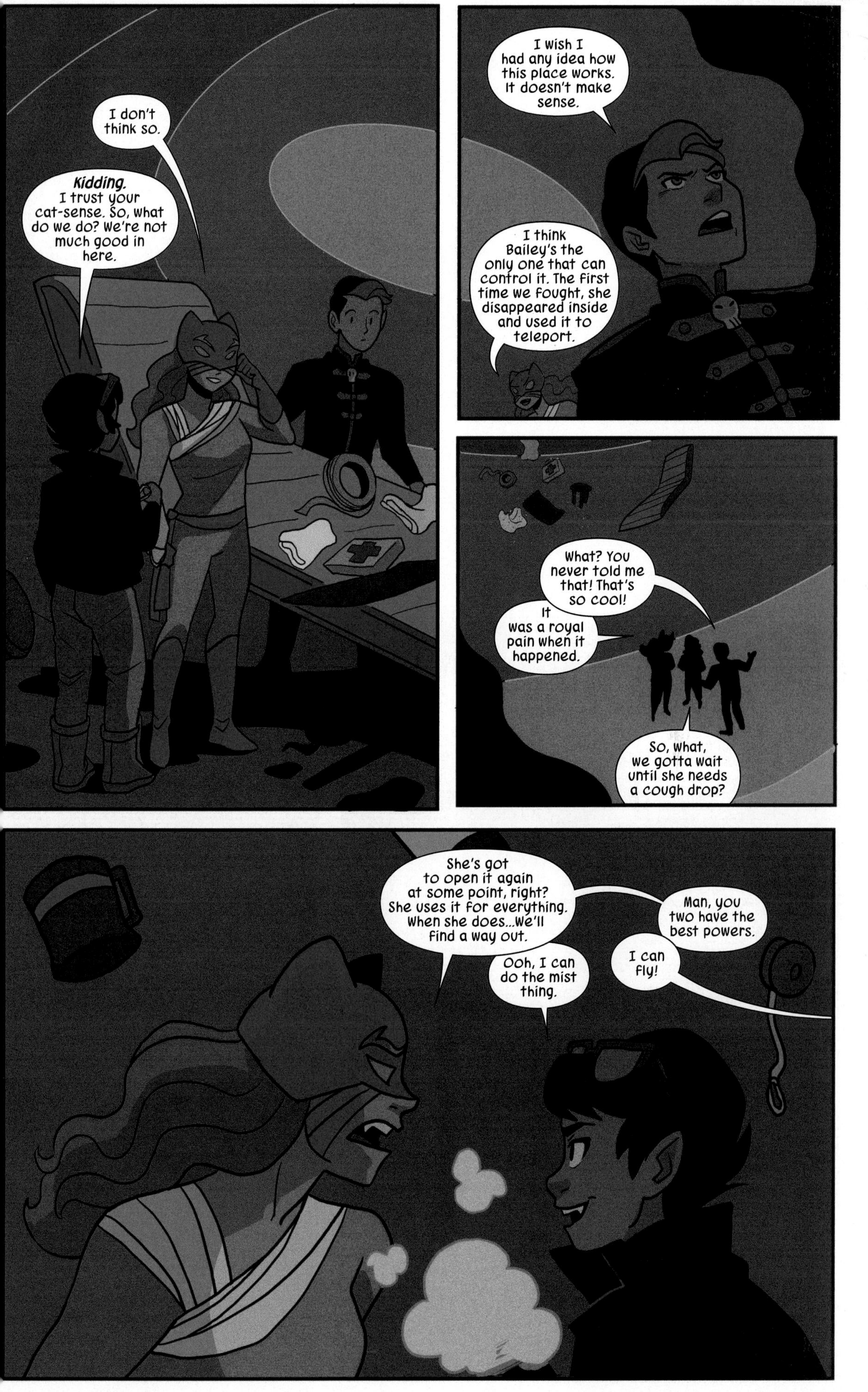
I don't think so.
Kidding. I trust your cat-sense. So, what do we do? We're not much good in here.
I wish I had any idea how this place works. It doesn't make sense.
I think Bailey's the only one that can control it. The first time we fought, she disappeared inside and used it to teleport.
What? You never told me that! That's so cool!
It was a royal pain when it happened.
So, what, we gotta wait until she needs a cough drop?
She's got to open it again at some point, right? She uses it for everything. When she does...we'll find a way out.
Man, you two have the best powers.
Ooh, I can do the mist thing.
I can fly!

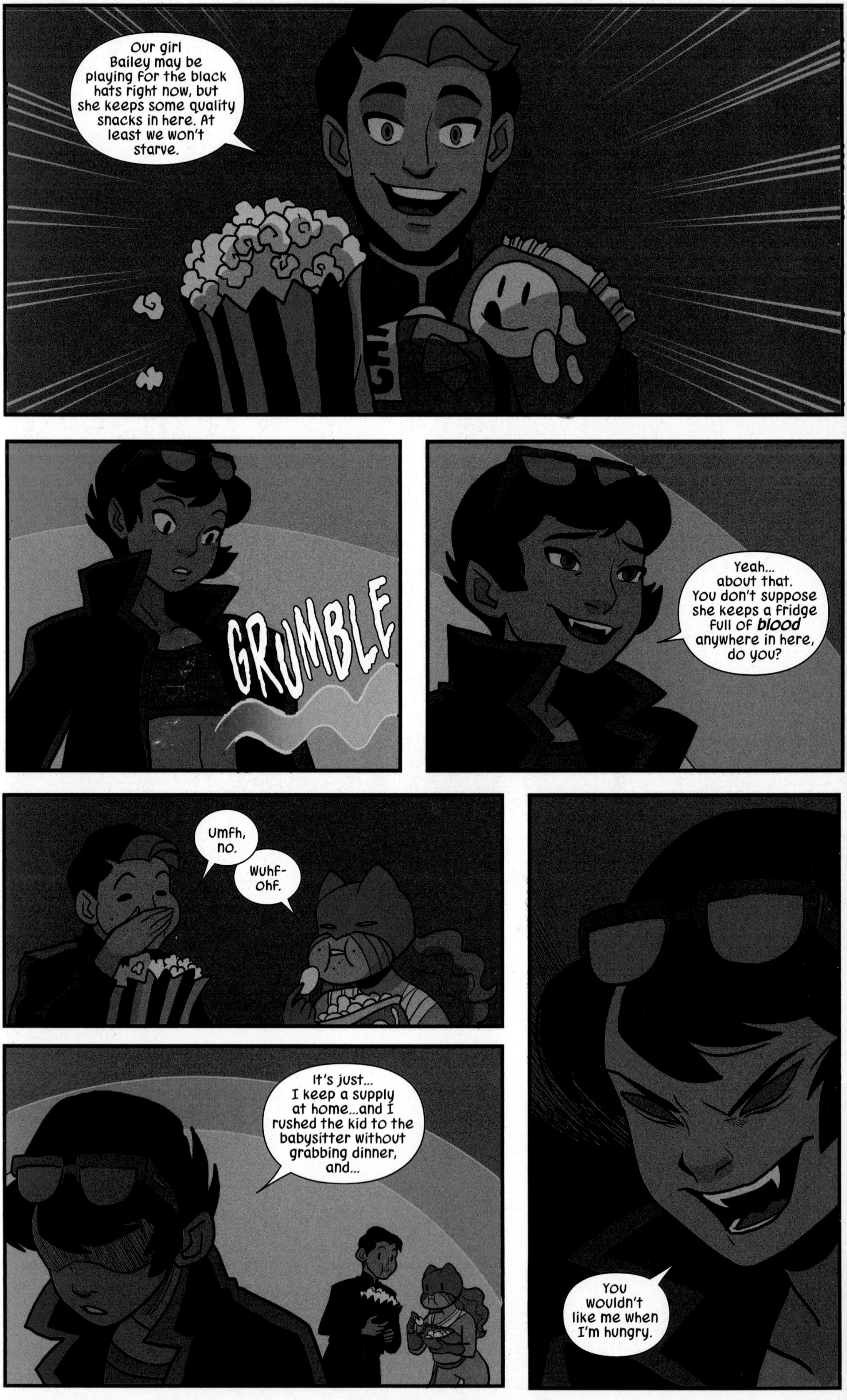
Our girl Bailey may be playing for the black hats right now, but she keeps some quality snacks in here. At least we won't starve.
GRUMBLE
Yeah... about that. You don't suppose she keeps a fridge full of *blood* anywhere in here, do you?
Umfh, no.
Wuhf-ohf.
It's just... I keep a supply at home...and I rushed the kid to the babysitter without grabbing dinner, and...
You wouldn't like me when I'm hungry.

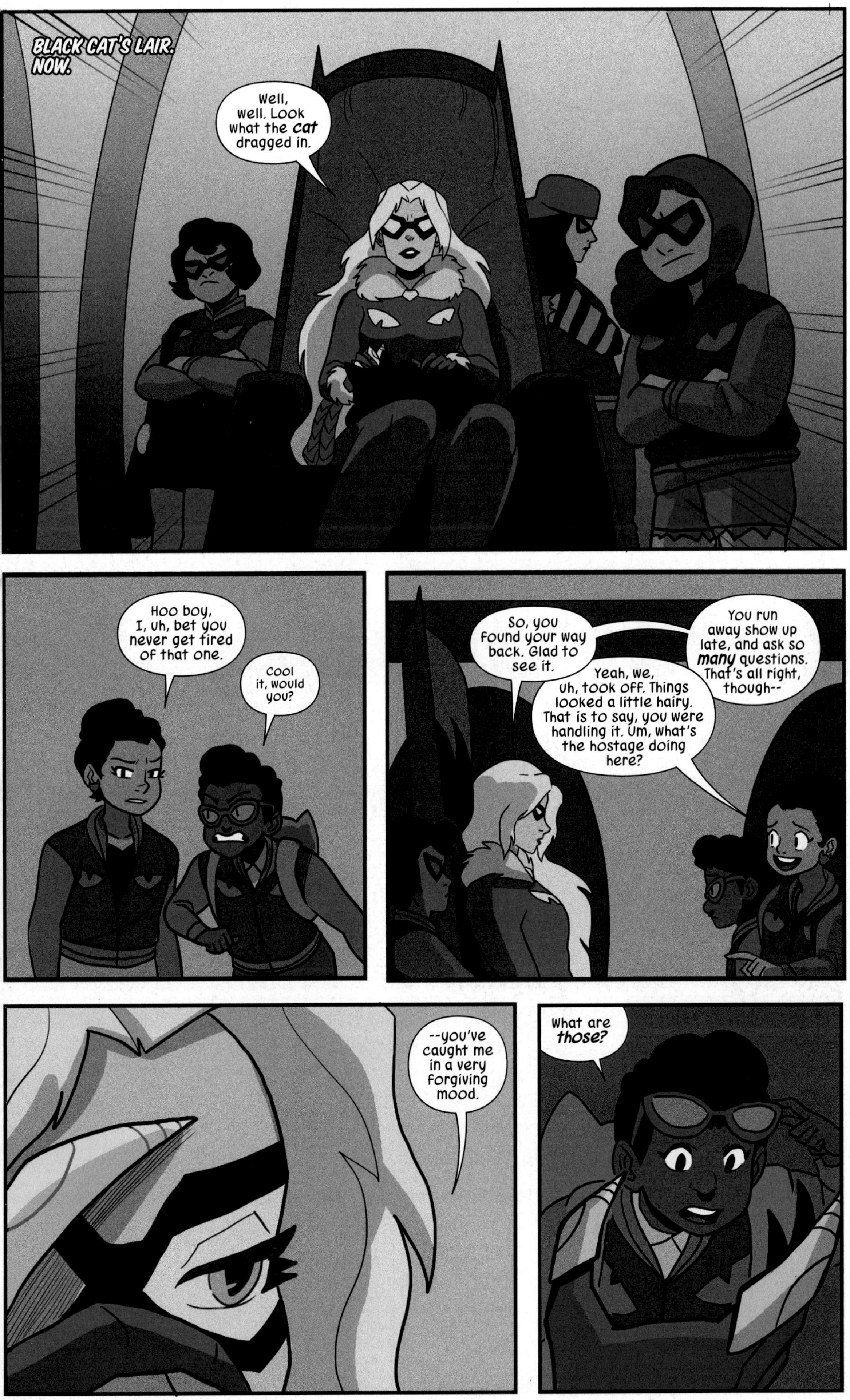
BLACK CAT'S LAIR. NOW.
Well, well. Look what the cat dragged in.
Hoo boy, I, uh, bet you never get tired of that one.
Cool it, would you?
So, you found your way back. Glad to see it.
Yeah, we, uh, took off. Things looked a little hairy. That is to say, you were handling it. Um, what's the hostage doing here?
You run away show up late, and ask so many questions. That's all right, though--
--you've caught me in a very forgiving mood.
What are those?

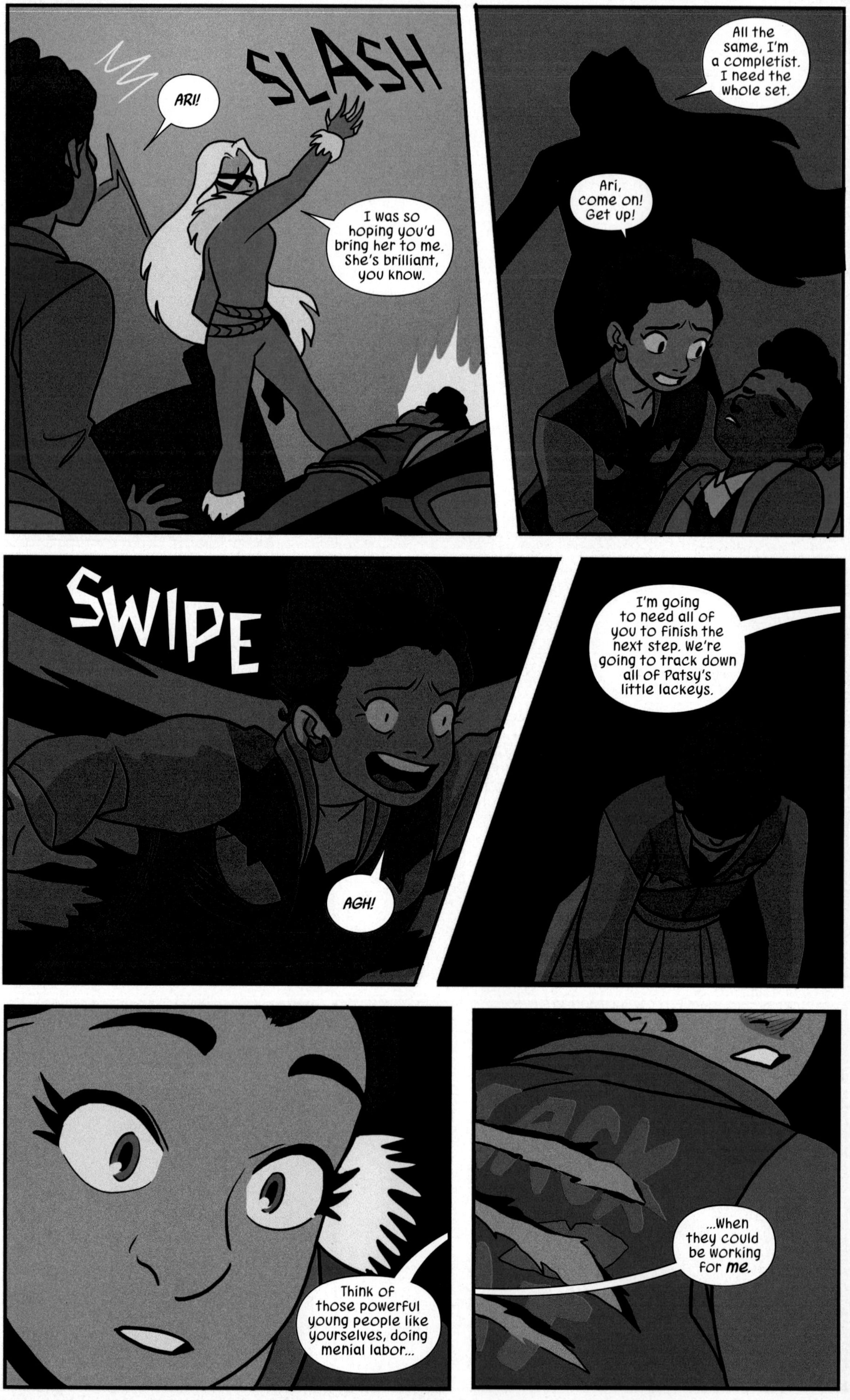
SLASH
ARI!
I was so hoping you'd bring her to me. She's brilliant, you know.
All the same, I'm a completist. I need the whole set.
Ari, come on! Get up!
SWIPE
AGH!
I'm going to need all of you to finish the next step. We're going to track down all of Patsy's little lackeys.
Think of those powerful young people like yourselves, doing menial labor...
...When they could be working for *me.*

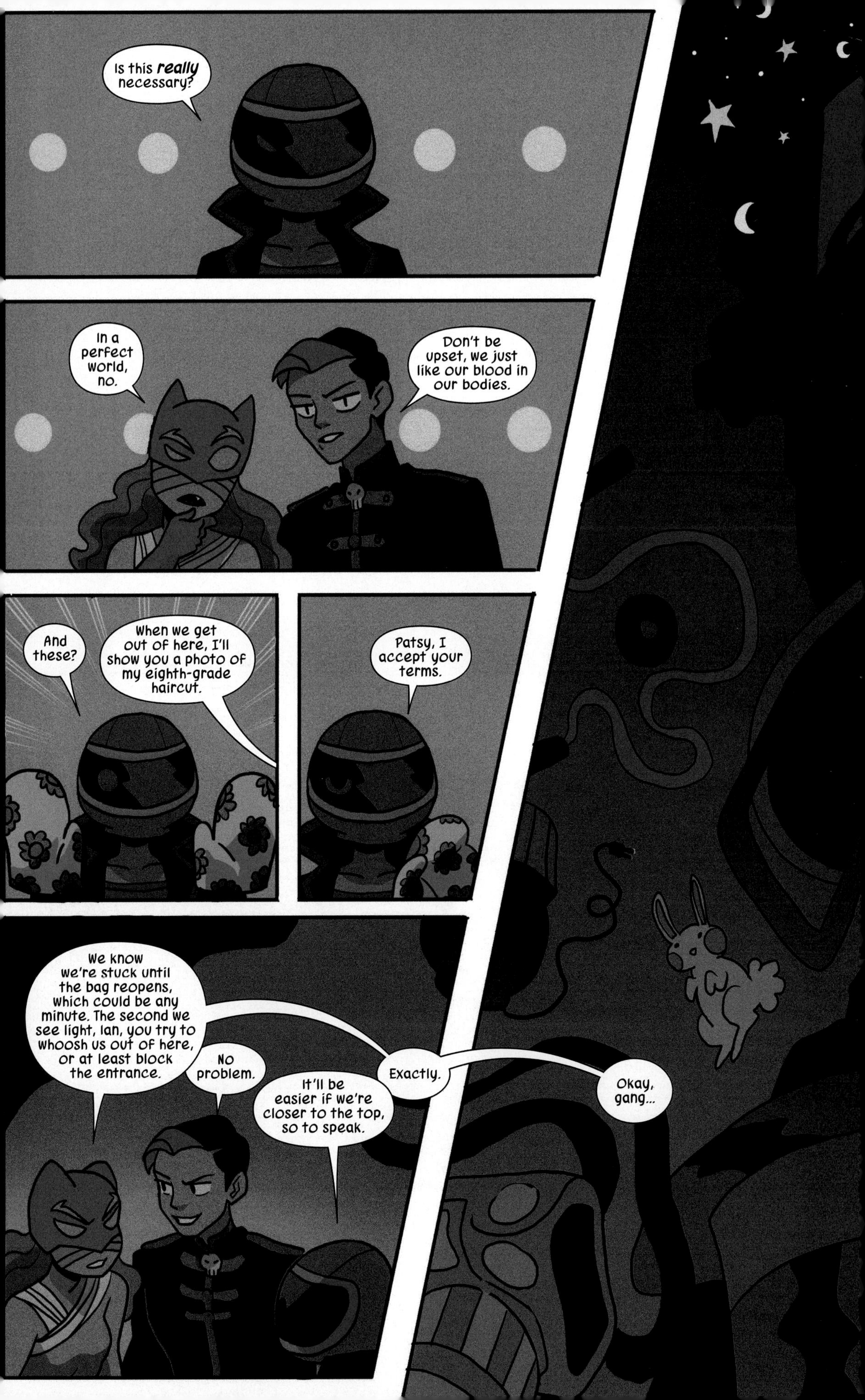

Is this *really* necessary?
In a perfect world, no.
Don't be upset, we just like our blood in our bodies.
And these?
When we get out of here, I'll show you a photo of my eighth-grade haircut.
Patsy, I accept your terms.
We know we're stuck until the bag reopens, which could be any minute. The second we see light, Ian, you try to whoosh us out of here, or at least block the entrance.
No problem.
It'll be easier if we're closer to the top, so to speak.
Exactly.
Okay, gang...

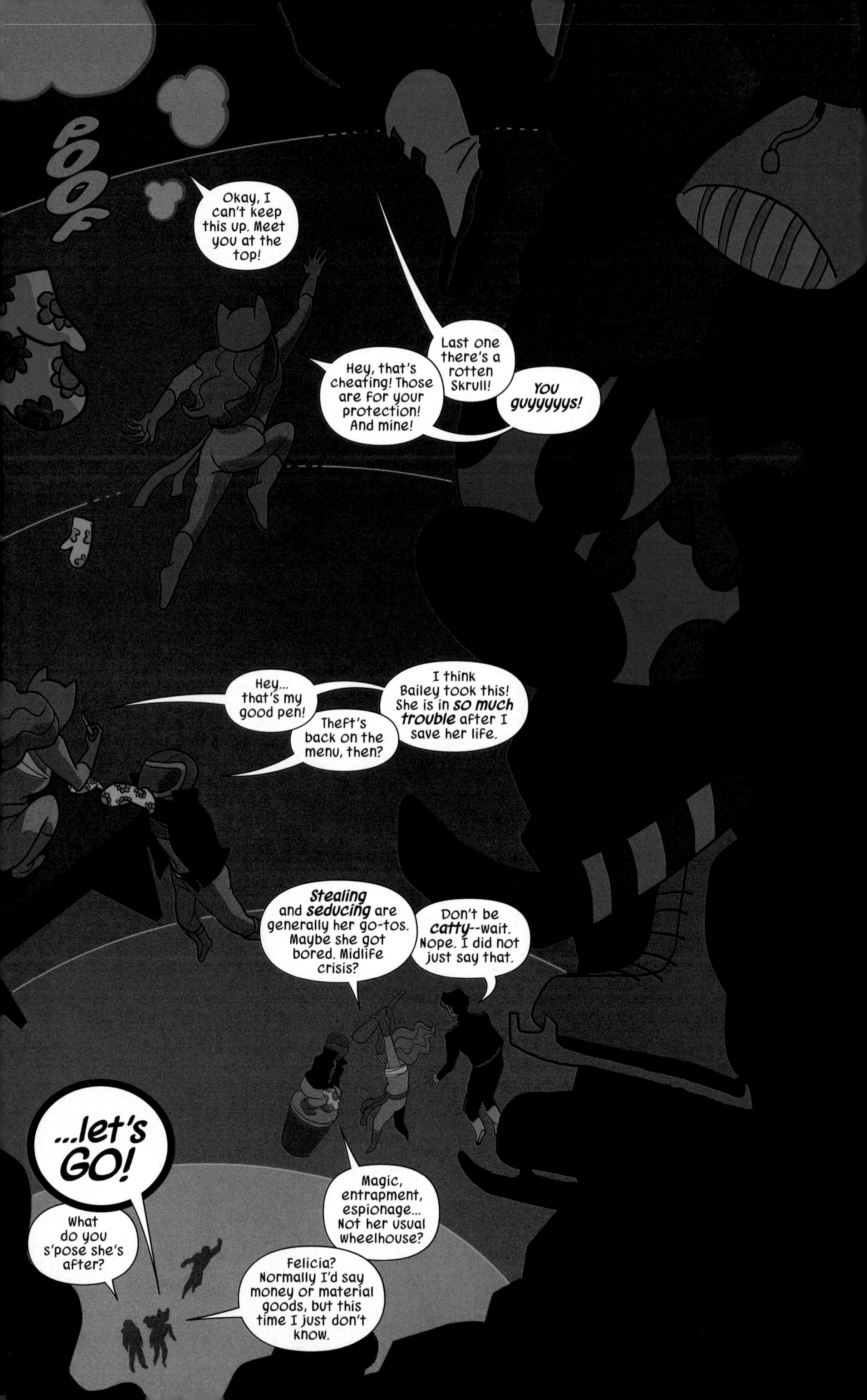
POOF
Okay, I can't keep this up. Meet you at the top!
Last one there's a rotten Skrull!
Hey, that's cheating! Those are for your protection! And mine!
YOU guyyyyys!
Hey... that's my good pen!
I think Bailey took this! She is in SO MUCH trouble after I save her life.
Theft's back on the menu, then?
Stealing and seducing are generally her go-tos. Maybe she got bored. Midlife crisis?
Don't be catty--wait. Nope. I did not just say that.
...let's GO!
What do you s'pose she's after?
Magic, entrapment, espionage... Not her usual wheelhouse?
Felicia? Normally I'd say money or material goods, but this time I just don't know.

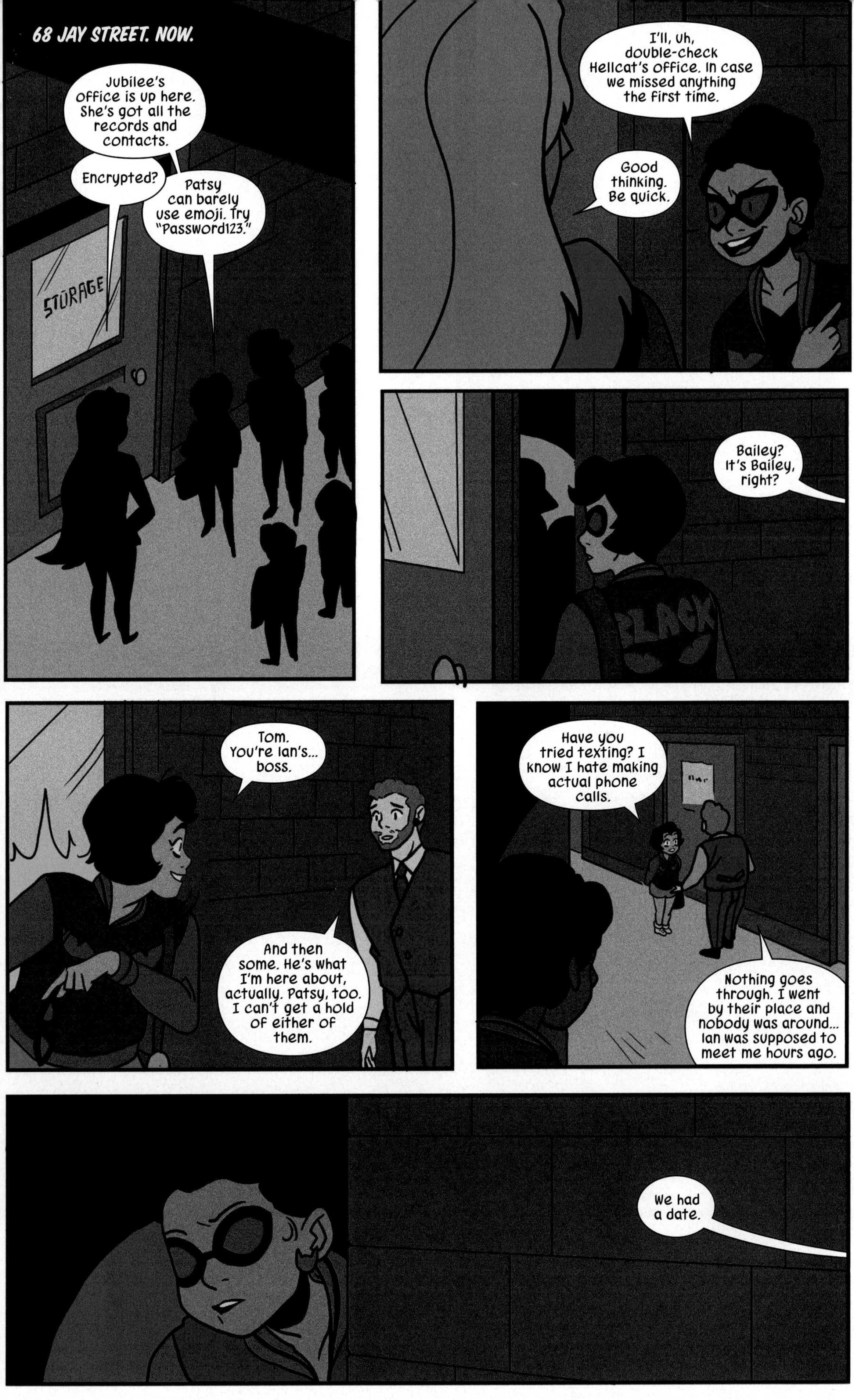
68 JAY STREET. NOW.
Jubilee's office is up here. She's got all the records and contacts.
Encrypted?
Patsy can barely use emoji. Try "Password123."
STORAGE
I'll, uh, double-check Hellcat's office. In case we missed anything the first time.
Good thinking. Be quick.
Bailey? It's Bailey, right?
BLACK
Tom. You're Ian's... boss.
And then some. He's what I'm here about, actually. Patsy, too. I can't get a hold of either of them.
Have you tried texting? I know I hate making actual phone calls.
Nothing goes through. I went by their place and nobody was around... Ian was supposed to meet me hours ago.
We had a date.

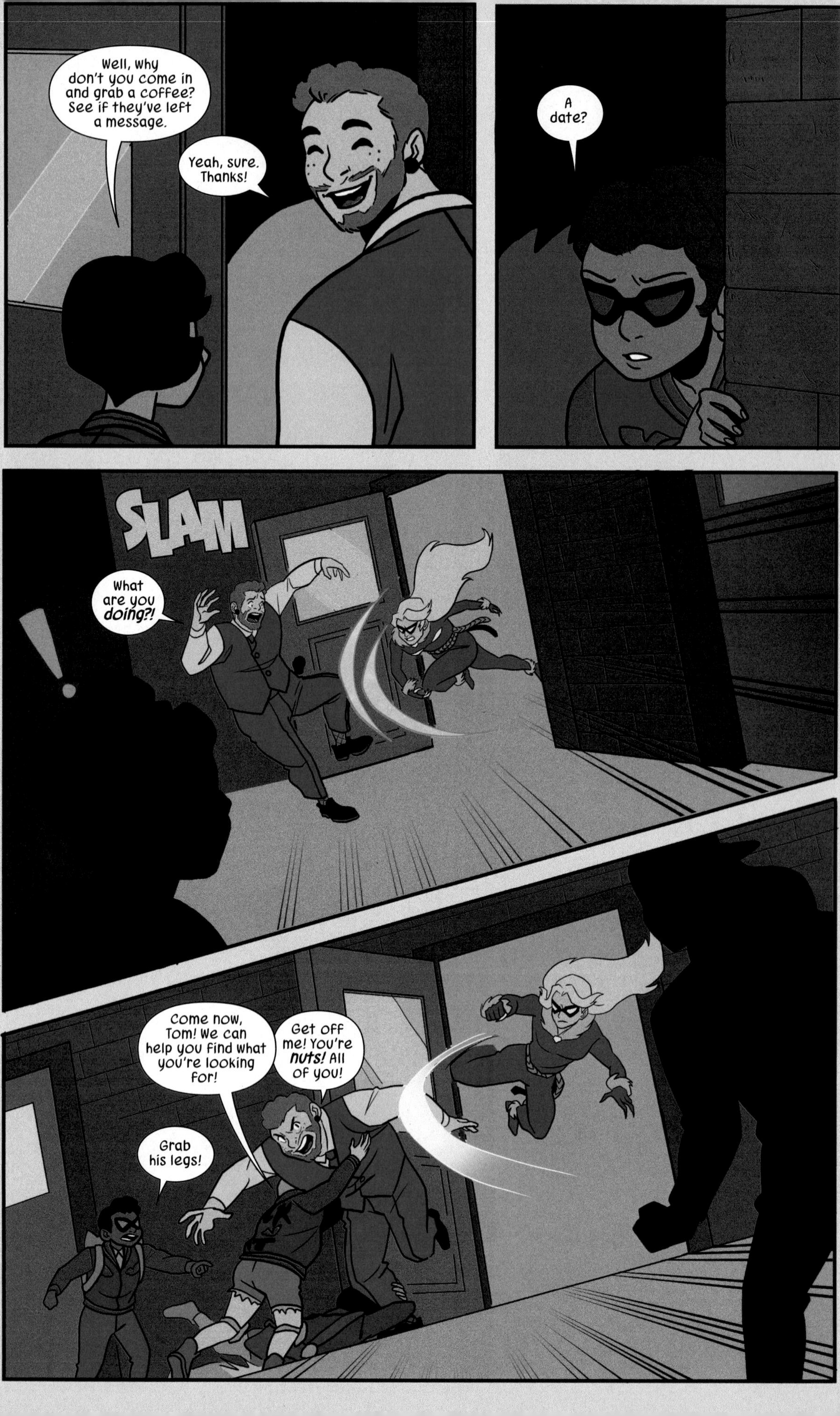
Well, why don't you come in and grab a coffee? See if they've left a message.
Yeah, sure. Thanks!
A date?
SLAM
!
What are you *doing?!*
Come now, Tom! We can help you find what you're looking for!
Get off me! You're *nuts!* All of you!
Grab his legs!

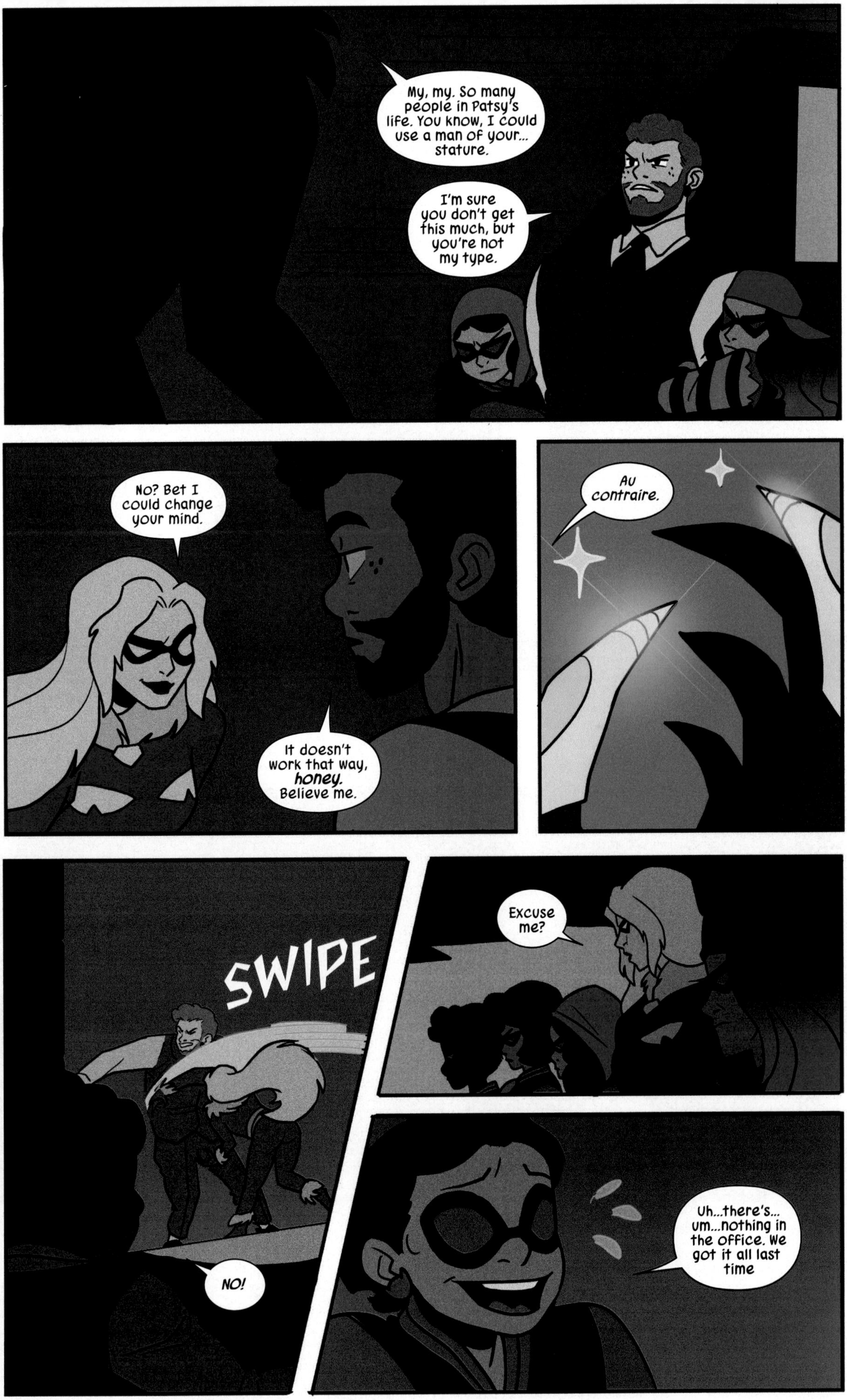
My, my. So many people in Patsy's life. You know, I could use a man of your... stature.
I'm sure you don't get this much, but you're not my type.
No? Bet I could change your mind.
It doesn't work that way, *honey.* Believe me.
Au contraire.
SWIPE
NO!
Excuse me?
Uh...there's... um...nothing in the office. We got it all last time

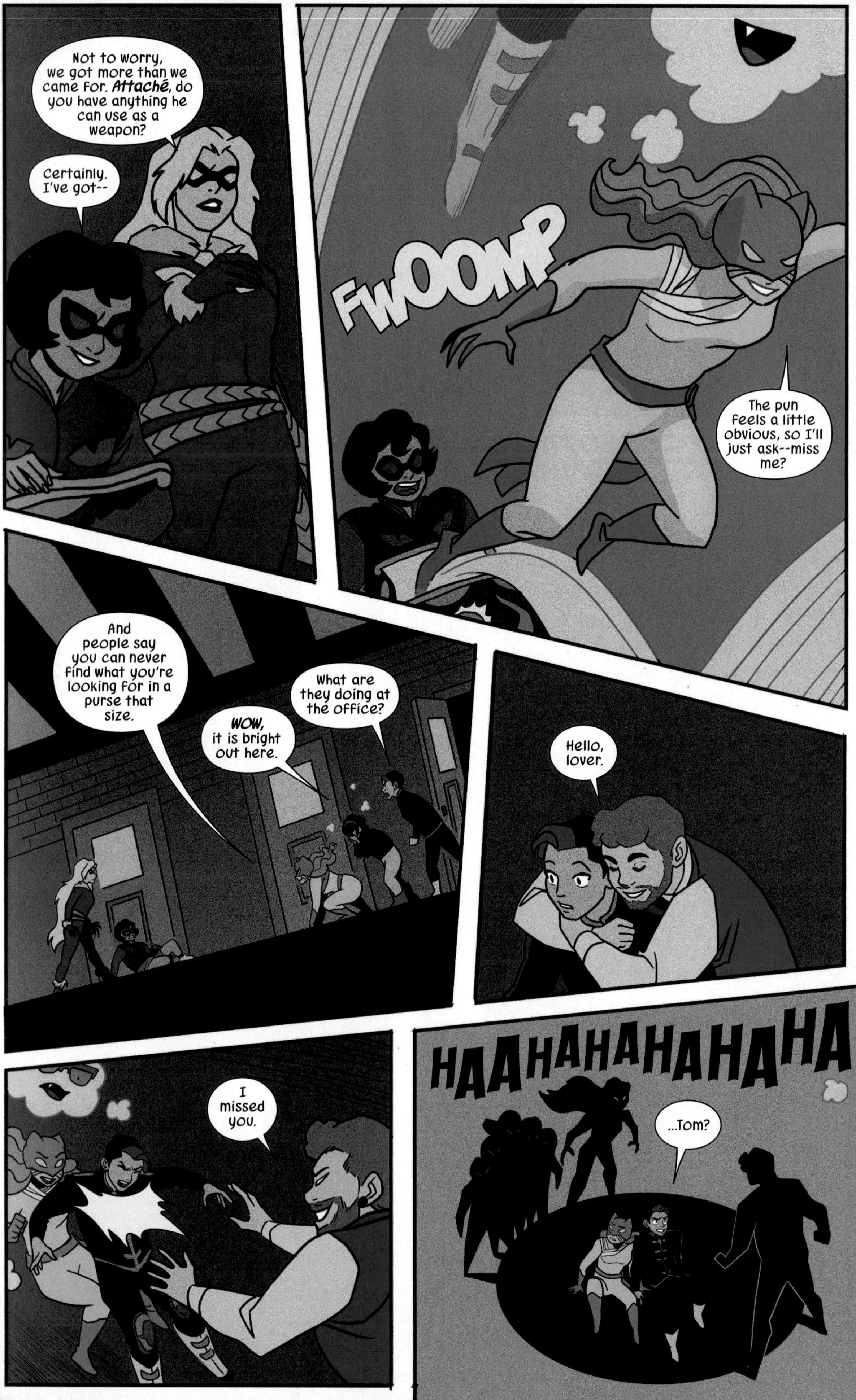
Not to worry, we got more than we came for. *Attaché*, do you have anything he can use as a weapon?
Certainly. I've got--
FWOOMP
The pun feels a little obvious, so I'll just ask--miss me?
And people say you can never find what you're looking for in a purse that size.
WOW, it is bright out here.
What are they doing at the office?
Hello, lover.
I missed you.
HAAHAHAHAHAHAHA
...Tom?

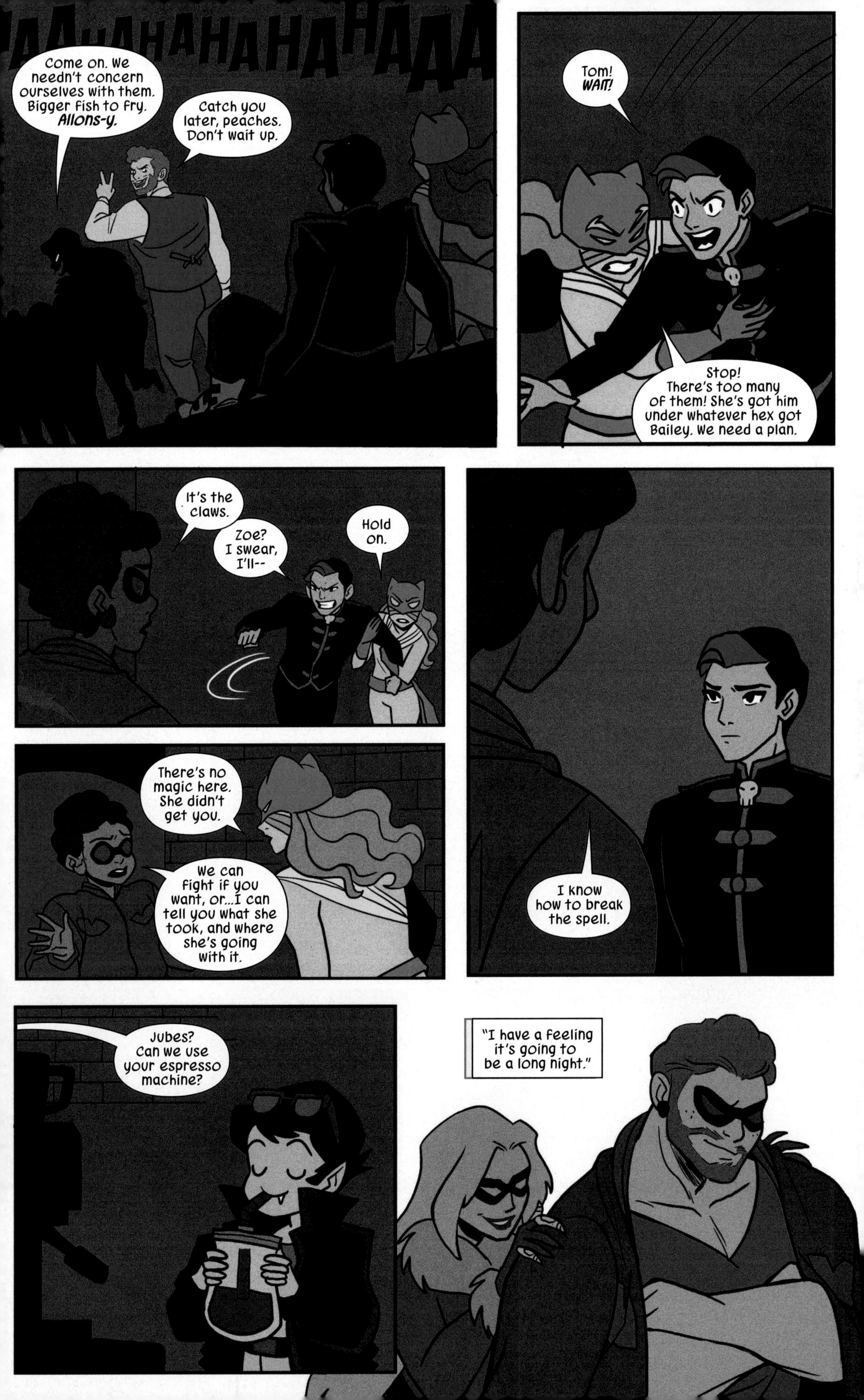
AAHAHAHAHAHAHAAA
Come on. We needn't concern ourselves with them. Bigger fish to fry. Allons-y.
Catch you later, peaches. Don't wait up.
Tom! WAIT!
Stop! There's too many of them! She's got him under whatever hex got Bailey. We need a plan.
It's the claws.
Zoe? I swear, I'll--
Hold on.
There's no magic here. She didn't get you.
We can fight if you want, or...I can tell you what she took, and where she's going with it.
I know how to break the spell.
Jubes? Can we use your espresso machine?
"I have a feeling it's going to be a long night."

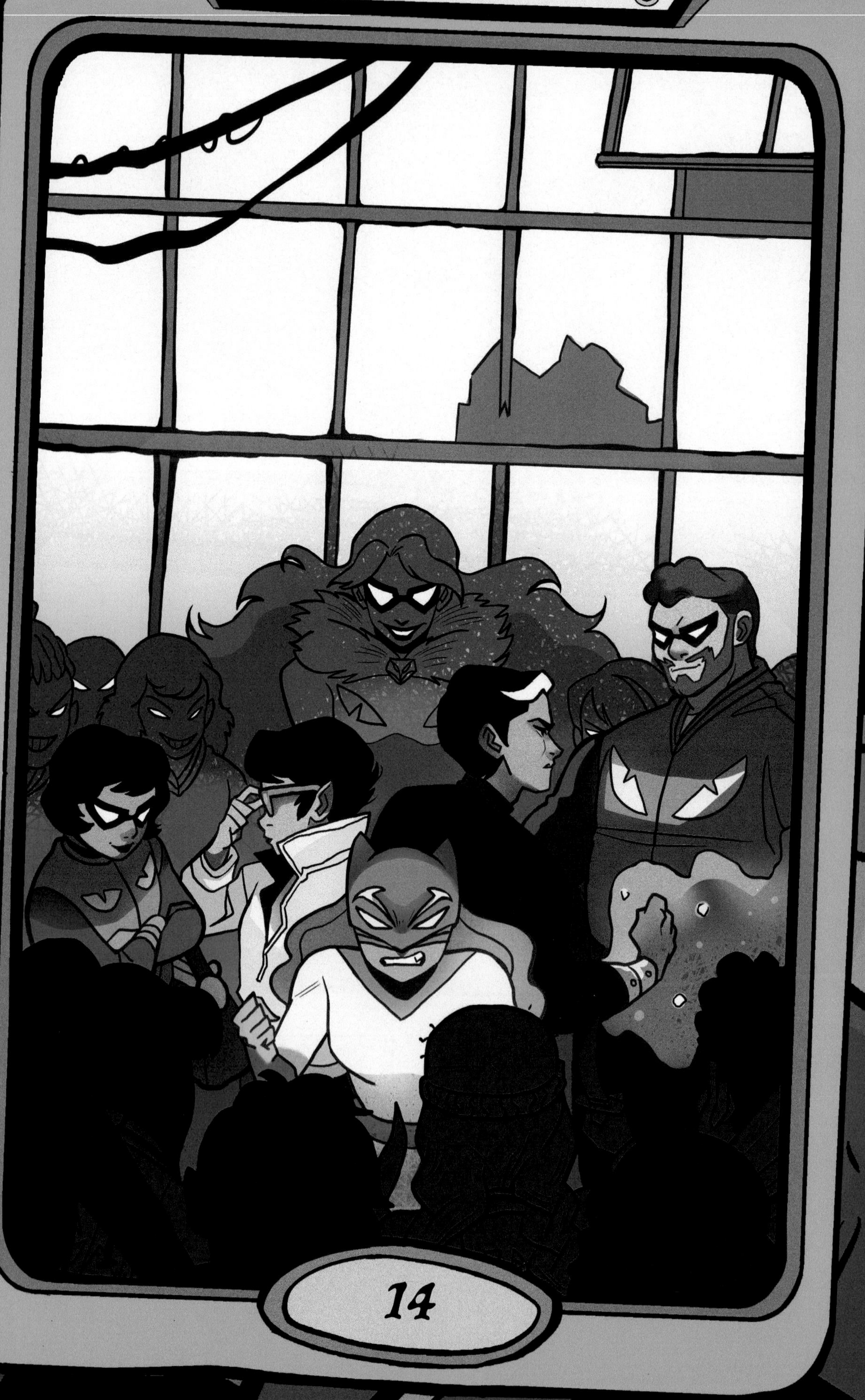
14

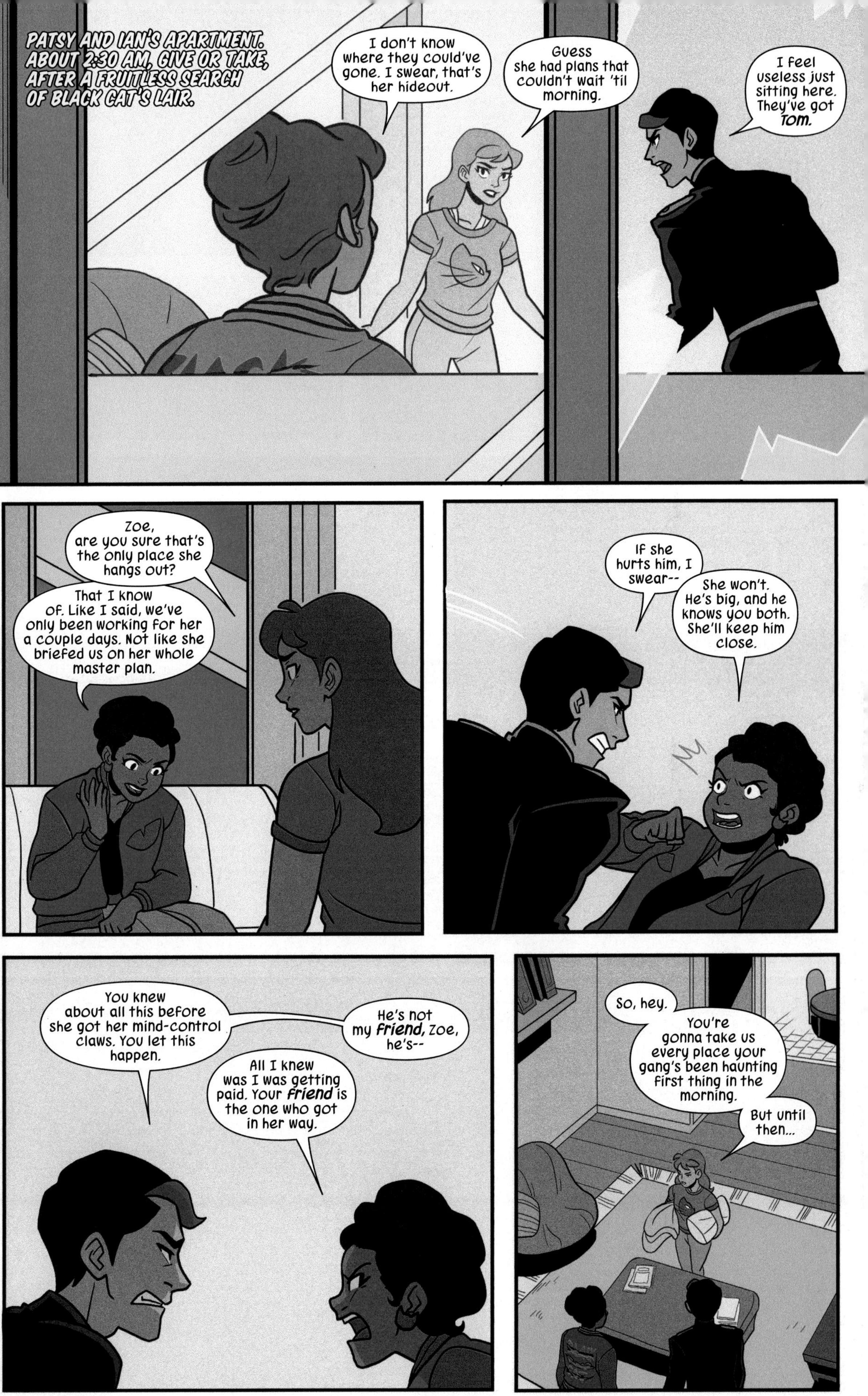
PATSY AND IAN'S APARTMENT. ABOUT 2:30 AM, GIVE OR TAKE, AFTER A FRUITLESS SEARCH OF BLACK CAT'S LAIR.
I don't know where they could've gone. I swear, that's her hideout.
Guess she had plans that couldn't wait 'til morning.
I feel useless just sitting here. They've got TOM.
Zoe, are you sure that's the only place she hangs out?
That I know of. Like I said, we've only been working for her a couple days. Not like she briefed us on her whole master plan.
If she hurts him, I swear--
She won't. He's big, and he knows you both. She'll keep him close.
You knew about all this before she got her mind-control claws. You let this happen.
He's not my friend, Zoe, he's--
All I knew was I was getting paid. Your friend is the one who got in her way.
So, hey.
You're gonna take us every place your gang's been haunting first thing in the morning.
But until then...

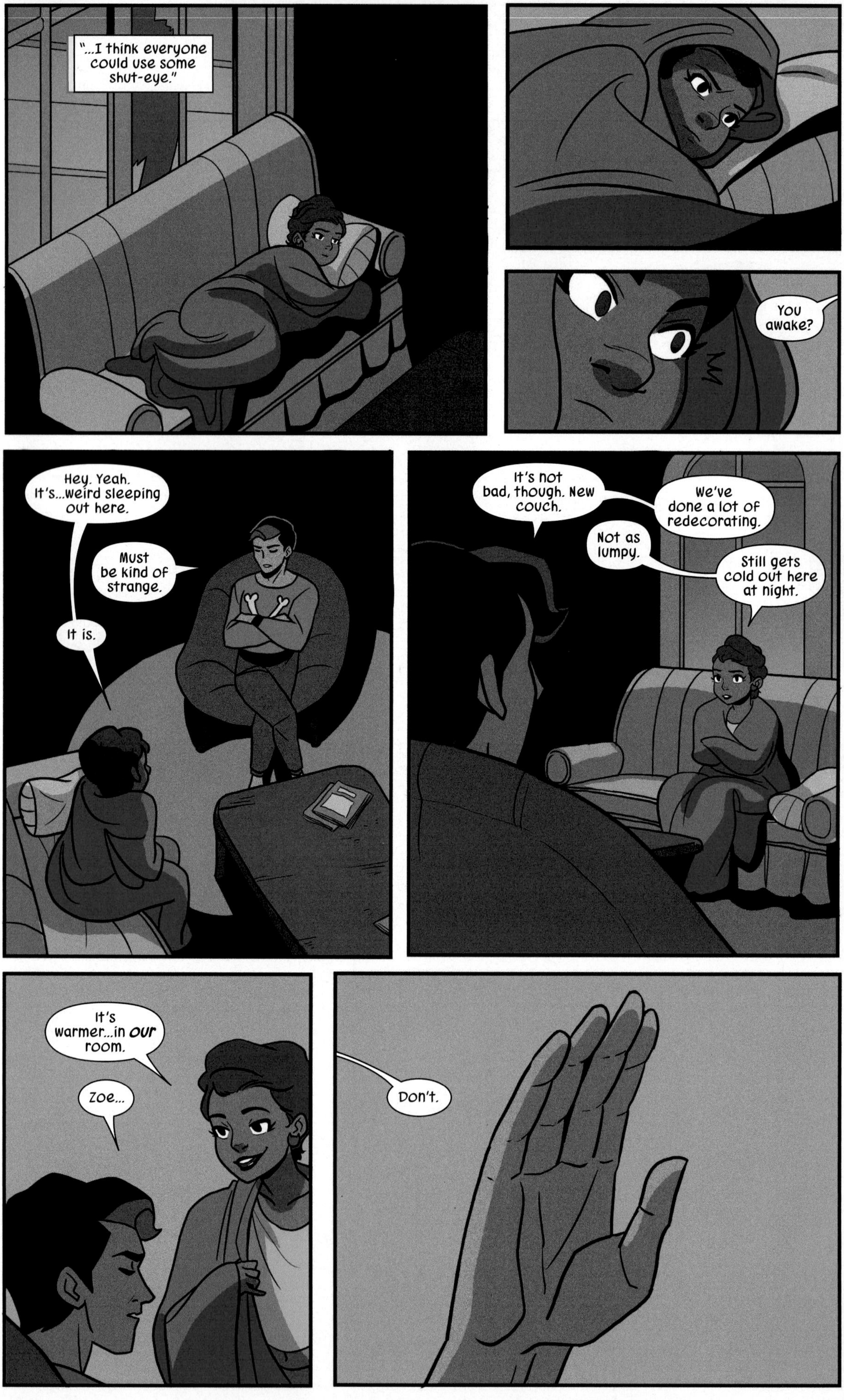
"...I think everyone could use some shut-eye."
You awake?
Hey. Yeah. It's...weird sleeping out here.
Must be kind of strange.
It is.
It's not bad, though. New couch.
We've done a lot of redecorating.
Not as lumpy.
Still gets cold out here at night.
It's warmer...in *our* room.
Zoe...
Don't.

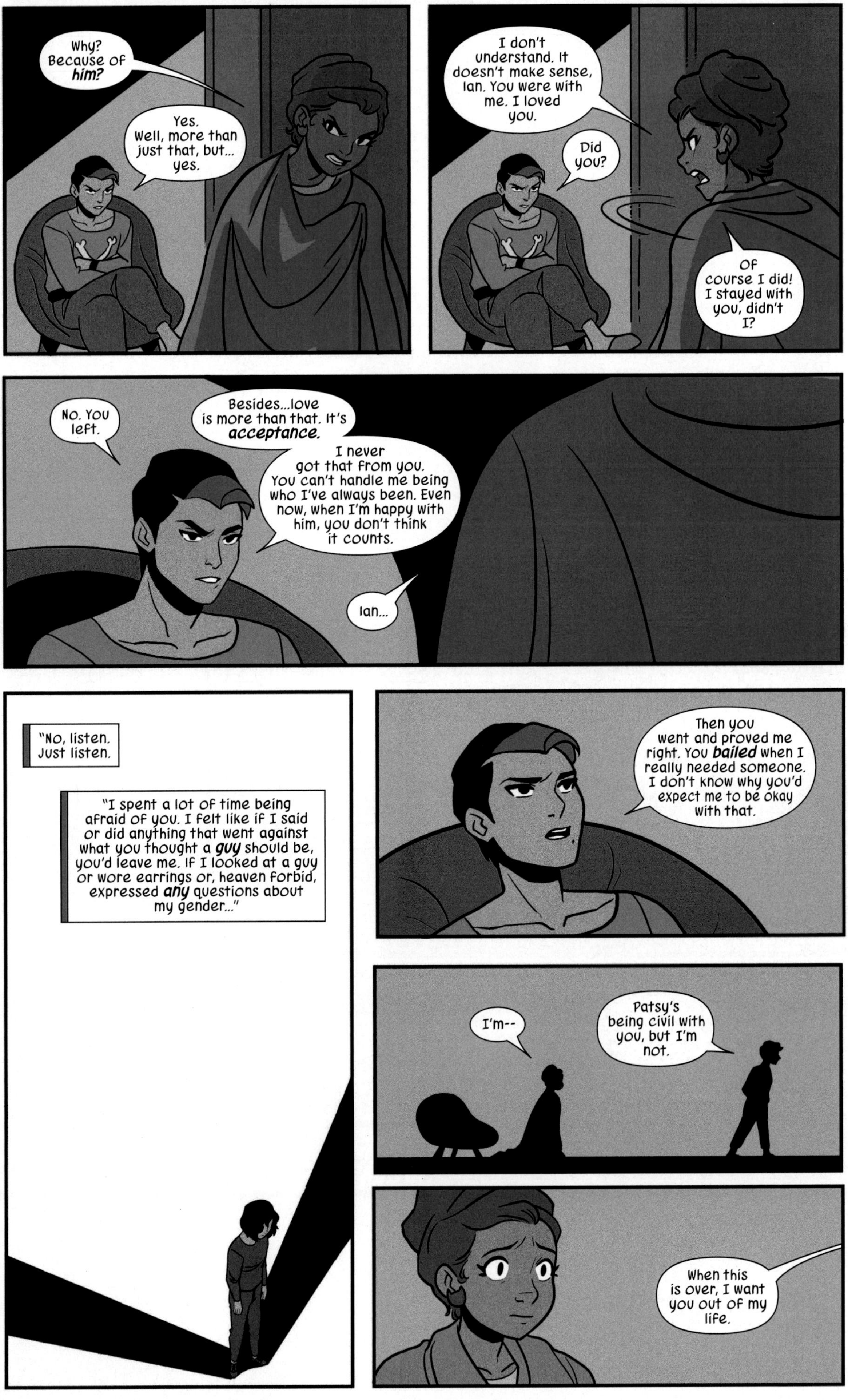
Why? Because of *him?*
Yes. Well, more than just that, but... yes.
I don't understand. It doesn't make sense, Ian. You were with me. I loved you.
Did you?
Of course I did! I stayed with you, didn't I?
No. You left.
Besides...love is more than that. It's *acceptance.*
I never got that from you. You can't handle me being who I've always been. Even now, when I'm happy with him, you don't think it counts.
Ian...
"No, listen. Just listen.
"I spent a lot of time being afraid of you. I felt like if I said or did anything that went against what you thought a *guy* should be, you'd leave me. If I looked at a guy or wore earrings or, heaven forbid, expressed *any* questions about my gender..."
Then you went and proved me right. You *bailed* when I really needed someone. I don't know why you'd expect me to be okay with that.
I'm--
Patsy's being civil with you, but I'm not.
When this is over, I want you out of my life.

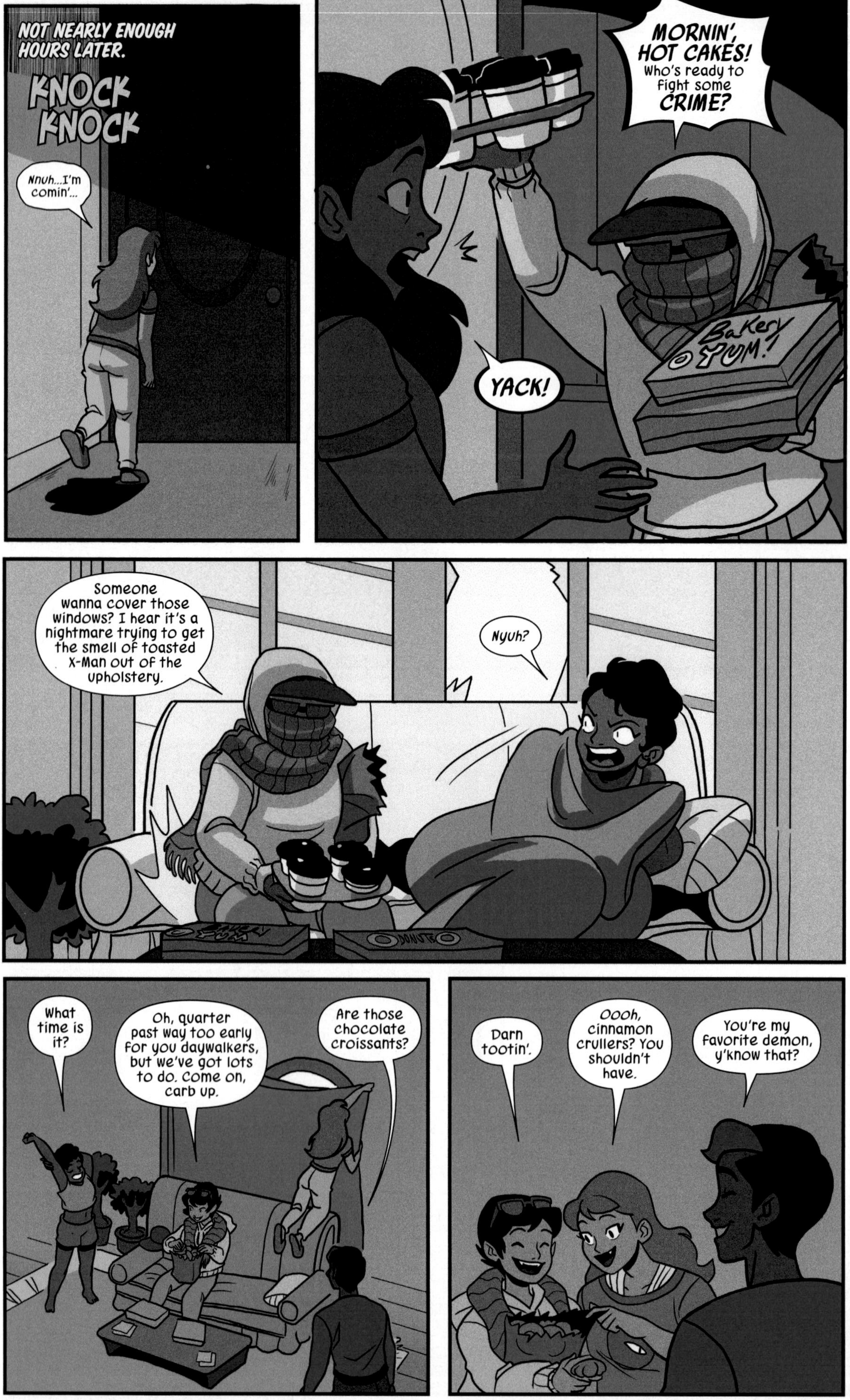
NOT NEARLY ENOUGH HOURS LATER.
KNOCK KNOCK
Nnuh...I'm comin'...
MORNIN', HOT CAKES! Who's ready to fight some CRIME?
YACK!
Someone wanna cover those windows? I hear it's a nightmare trying to get the smell of toasted X-Man out of the upholstery.
Nyuh?
What time is it?
Oh, quarter past way too early for you daywalkers, but we've got lots to do. Come on, carb up.
Are those chocolate croissants?
Darn tootin'.
Oooh, cinnamon crullers? You shouldn't have.
You're my favorite demon, y'know that?
Bakery YUM!

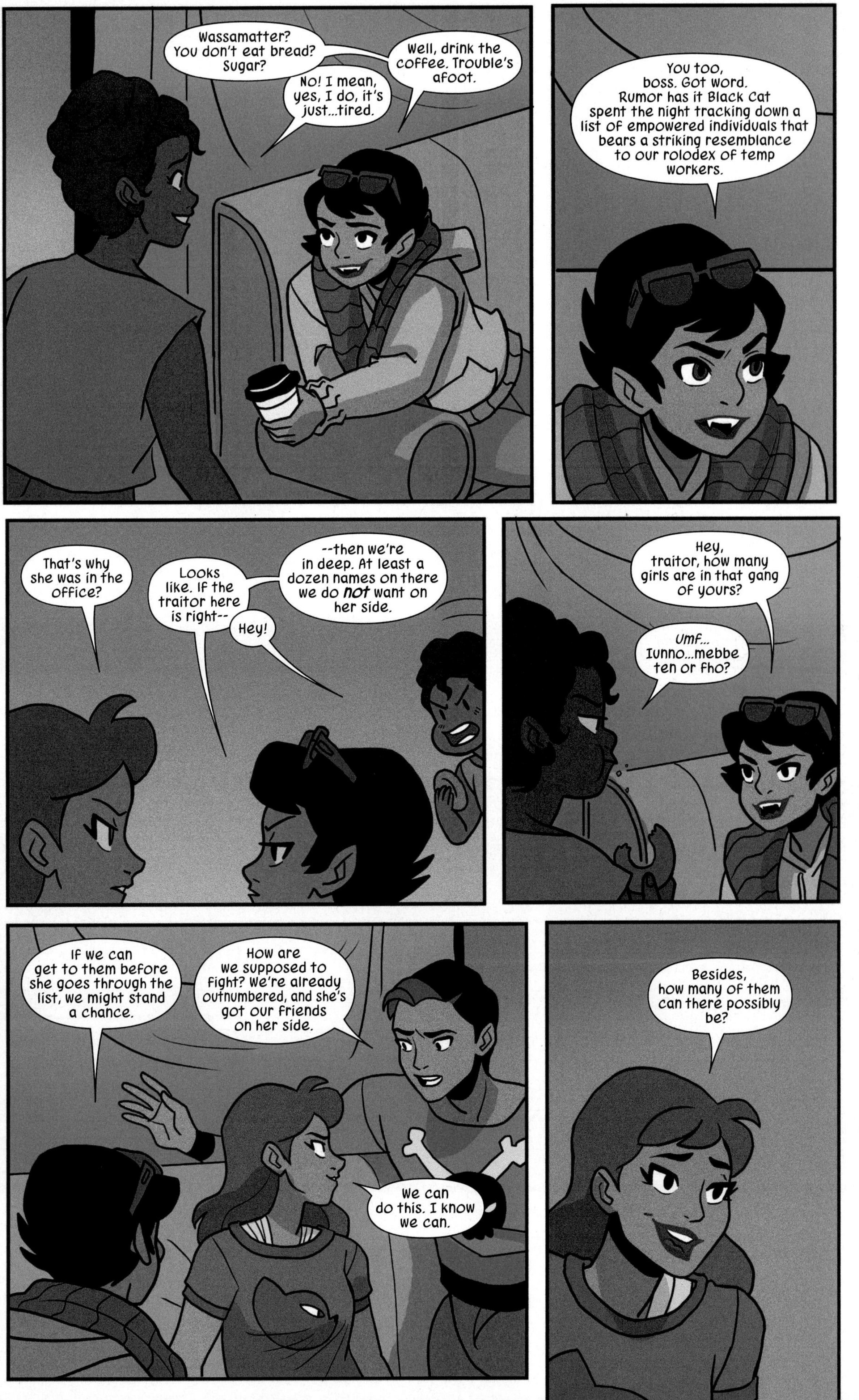
Wassamatter? You don't eat bread? Sugar?
No! I mean, yes, I do, it's just...tired.
Well, drink the coffee. Trouble's afoot.
You too, boss. Got word. Rumor has it Black Cat spent the night tracking down a list of empowered individuals that bears a striking resemblance to our rolodex of temp workers.
That's why she was in the office?
Looks like. If the traitor here is right--
Hey!
--then we're in deep. At least a dozen names on there we do *not* want on her side.
Hey, traitor, how many girls are in that gang of yours?
Umf... Iunno...mebbe ten or fho?
If we can get to them before she goes through the list, we might stand a chance.
How are we supposed to fight? We're already outnumbered, and she's got our friends on her side.
We can do this. I know we can.
Besides, how many of them can there possibly be?

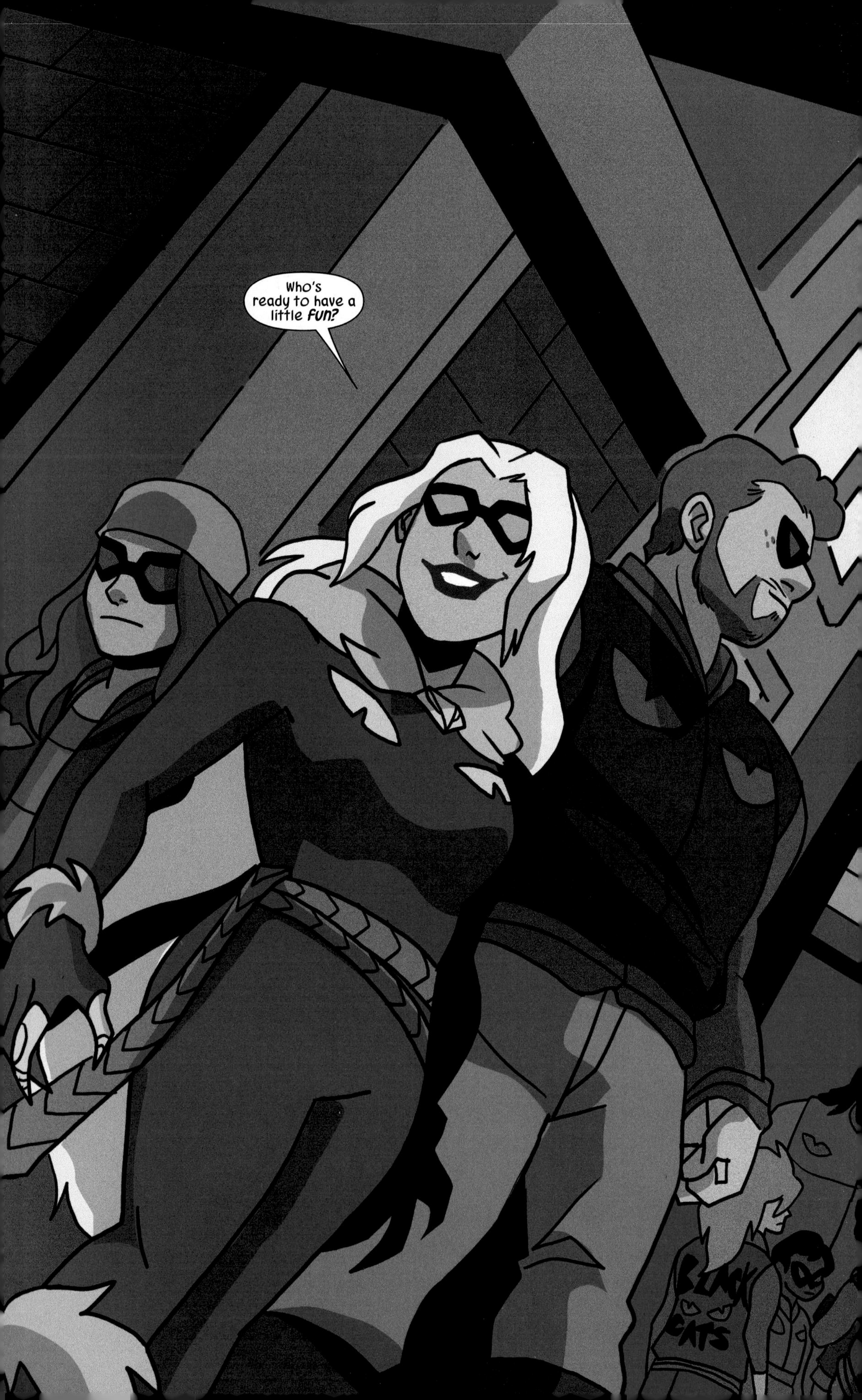
Who's ready to have a little *FUN?*
BLACK CATS

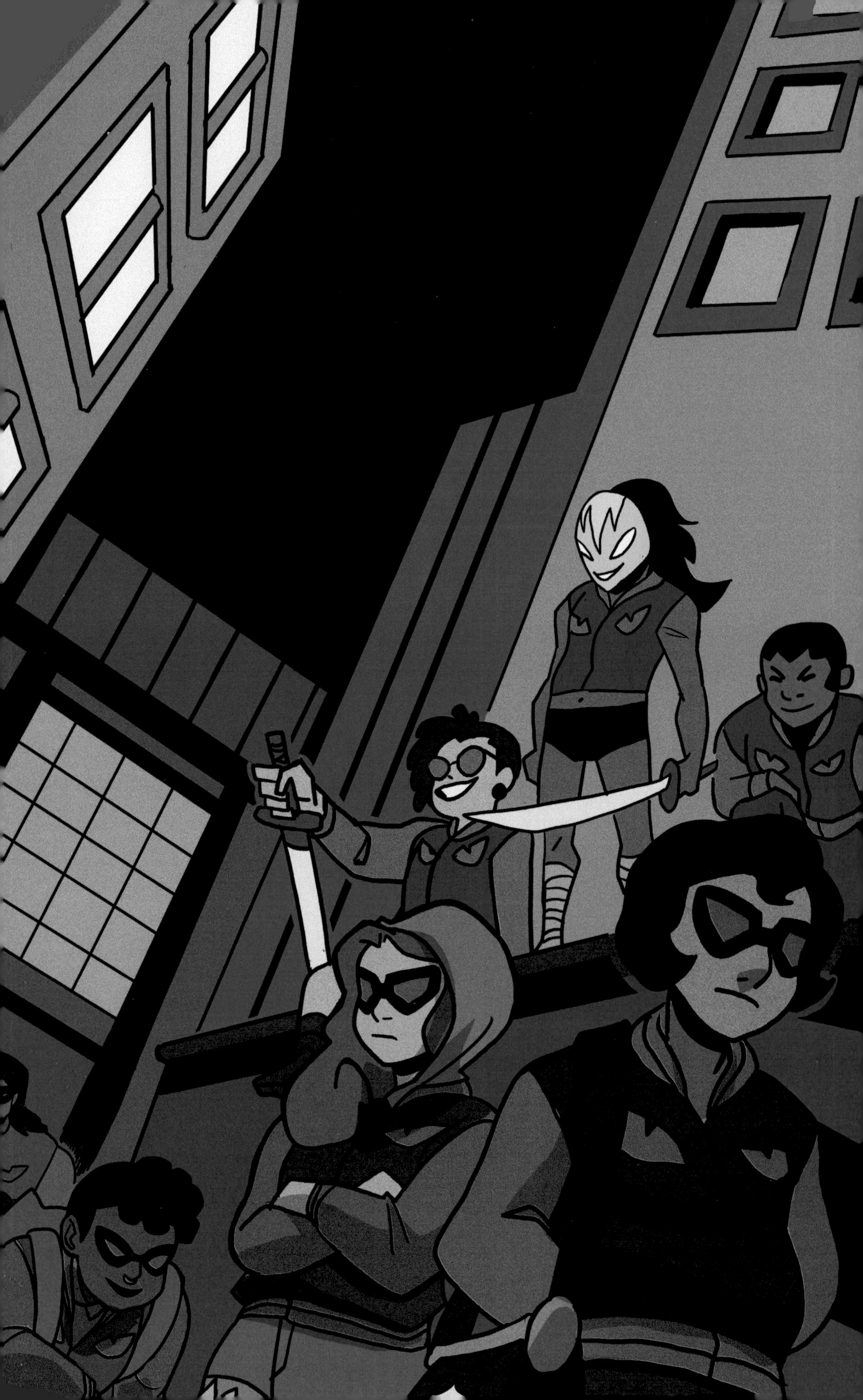

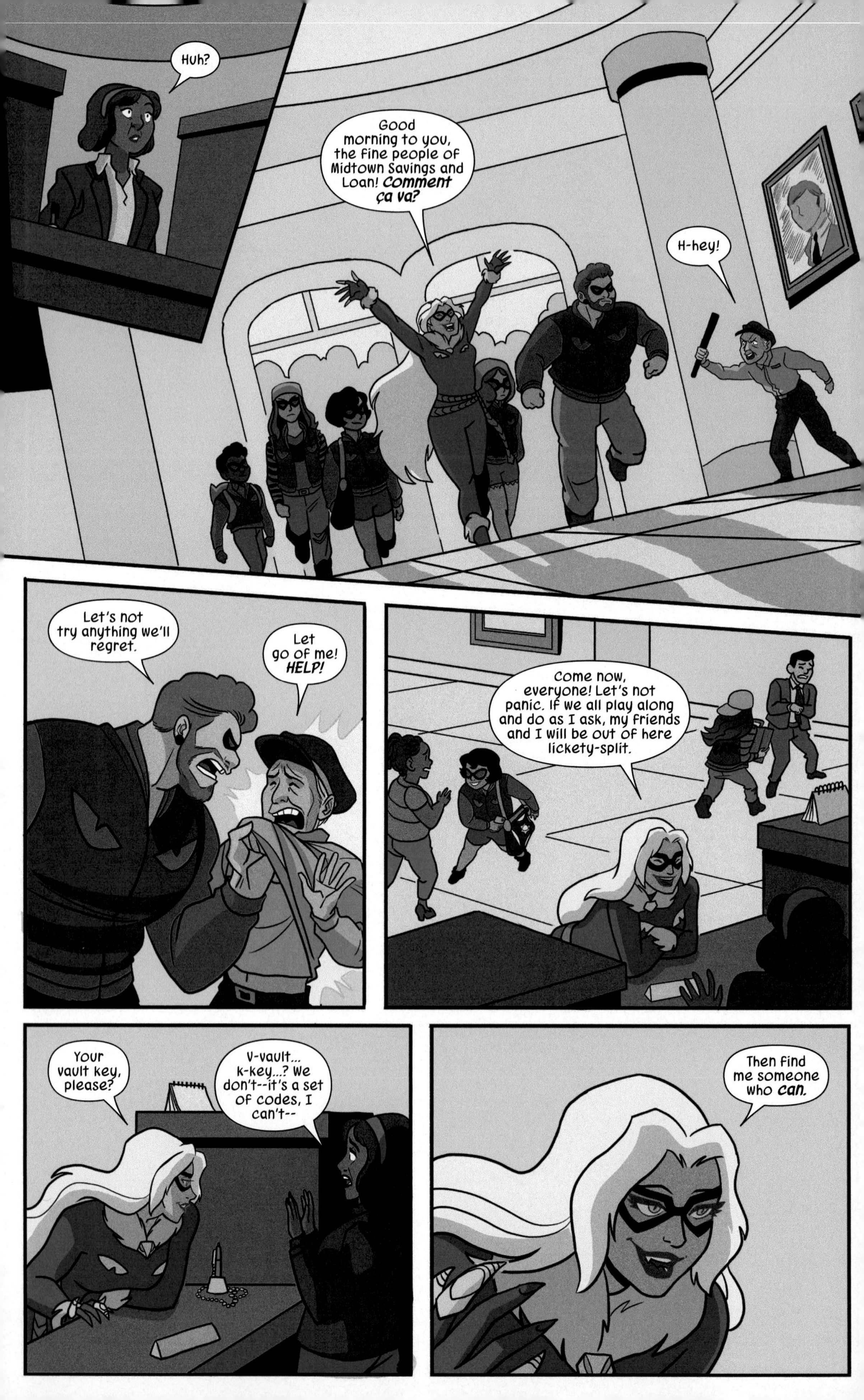
Huh?
Good morning to you, the fine people of Midtown Savings and Loan! *Comment ça va?*
H-hey!
Let's not try anything we'll regret.
Let go of me! *HELP!*
Come now, everyone! Let's not panic. If we all play along and do as I ask, my friends and I will be out of here lickety-split.
Your vault key, please?
V-vault... k-key...? We don't--it's a set of codes, I can't--
Then find me someone who *can.*

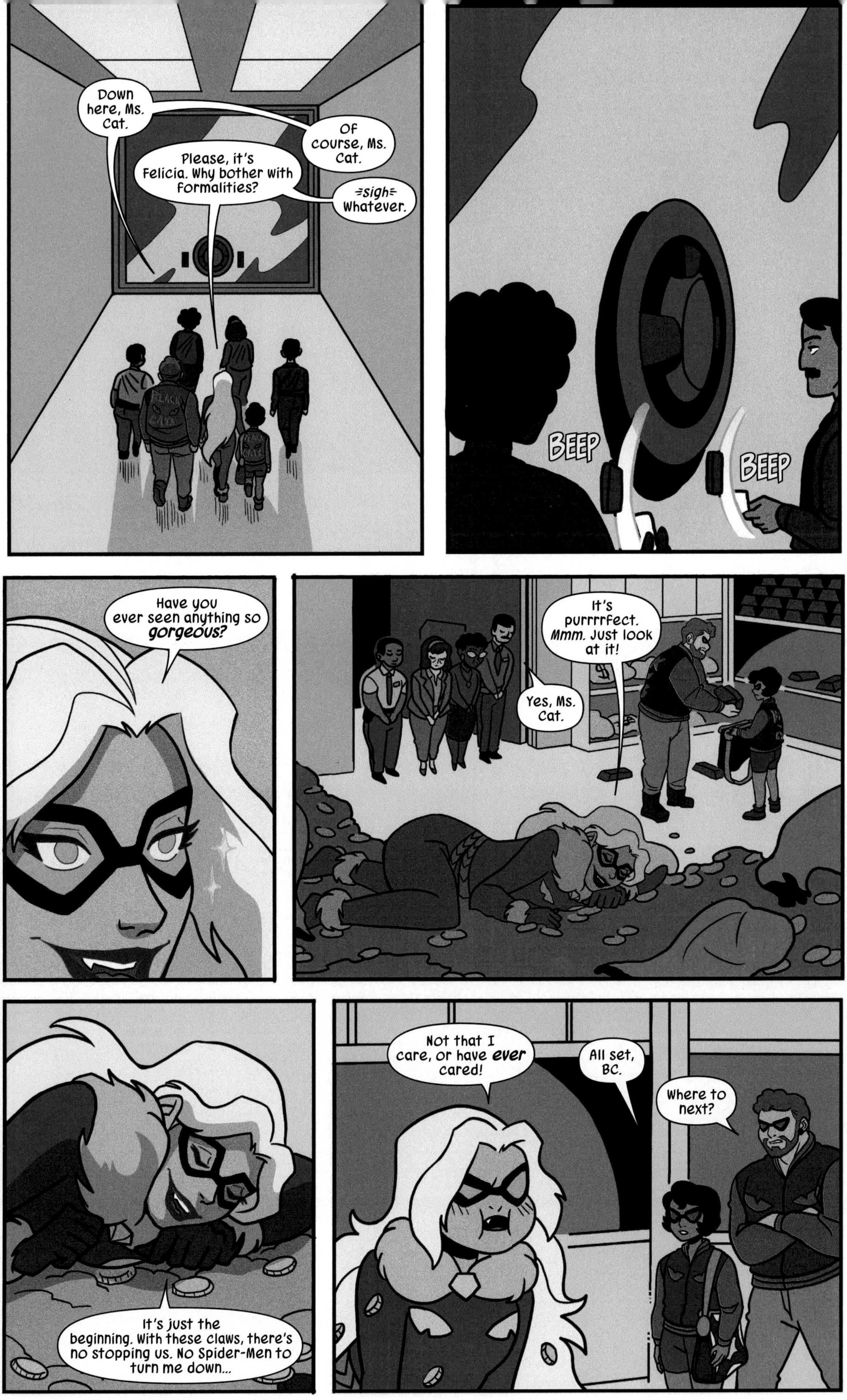
Down here, Ms. Cat.
Of course, Ms. Cat.
Please, it's Felicia. Why bother with formalities?
=sigh= Whatever.
BEEP
BEEP
Have you ever seen anything so *gorgeous?*
It's purrrrfect. Mmm. Just look at it!
Yes, Ms. Cat.
It's just the beginning. With these claws, there's no stopping us. No Spider-Men to turn me down...
Not that I care, or have *ever* cared!
All set, BC.
Where to next?

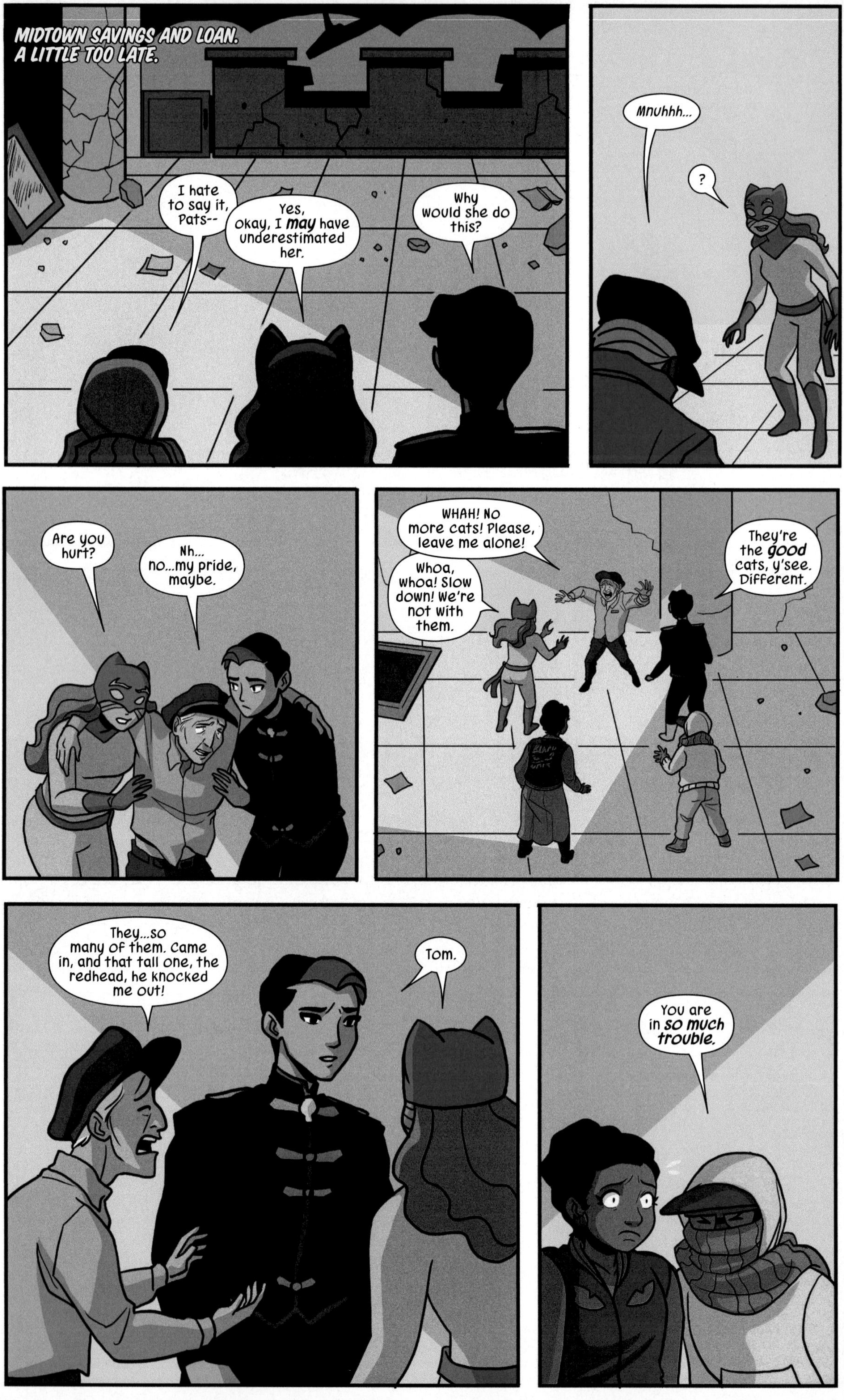
MIDTOWN SAVINGS AND LOAN. A LITTLE TOO LATE.
I hate to say it, Pats--
Yes, Okay, I may have underestimated her.
Why would she do this?
Mnuhhh...
?
Are you hurt?
Nh... no...my pride, maybe.
WHAH! No more cats! Please, leave me alone!
Whoa, whoa! Slow down! We're not with them.
They're the good cats, y'see. Different.
They...so many of them. Came in, and that tall one, the redhead, he knocked me out!
Tom.
You are in so much trouble.

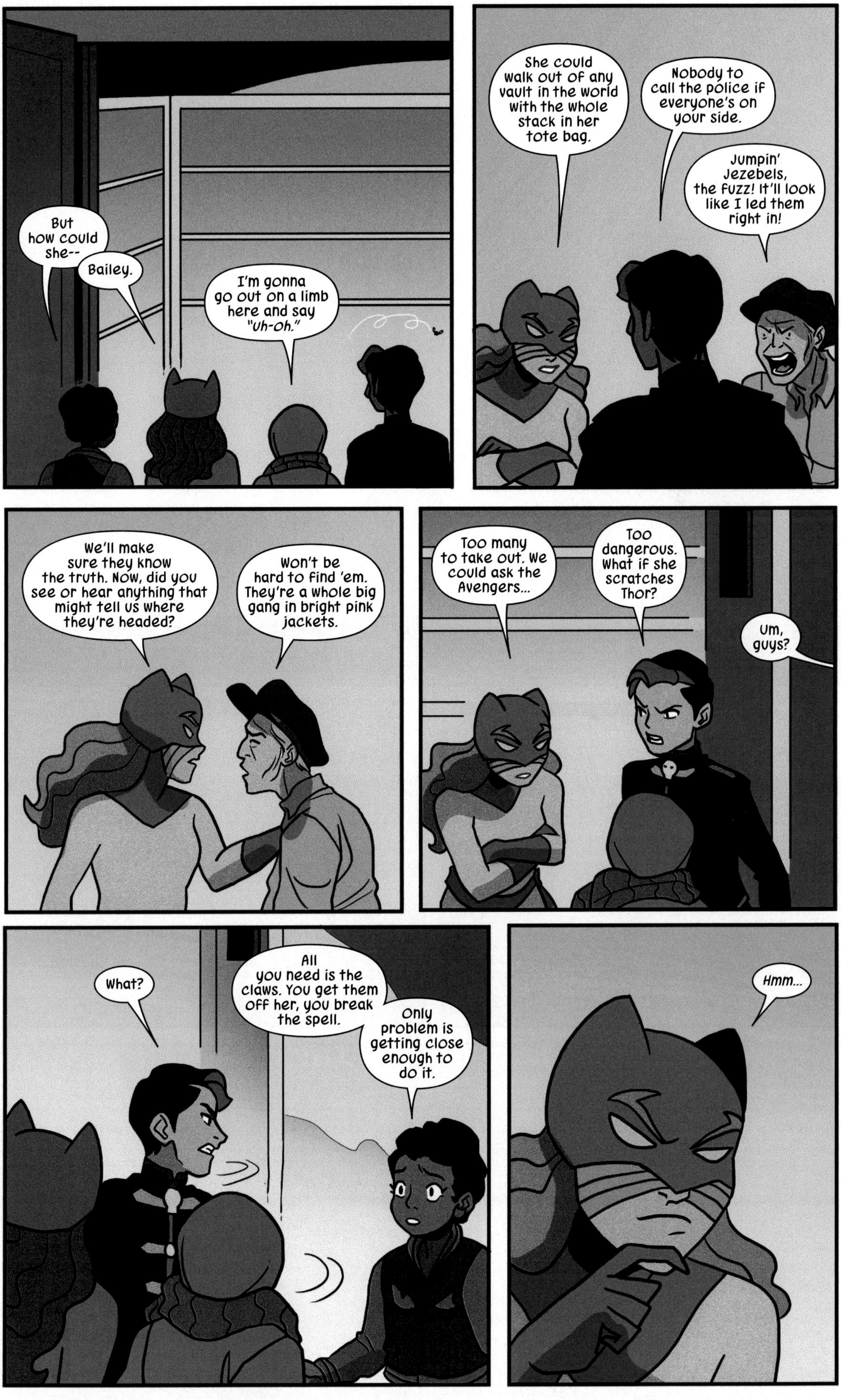
But how could she--
Bailey.
I'm gonna go out on a limb here and say "Uh-Oh."
She could walk out of any vault in the world with the whole stack in her tote bag.
Nobody to call the police if everyone's on your side.
Jumpin' Jezebels, the fuzz! It'll look like I led them right in!
We'll make sure they know the truth. Now, did you see or hear anything that might tell us where they're headed?
Won't be hard to find 'em. They're a whole big gang in bright pink jackets.
Too many to take out. We could ask the Avengers...
Too dangerous. What if she scratches Thor?
Um, guys?
What?
All you need is the claws. You get them off her, you break the spell.
Only problem is getting close enough to do it.
Hmm...

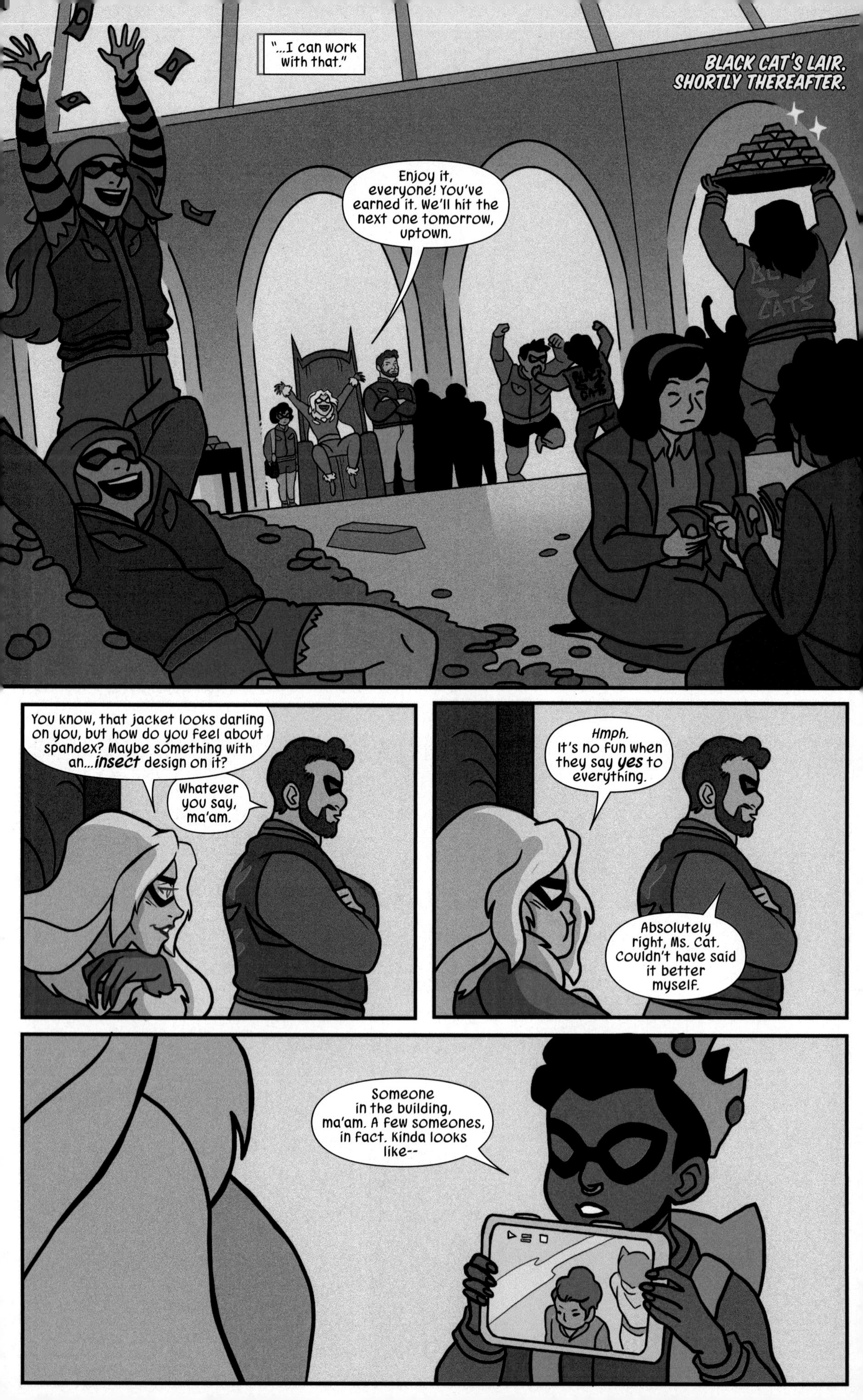
"...I can work with that."
BLACK CAT'S LAIR. SHORTLY THEREAFTER.
Enjoy it, everyone! You've earned it. We'll hit the next one tomorrow, uptown.
You know, that jacket looks darling on you, but how do you feel about spandex? Maybe something with an...*insect* design on it?
Whatever you say, ma'am.
Hmph. It's no fun when they say *yes* to everything.
Absolutely right, Ms. Cat. Couldn't have said it better myself.
Someone in the building, ma'am. A few someones, in fact. Kinda looks like--

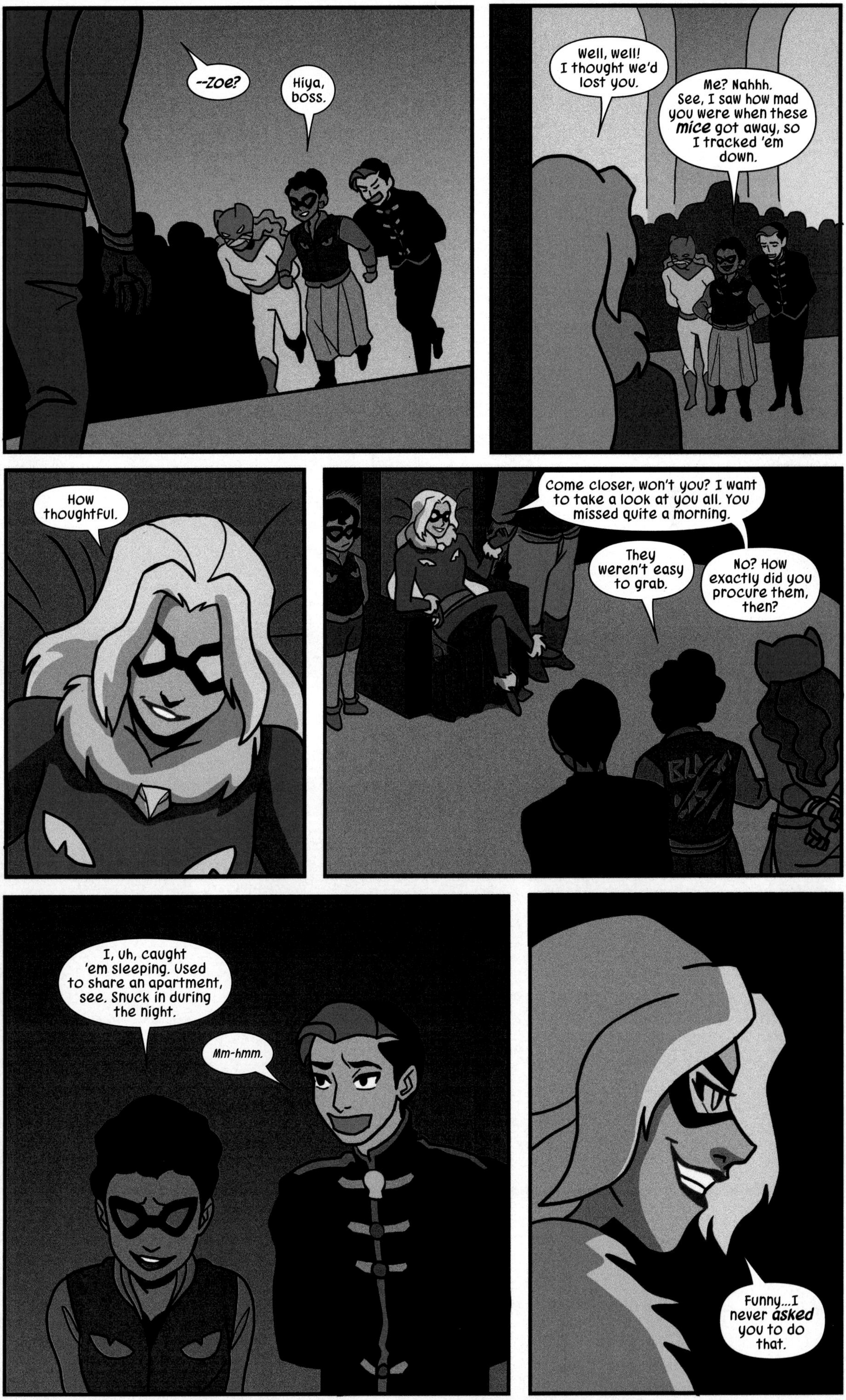
--Zoe?
Hiya, boss.
Well, well! I thought we'd lost you.
Me? Nahhh. See, I saw how mad you were when these *mice* got away, so I tracked 'em down.
How thoughtful.
Come closer, won't you? I want to take a look at you all. You missed quite a morning.
They weren't easy to grab.
No? How exactly did you procure them, then?
I, uh, caught 'em sleeping. Used to share an apartment, see. Snuck in during the night.
Mm-hmm.
Funny...I never *asked* you to do that.

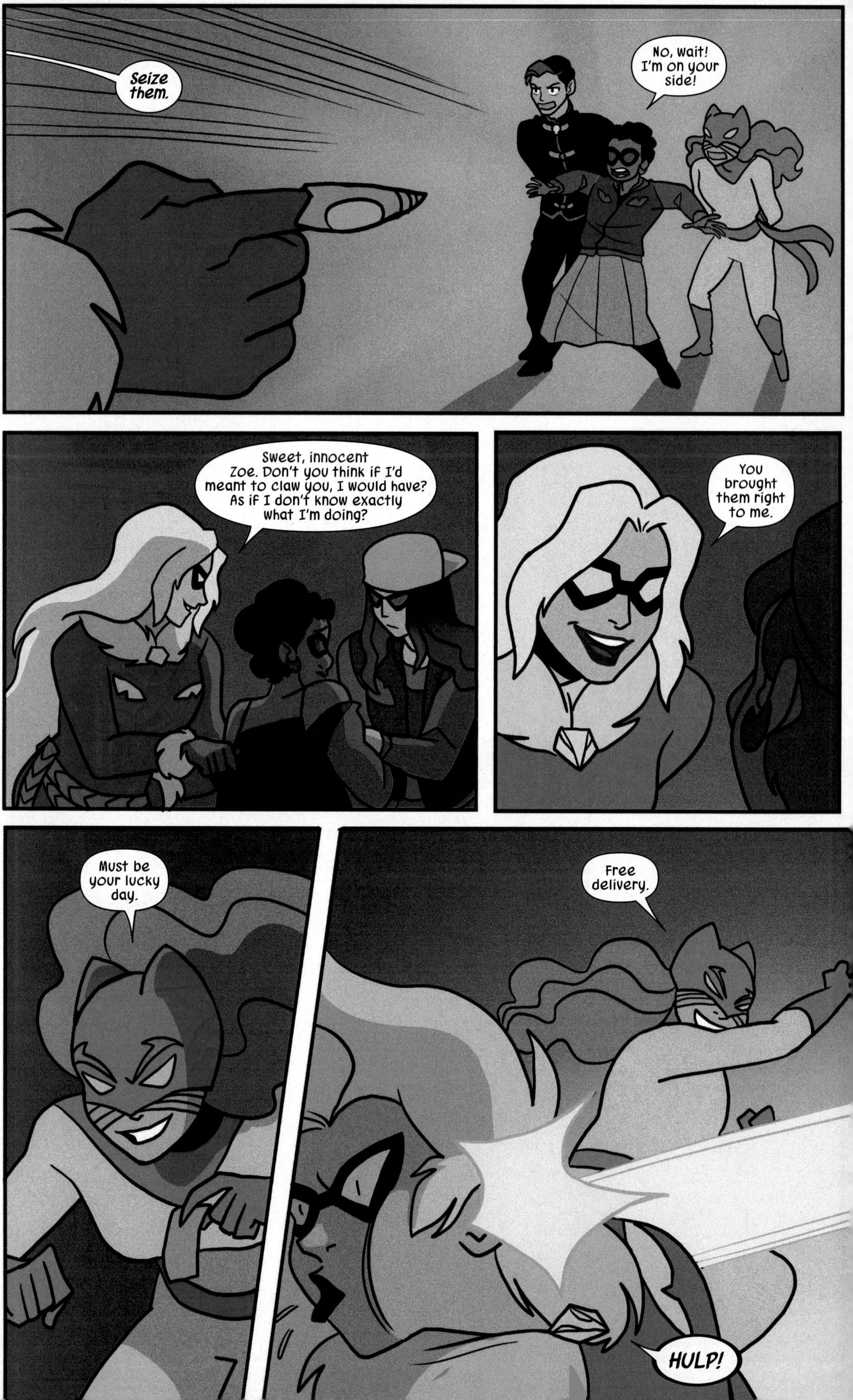
Seize them.
No, wait! I'm on your side!
Sweet, innocent Zoe. Don't you think if I'd meant to claw you, I would have? As if I don't know exactly what I'm doing?
You brought them right to me.
Must be your lucky day.
Free delivery.
HULP!

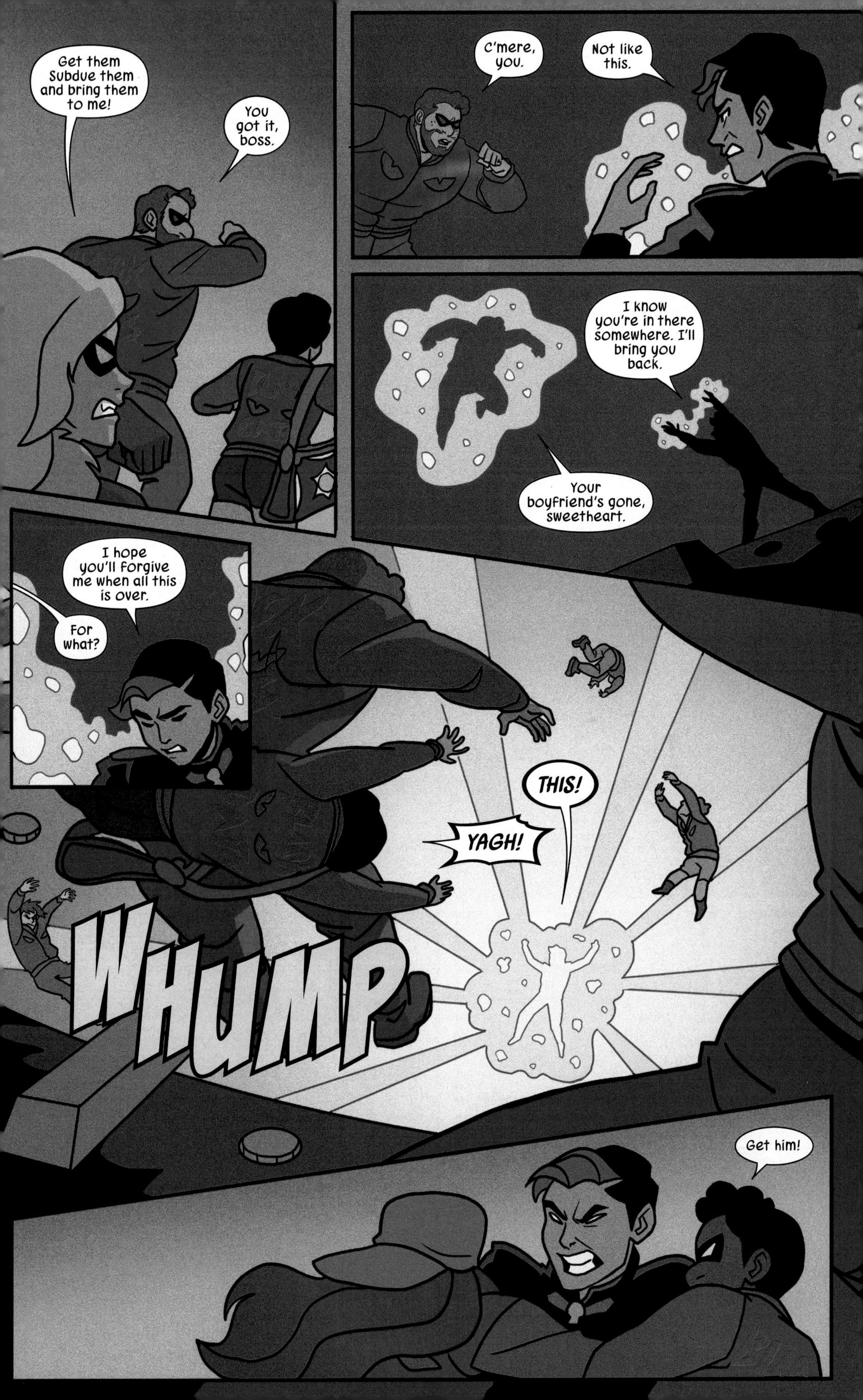
Get them
Subdue them
and bring them
to me!
You
got it,
boss.
C'mere,
you.
Not like
this.
I know
you're in there
somewhere. I'll
bring you
back.
Your
boyfriend's gone,
sweetheart.
I hope
you'll forgive
me when all this
is over.
For
what?
THIS!
YAGH!
WHUMP
Get him!

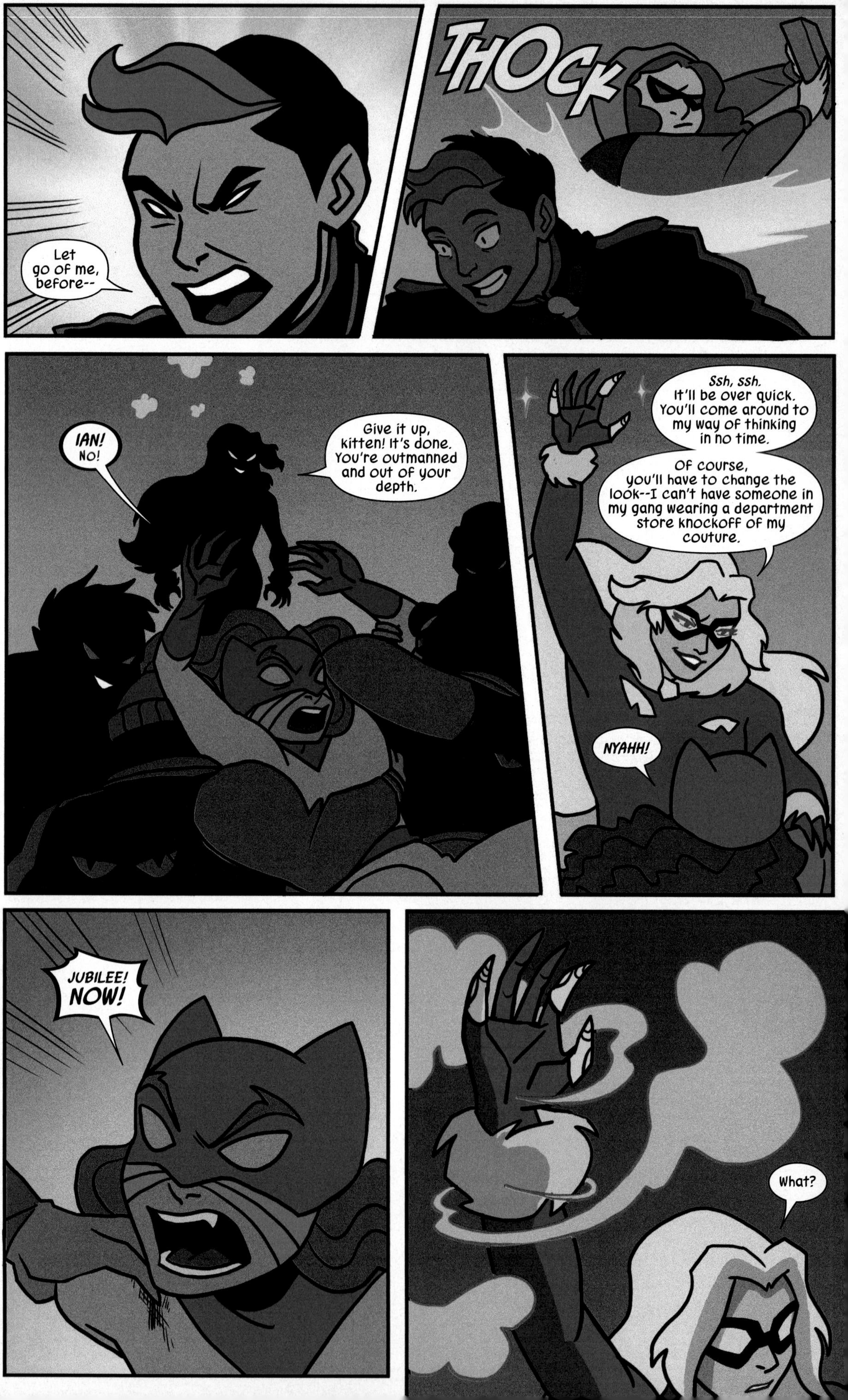
Let go of me, before--
THOCK
IAN! NO!
Give it up, kitten! It's done. You're outmanned and out of your depth.
Ssh, ssh. It'll be over quick. You'll come around to my way of thinking in no time.
Of course, you'll have to change the look--I can't have someone in my gang wearing a department store knockoff of my couture.
NYAHH!
JUBILEE! NOW!
What?

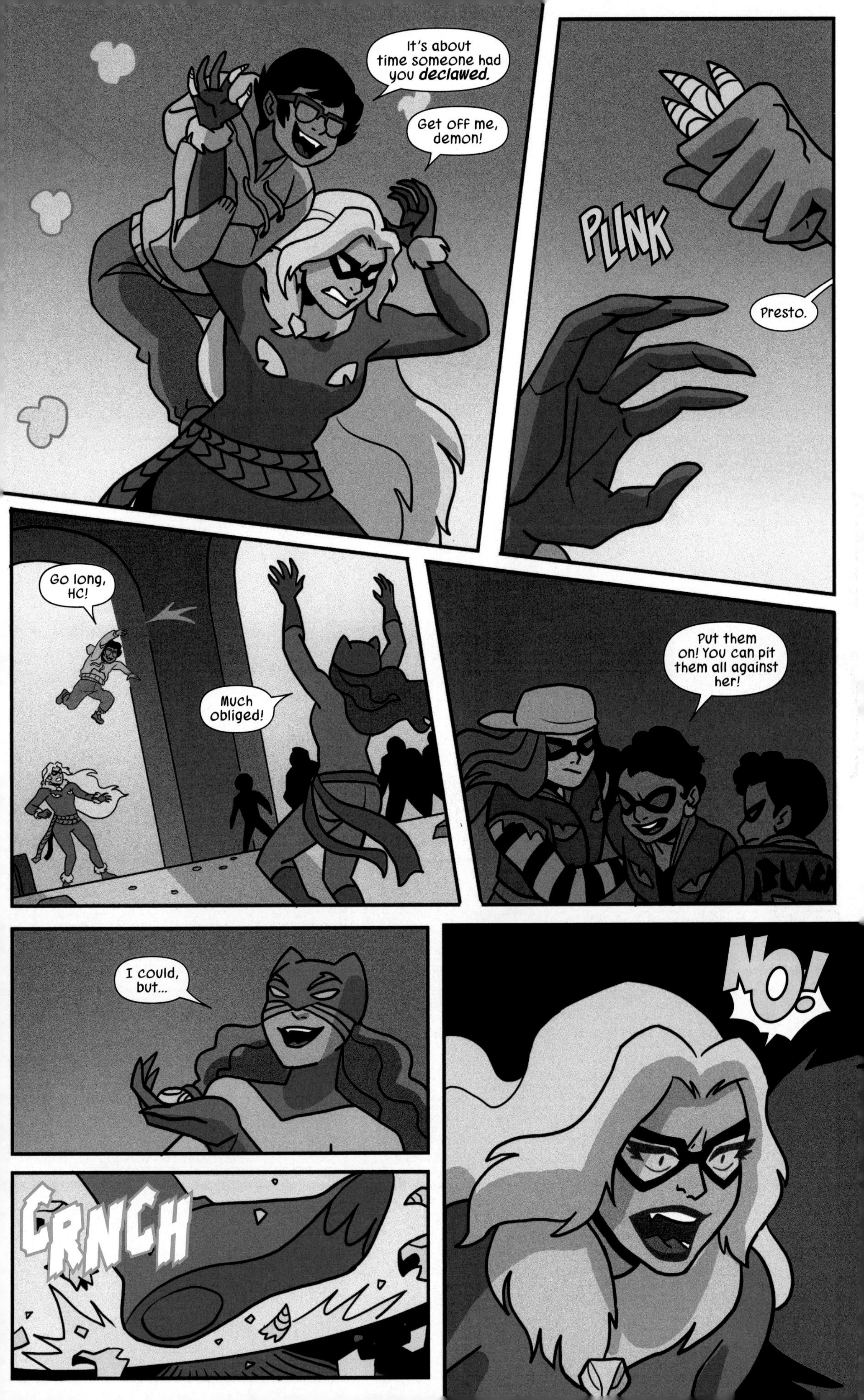

It's about time someone had you declawed.
Get off me, demon!
PLINK
Presto.
Go long, HC!
Much obliged!
Put them on! You can pit them all against her!
I could, but...
CRNCH
NO!

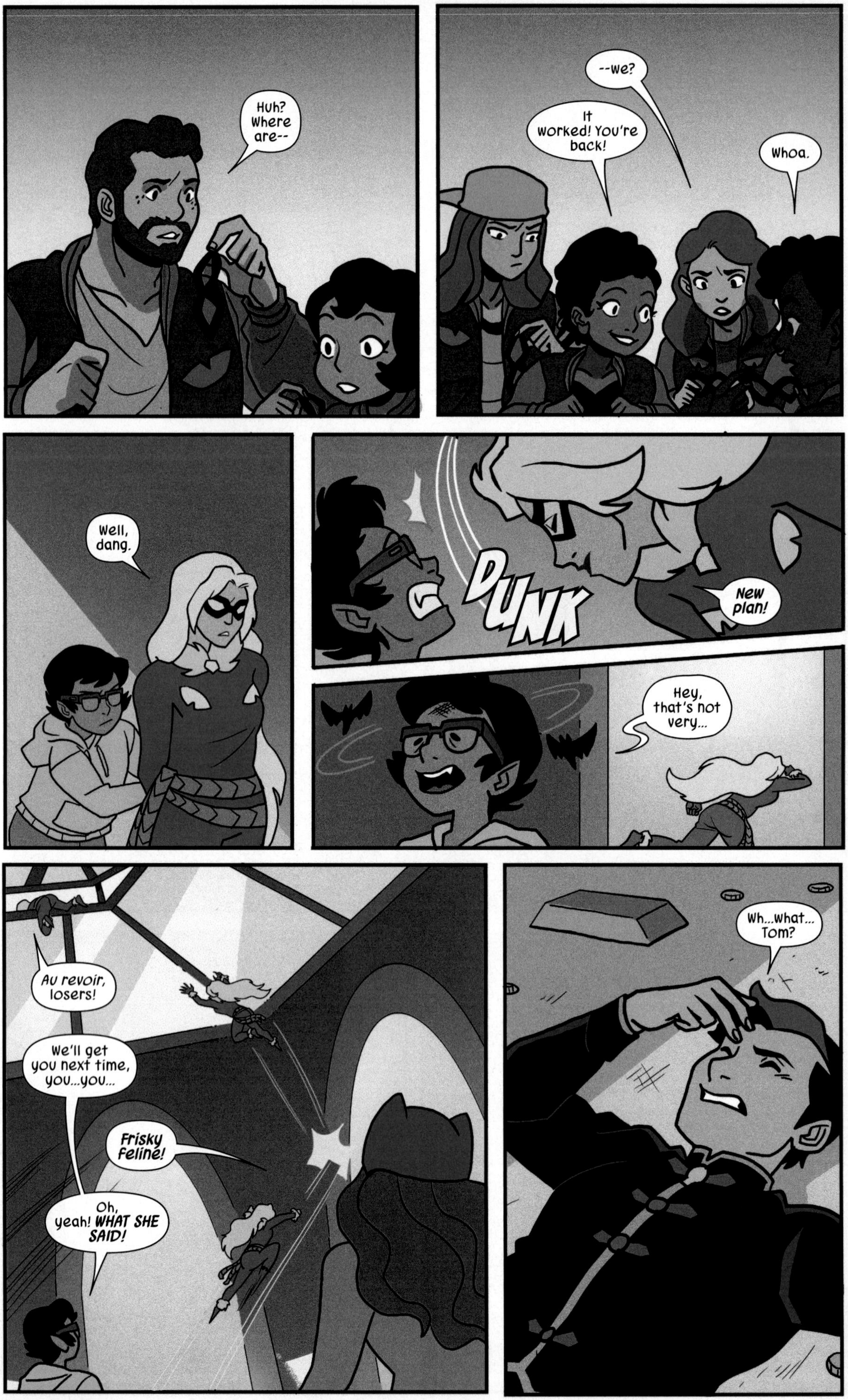

Huh? Where are--
It worked! You're back!
--we?
Whoa.
Well, dang.
DUNK
New plan!
Hey, that's not very...
Au revoir, losers!
We'll get you next time, you...you...
Frisky Feline!
Oh, yeah! WHAT SHE SAID!
Wh...what... Tom?

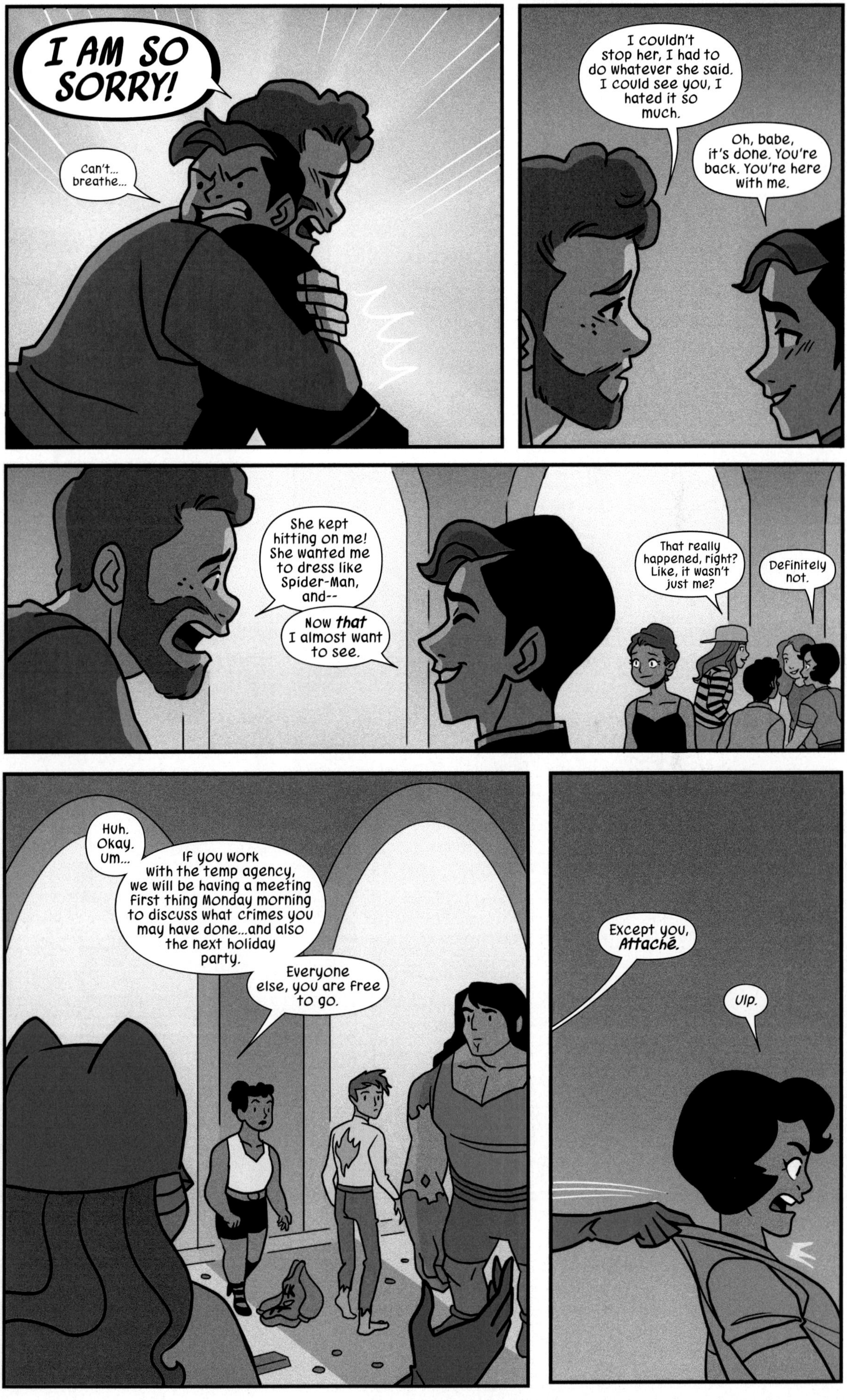
I AM SO SORRY!
Can't... breathe...
I couldn't stop her, I had to do whatever she said. I could see you, I hated it so much.
Oh, babe, it's done. You're back. You're here with me.
She kept hitting on me! She wanted me to dress like Spider-Man, and--
Now *that* I almost want to see.
That really happened, right? Like, it wasn't just me?
Definitely not.
Huh. Okay. Um...
If you work with the temp agency, we will be having a meeting first thing Monday morning to discuss what crimes you may have done...and also the next holiday party.
Everyone else, you are free to go.
Except you, *Attaché.*
Ulp.

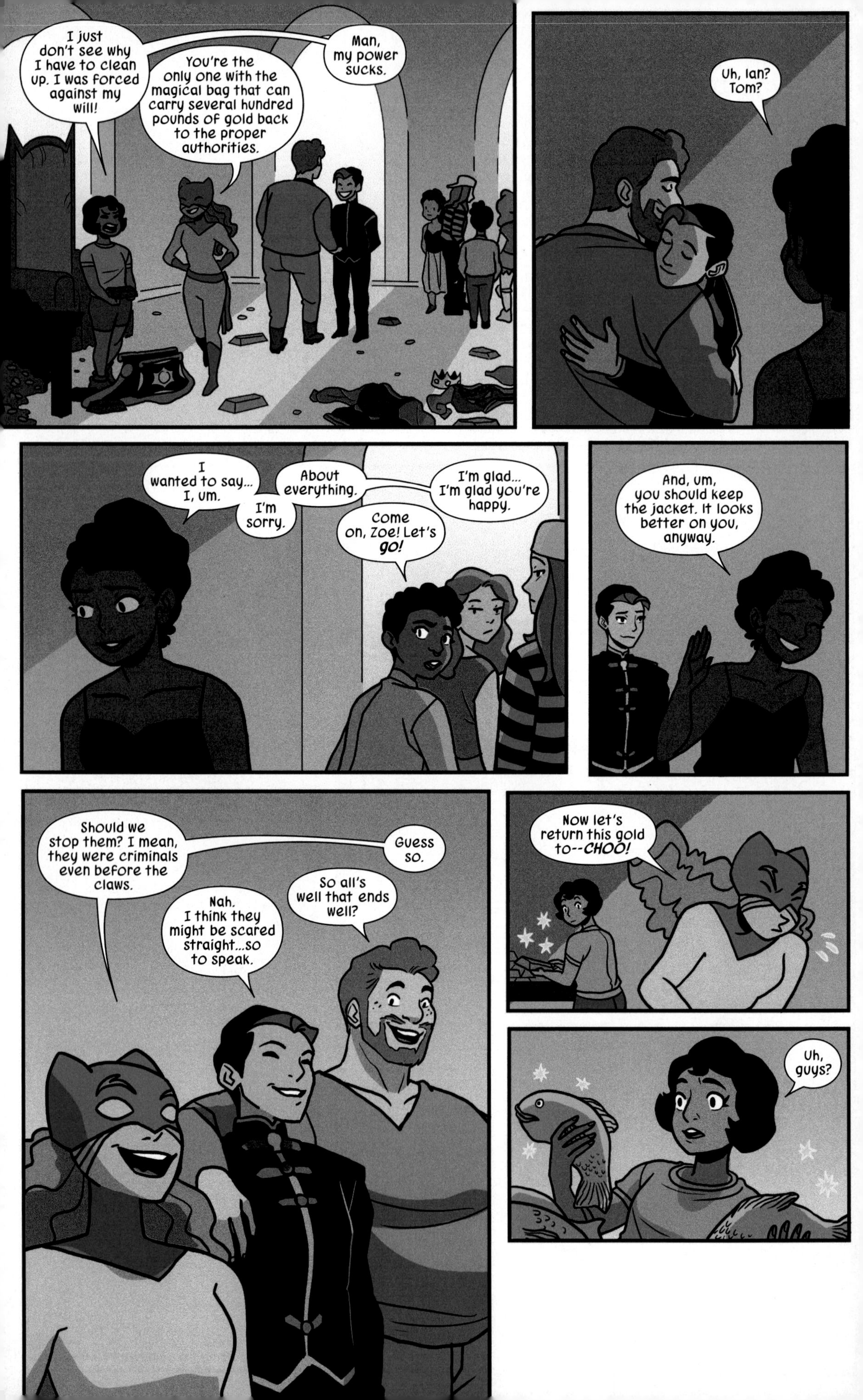
I just don't see why I have to clean up. I was forced against my will!
You're the only one with the magical bag that can carry several hundred pounds of gold back to the proper authorities.
Man, my power sucks.
Uh, Ian? Tom?
I wanted to say... I, um.
I'm sorry.
About everything.
I'm glad... I'm glad you're happy.
Come on, Zoe! Let's **go!**
And, um, you should keep the jacket. It looks better on you, anyway.
Should we stop them? I mean, they were criminals even before the claws.
Guess so.
Nah. I think they might be scared straight...so to speak.
So all's well that ends well?
Now let's return this gold to--***CHOO!***
Uh, guys?

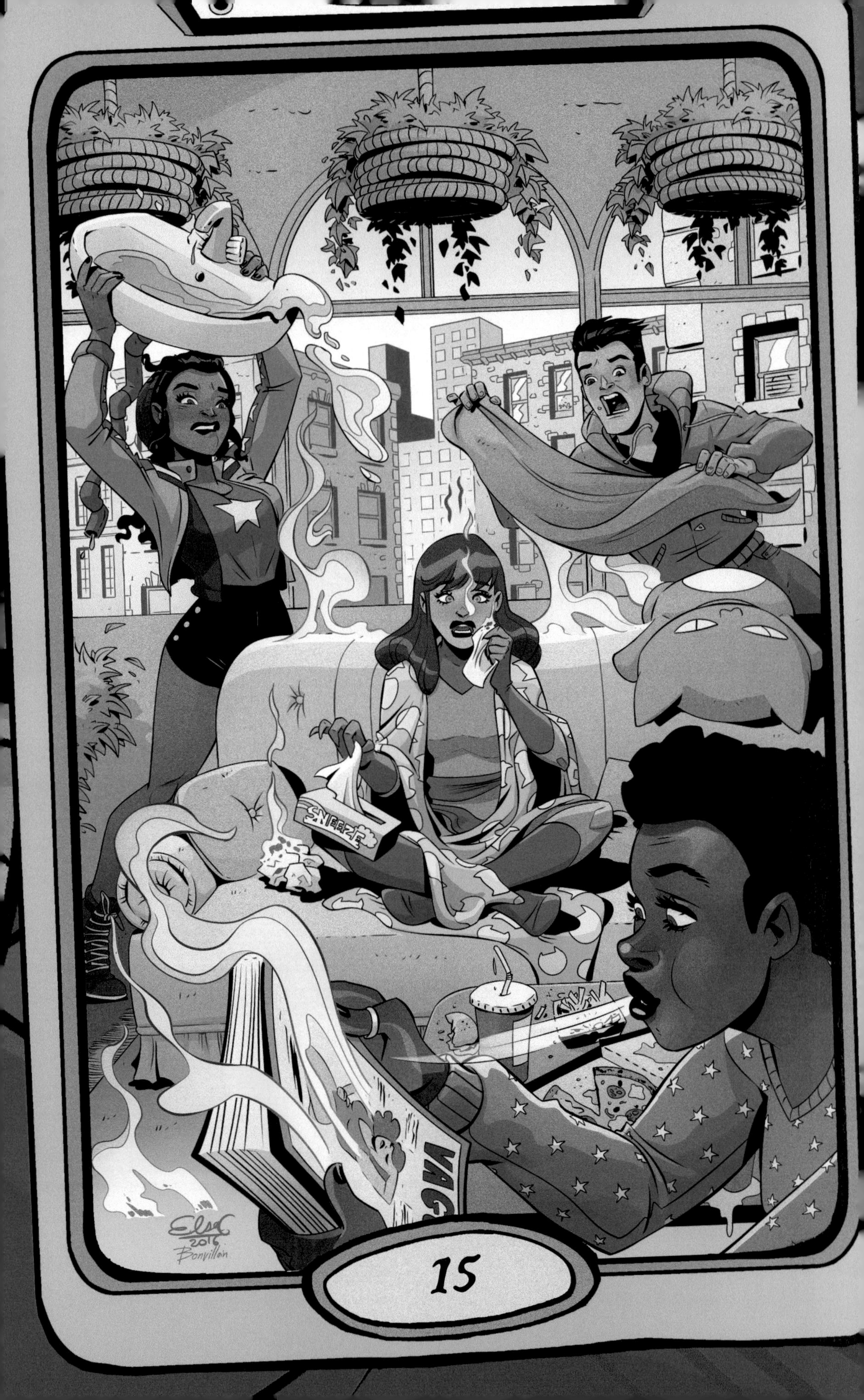

SNEEZE
Elsa 2016 Bonvillain
15

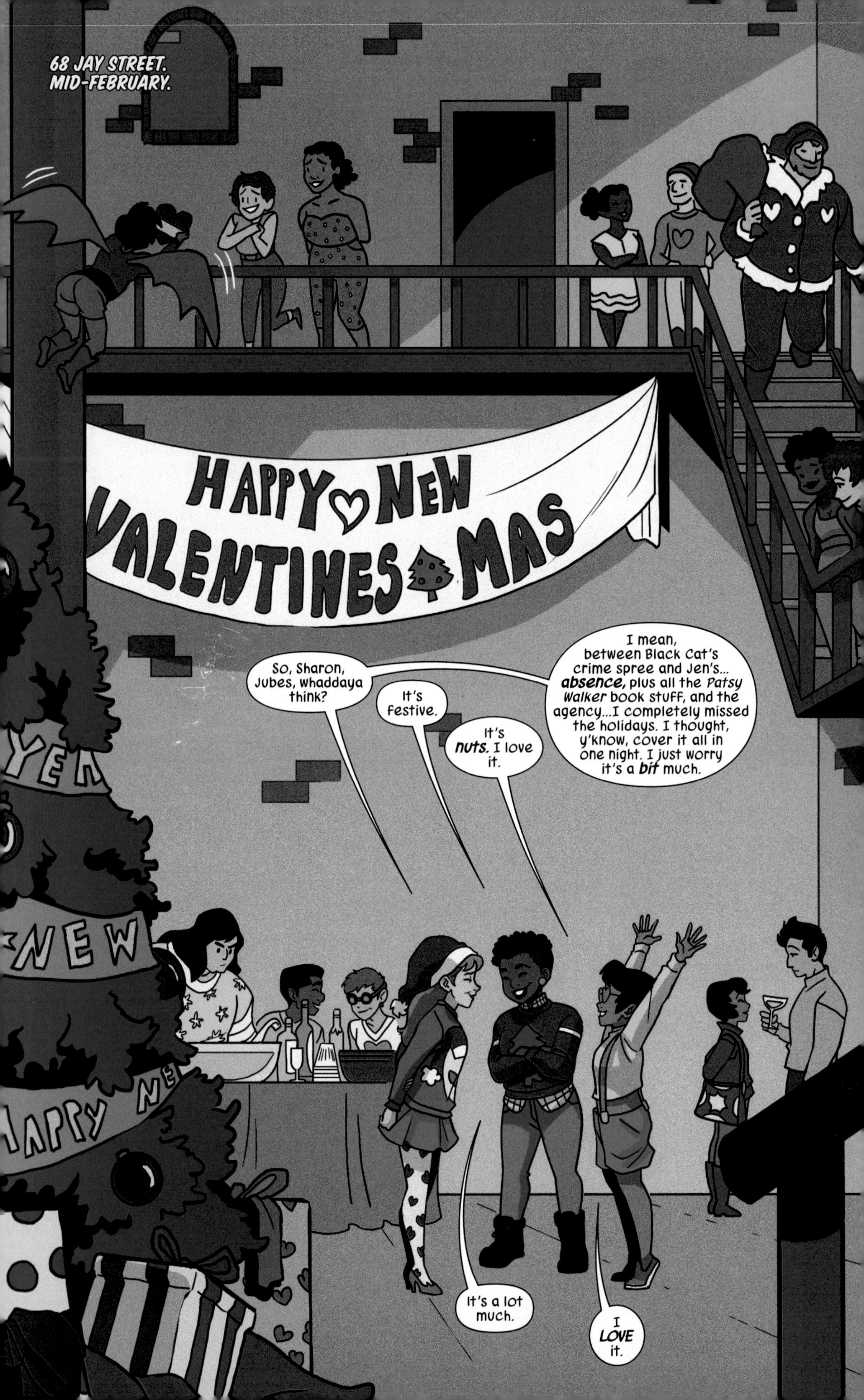
68 JAY STREET.
MID-FEBRUARY.
HAPPY NEW VALENTINES MAS
So, Sharon, Jubes, whaddaya think?
I mean, between Black Cat's crime spree and Jen's... **absence,** plus all the *Patsy Walker* book stuff, and the agency...I completely missed the holidays. I thought, y'know, cover it all in one night. I just worry it's a **bit** much.
It's festive.
It's **nuts.** I love it.
It's a lot much.
I **LOVE** it.
YEA
NEW
HAPPY NE

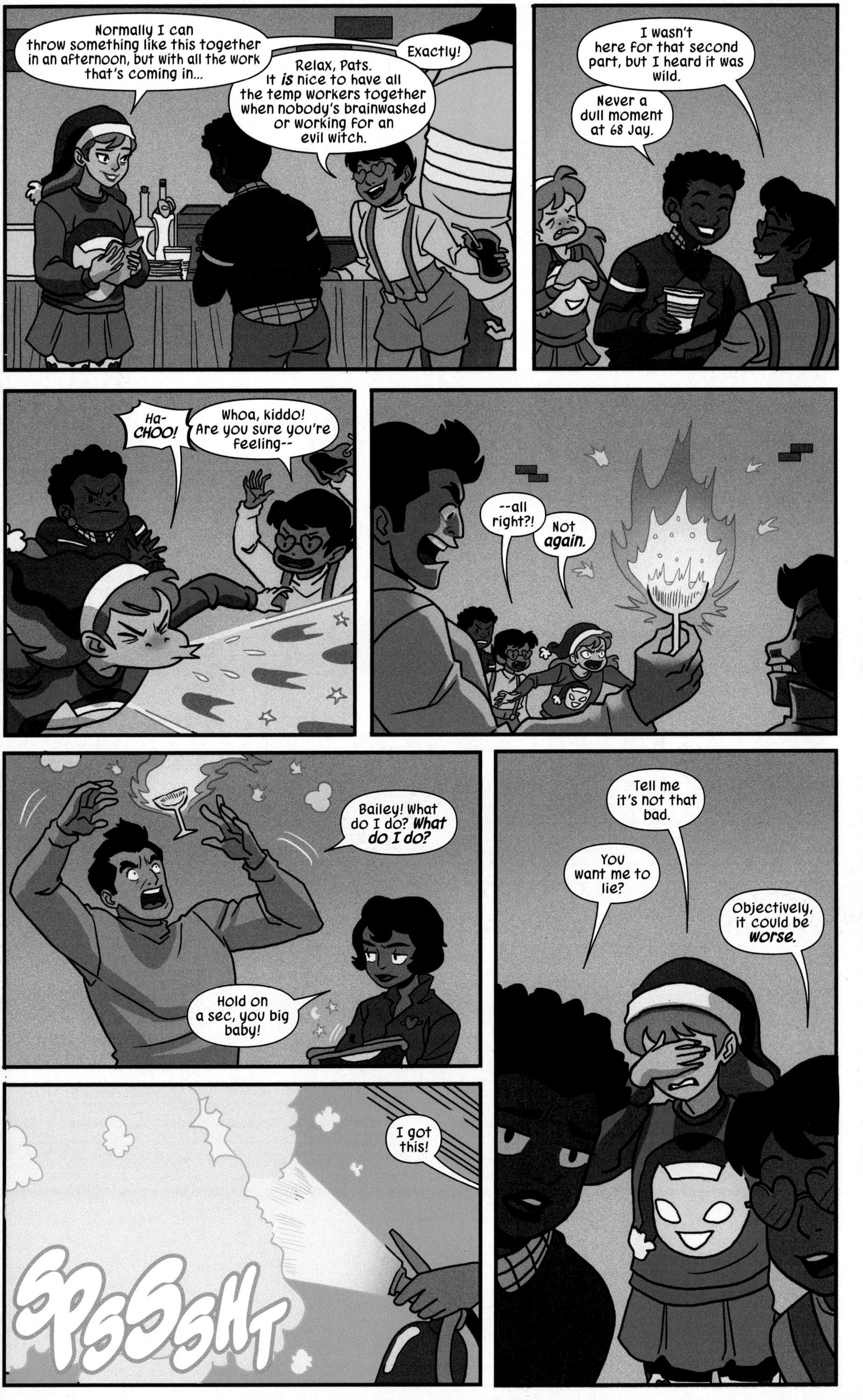

Normally I can throw something like this together in an afternoon, but with all the work that's coming in...
Exactly!
Relax, Pats. It *is* nice to have all the temp workers together when nobody's brainwashed or working for an evil witch.
I wasn't here for that second part, but I heard it was wild.
Never a dull moment at 68 Jay.
Ha-CHOO!
Whoa, kiddo! Are you sure you're feeling--
--all right?!
Not *again.*
Bailey! What do I do? *What do I do?*
Hold on a sec, you big baby!
I got this!
SPSSSHT
Tell me it's not that bad.
You want me to lie?
Objectively, it could be *worse.*

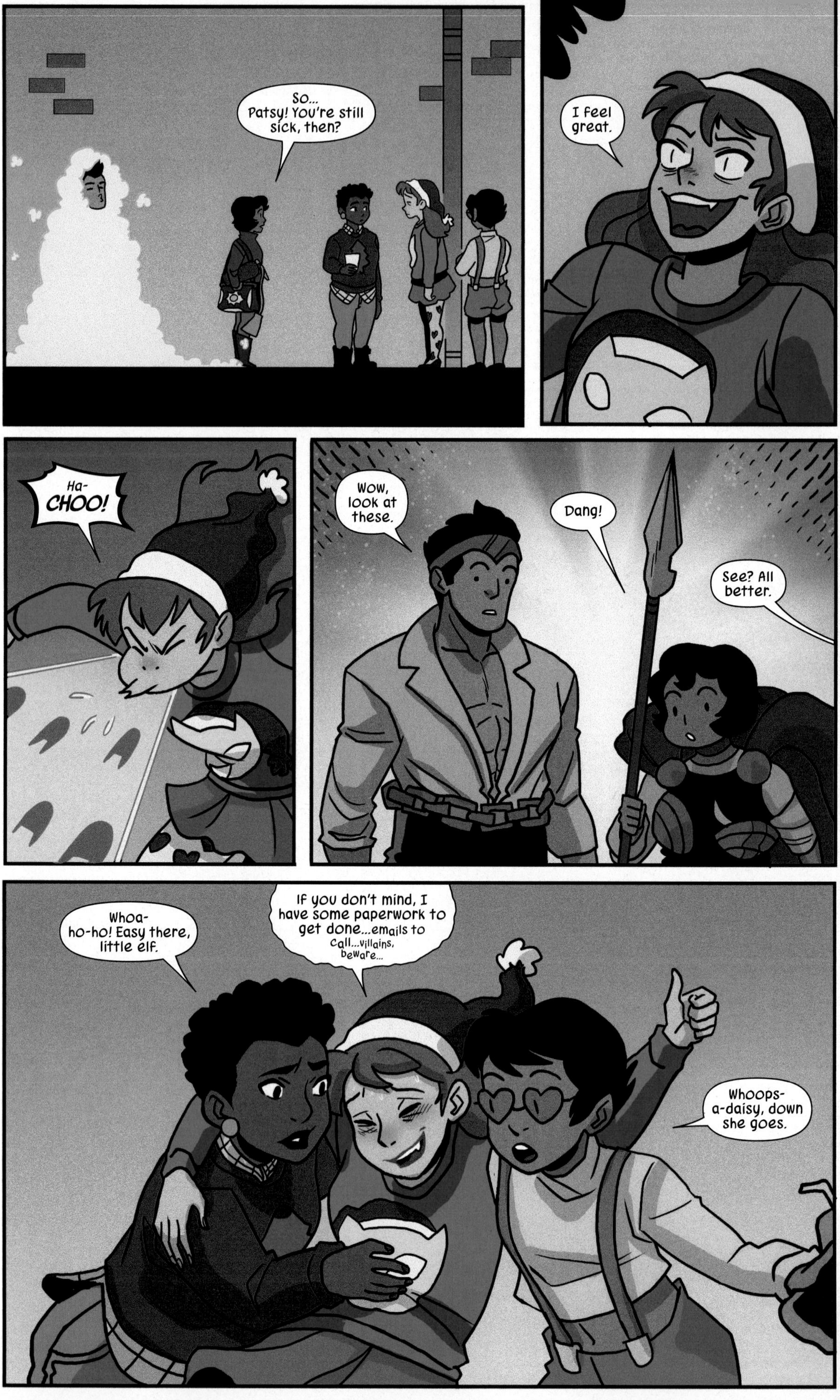
So... Patsy! You're still sick, then?
I feel great.
Ha- CHOO!
Wow, look at these.
Dang!
See? All better.
Whoa- ho-ho! Easy there, little elf.
If you don't mind, I have some paperwork to get done...emails to call...villains, beware...
Whoops- a-daisy, down she goes.

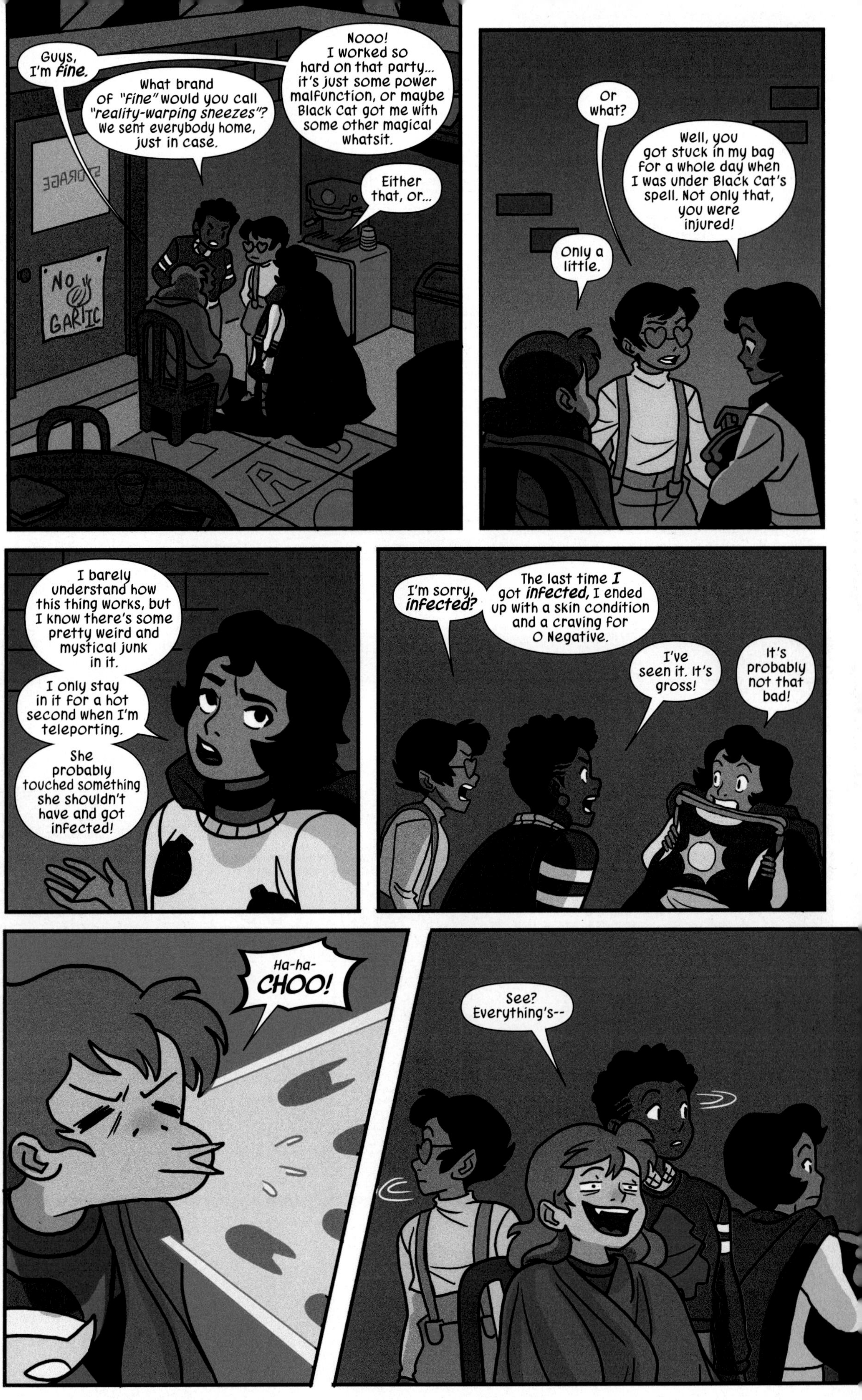
Guys, I'm fine.
What brand of "fine" would you call "reality-warping sneezes"? We sent everybody home, just in case.
Nooo! I worked so hard on that party... it's just some power malfunction, or maybe Black Cat got me with some other magical whatsit.
Either that, or...
STORAGE
No GARLIC
Or what?
Well, you got stuck in my bag for a whole day when I was under Black Cat's spell. Not only that, you were injured!
Only a little.
I barely understand how this thing works, but I know there's some pretty weird and mystical junk in it.
I only stay in it for a hot second when I'm teleporting.
She probably touched something she shouldn't have and got infected!
I'm sorry, infected?
The last time I got infected, I ended up with a skin condition and a craving for O Negative.
I've seen it. It's gross!
It's probably not that bad!
Ha-ha-CHOO!
See? Everything's--

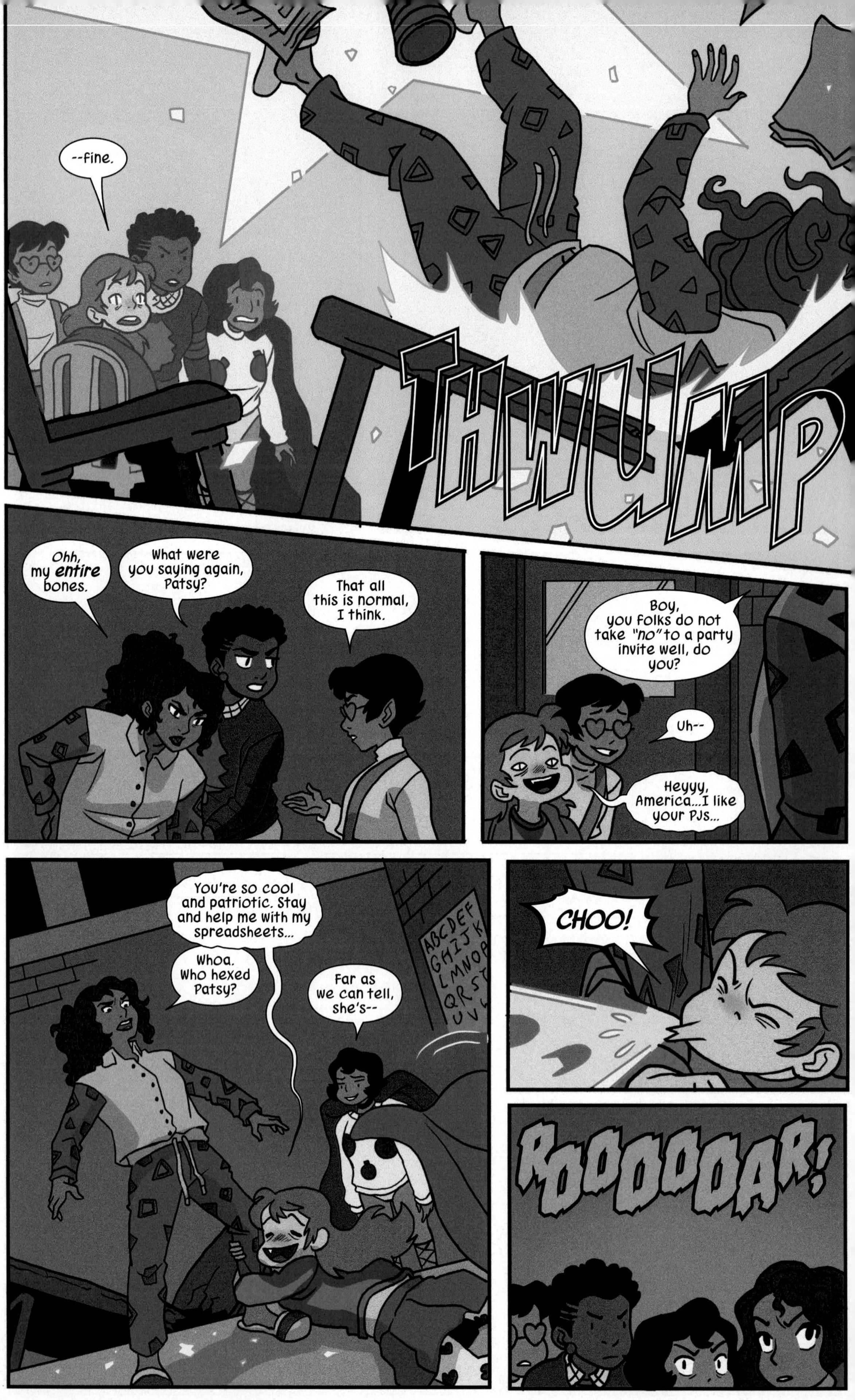
--fine.
THWUMP
Ohh, my entire bones.
What were you saying again, Patsy?
That all this is normal, I think.
Boy, you folks do not take "no" to a party invite well, do you?
Uh--
Heyyy, America...I like your PJs...
You're so cool and patriotic. Stay and help me with my spreadsheets...
Whoa. Who hexed Patsy?
Far as we can tell, she's--
CHOO!
ROOOOOAR!

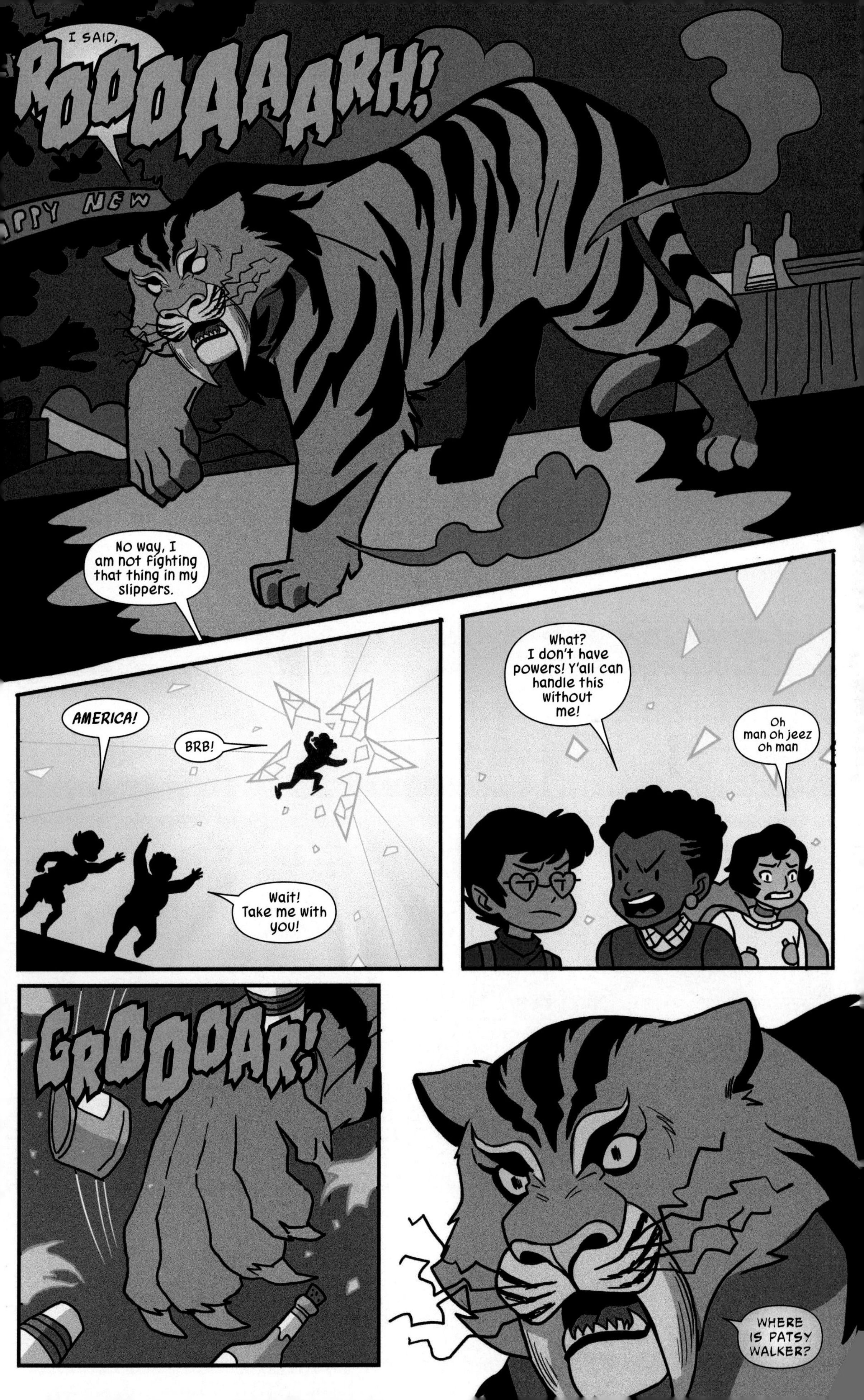
I SAID,
ROOOAAAARH!
APPY NEW
No way, I am not fighting that thing in my slippers.
AMERICA!
BRB!
Wait! Take me with you!
What? I don't have powers! Y'all can handle this without me!
Oh man oh jeez oh man
GROOOAR!
WHERE IS PATSY WALKER?

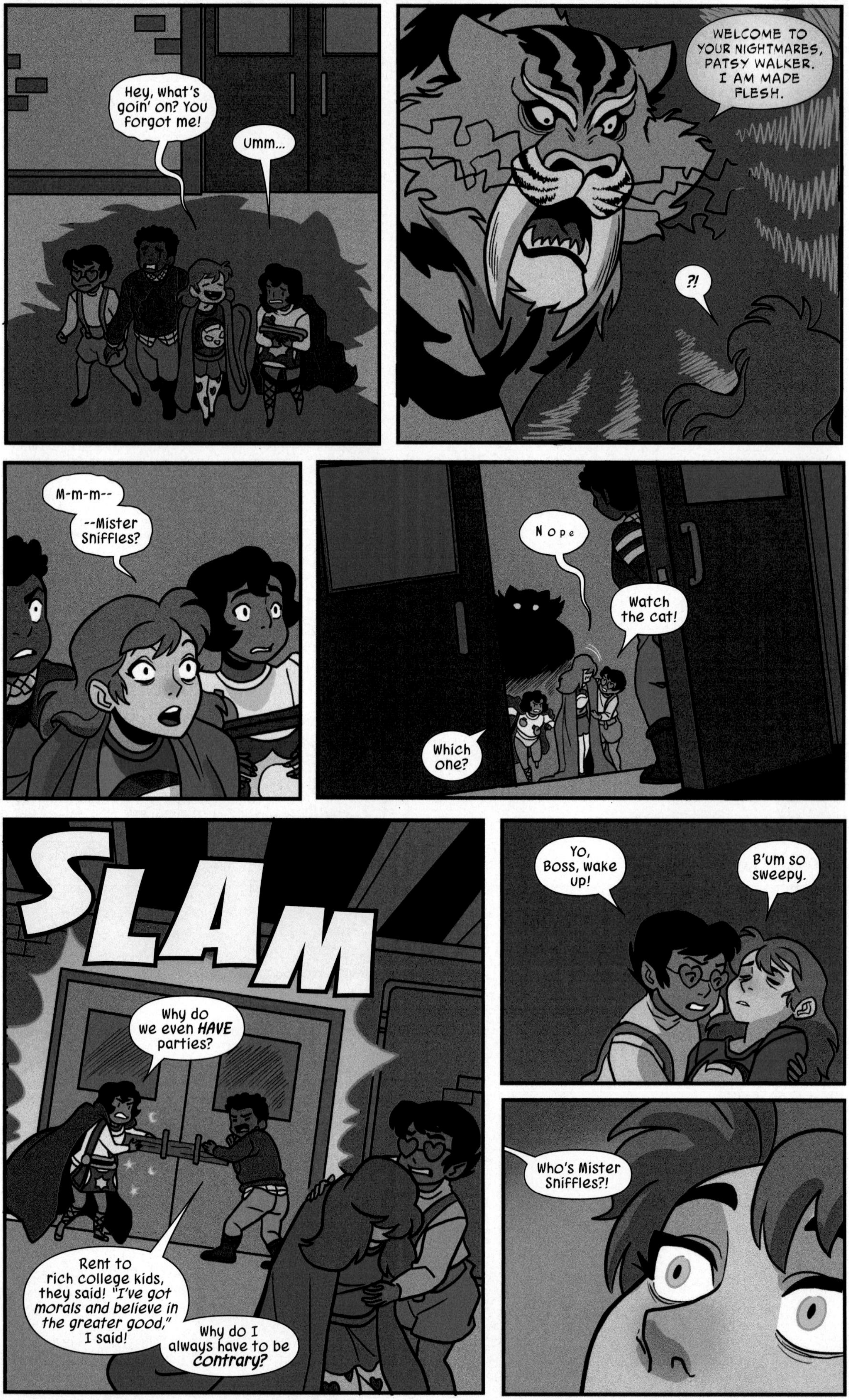
Hey, what's goin' on? You forgot me!
Umm...
WELCOME TO YOUR NIGHTMARES, PATSY WALKER. I AM MADE FLESH.
?!
M-m-m--
--Mister Sniffles?
Nope
Watch the cat!
Which one?
SLAM
Why do we even HAVE parties?
Rent to rich college kids, they said! "I've got morals and believe in the greater good," I said!
Why do I always have to be contrary?
Yo, Boss, wake up!
B'um so sweepy.
Who's Mister Sniffles?!

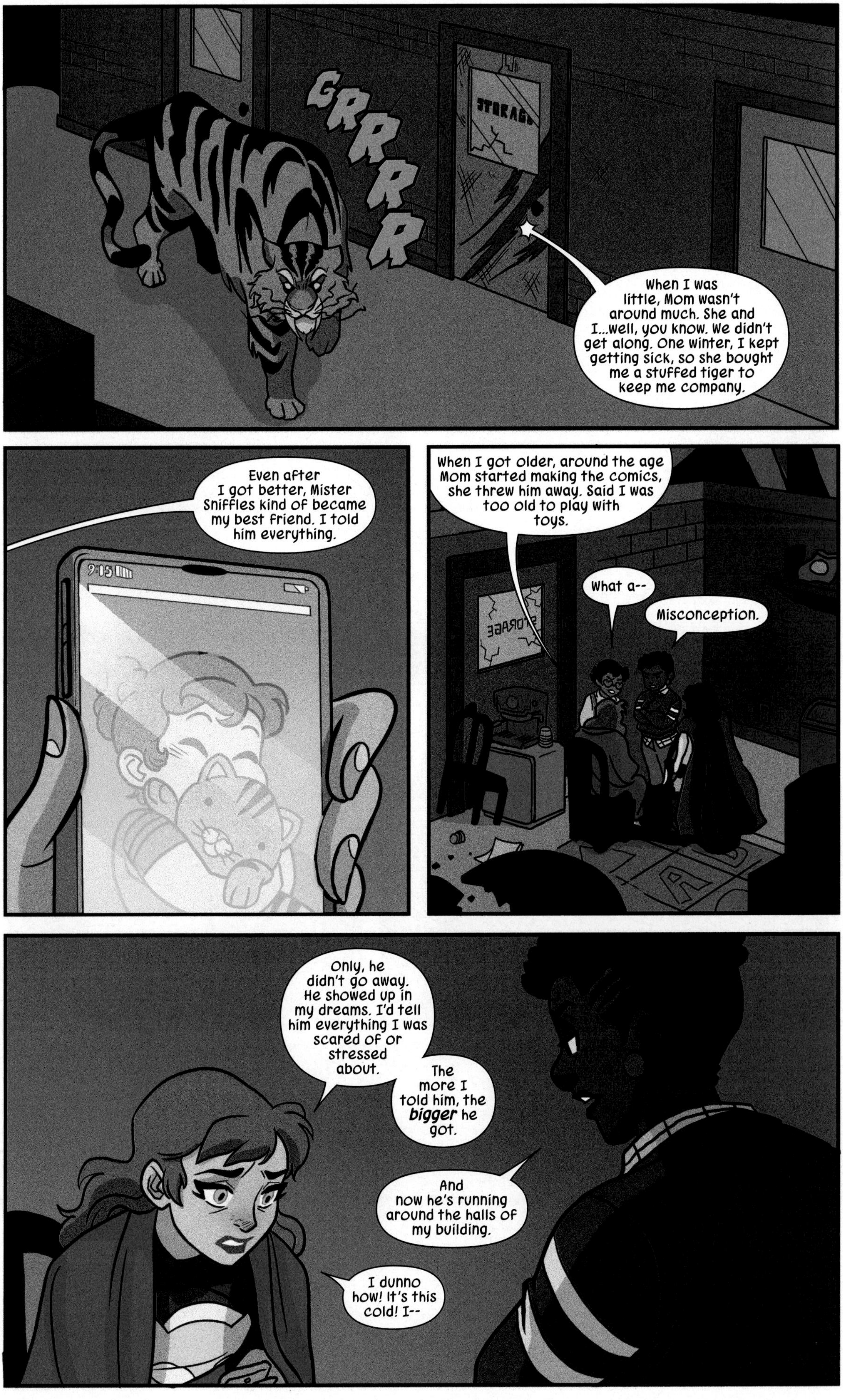
GRRRR
STORAGE
When I was little, Mom wasn't around much. She and I...well, you know. We didn't get along. One winter, I kept getting sick, so she bought me a stuffed tiger to keep me company.
Even after I got better, Mister Sniffles kind of became my best friend. I told him everything.
9:15
When I got older, around the age Mom started making the comics, she threw him away. Said I was too old to play with toys.
STORAGE
What a--
Misconception.
Only, he didn't go away. He showed up in my dreams. I'd tell him everything I was scared of or stressed about.
The more I told him, the *bigger* he got.
And now he's running around the halls of my building.
I dunno how! It's this cold! I--

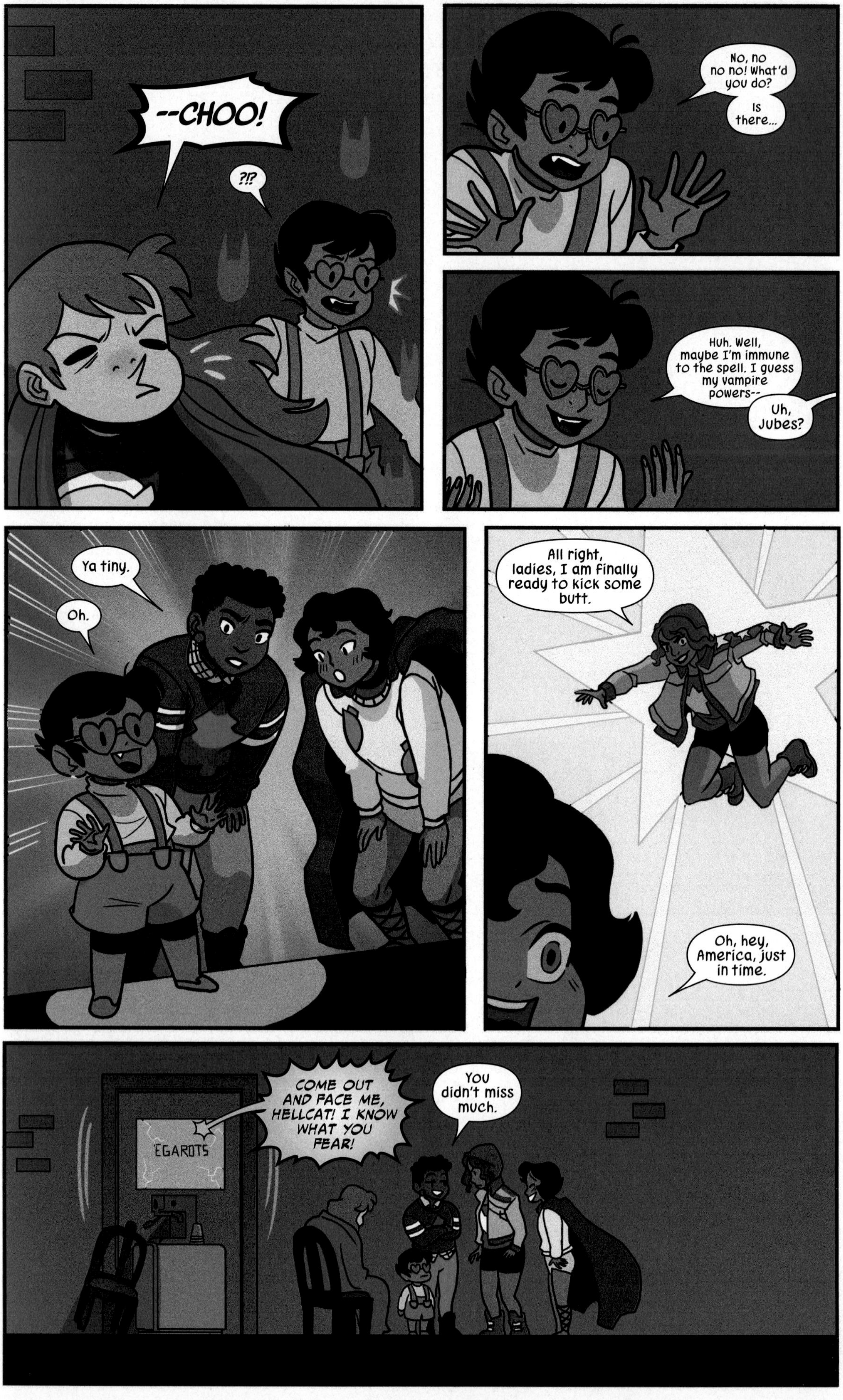
--CHOO!
?!?
No, no no no! What'd you do?
Is there...
Huh. Well, maybe I'm immune to the spell. I guess my vampire powers--
Uh, Jubes?
Ya tiny.
Oh.
All right, ladies, I am finally ready to kick some butt.
Oh, hey, America, just in time.
COME OUT AND FACE ME, HELLCAT! I KNOW WHAT YOU FEAR!
EGAROTS
You didn't miss much.

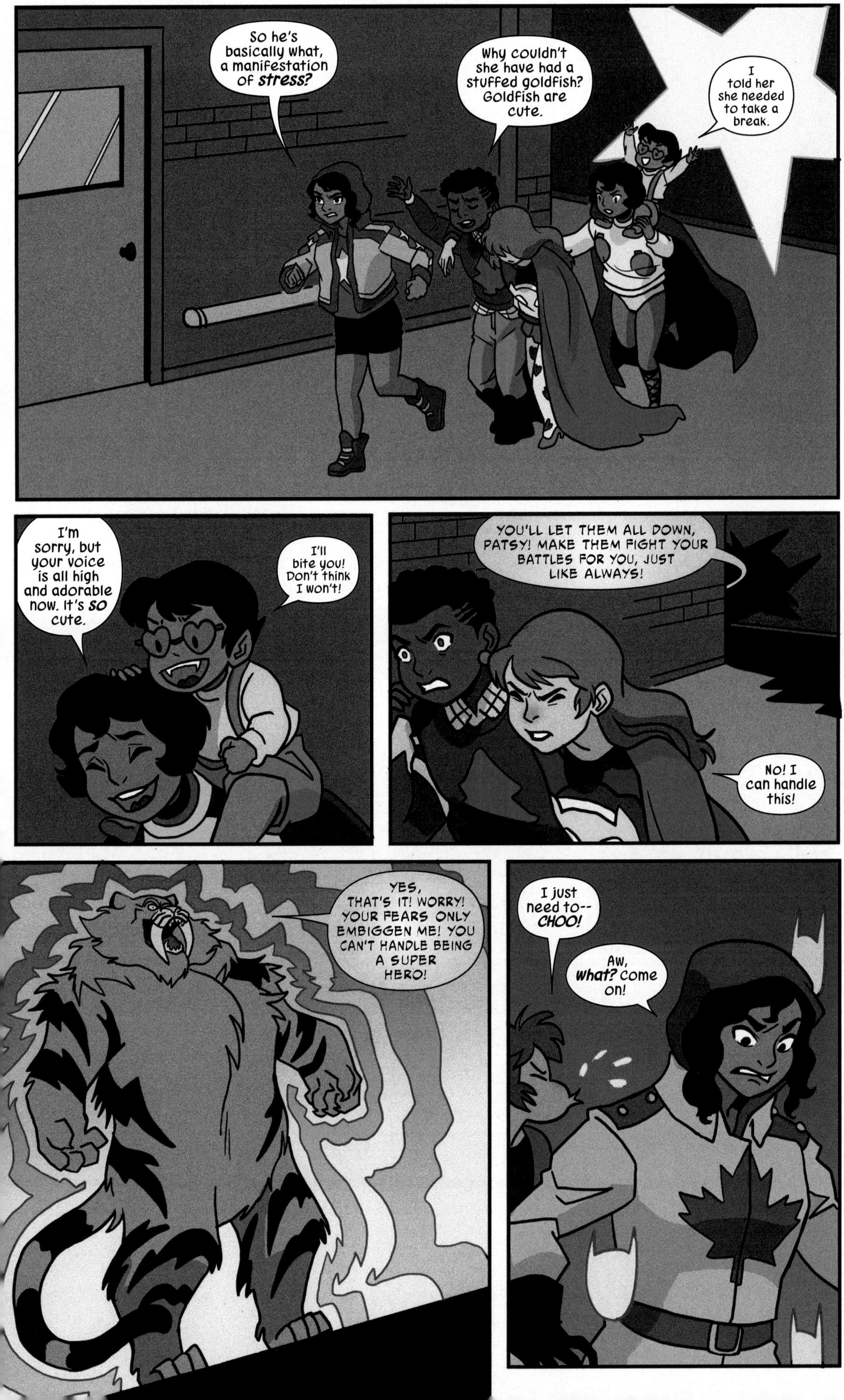
So he's basically what, a manifestation of ***stress?***
Why couldn't she have had a stuffed goldfish? Goldfish are cute.
I told her she needed to take a break.
I'm sorry, but your voice is all high and adorable now. It's ***SO*** cute.
I'll bite you! Don't think I won't!
YOU'LL LET THEM ALL DOWN, PATSY! MAKE THEM FIGHT YOUR BATTLES FOR YOU, JUST LIKE ALWAYS!
No! I can handle this!
YES, THAT'S IT! WORRY! YOUR FEARS ONLY EMBIGGEN ME! YOU CAN'T HANDLE BEING A SUPER HERO!
I just need to-- ***CHOO!***
Aw, ***what?*** Come on!

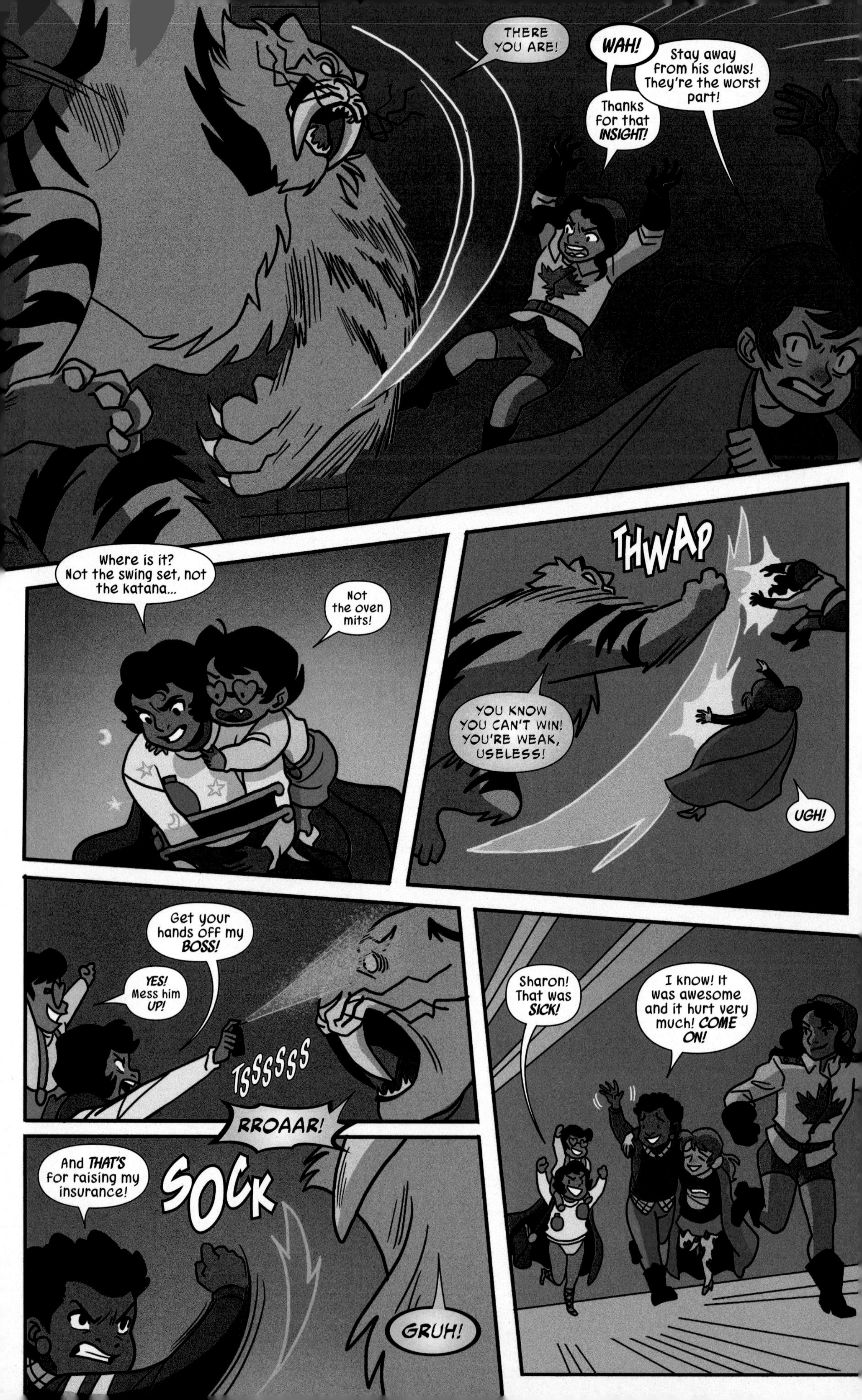
THERE YOU ARE!
WAH!
Thanks for that INSIGHT!
Stay away from his claws! They're the worst part!
Where is it? Not the swing set, not the katana...
Not the oven mits!
THWAP
YOU KNOW YOU CAN'T WIN! YOU'RE WEAK, USELESS!
UGH!
Get your hands off my BOSS!
YES! Mess him UP!
TSSSSSS
RROAAR!
And THAT'S for raising my insurance!
SOCK
GRUH!
Sharon! That was SICK!
I know! It was awesome and it hurt very much! COME ON!

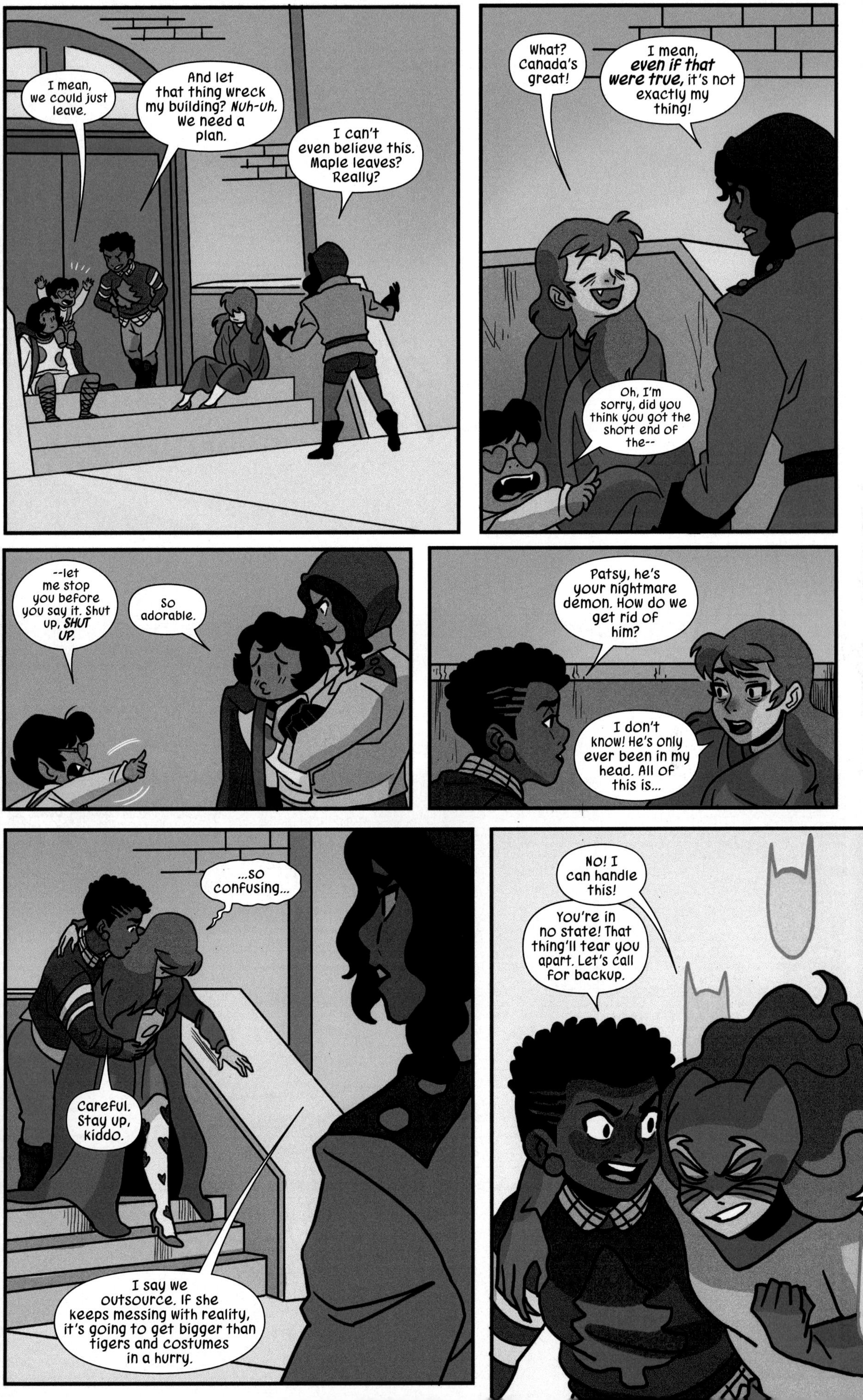
I mean, we could just leave.
And let that thing wreck my building? Nuh-Uh. We need a plan.
I can't even believe this. Maple leaves? Really?
What? Canada's great!
I mean, even if that were true, it's not exactly my thing!
Oh, I'm sorry, did you think you got the short end of the--
--let me stop you before you say it. Shut up, SHUT UP.
So adorable.
Patsy, he's your nightmare demon. How do we get rid of him?
I don't know! He's only ever been in my head. All of this is...
...so confusing...
Careful. Stay up, kiddo.
I say we outsource. If she keeps messing with reality, it's going to get bigger than tigers and costumes in a hurry.
No! I can handle this!
You're in no state! That thing'll tear you apart. Let's call for backup.

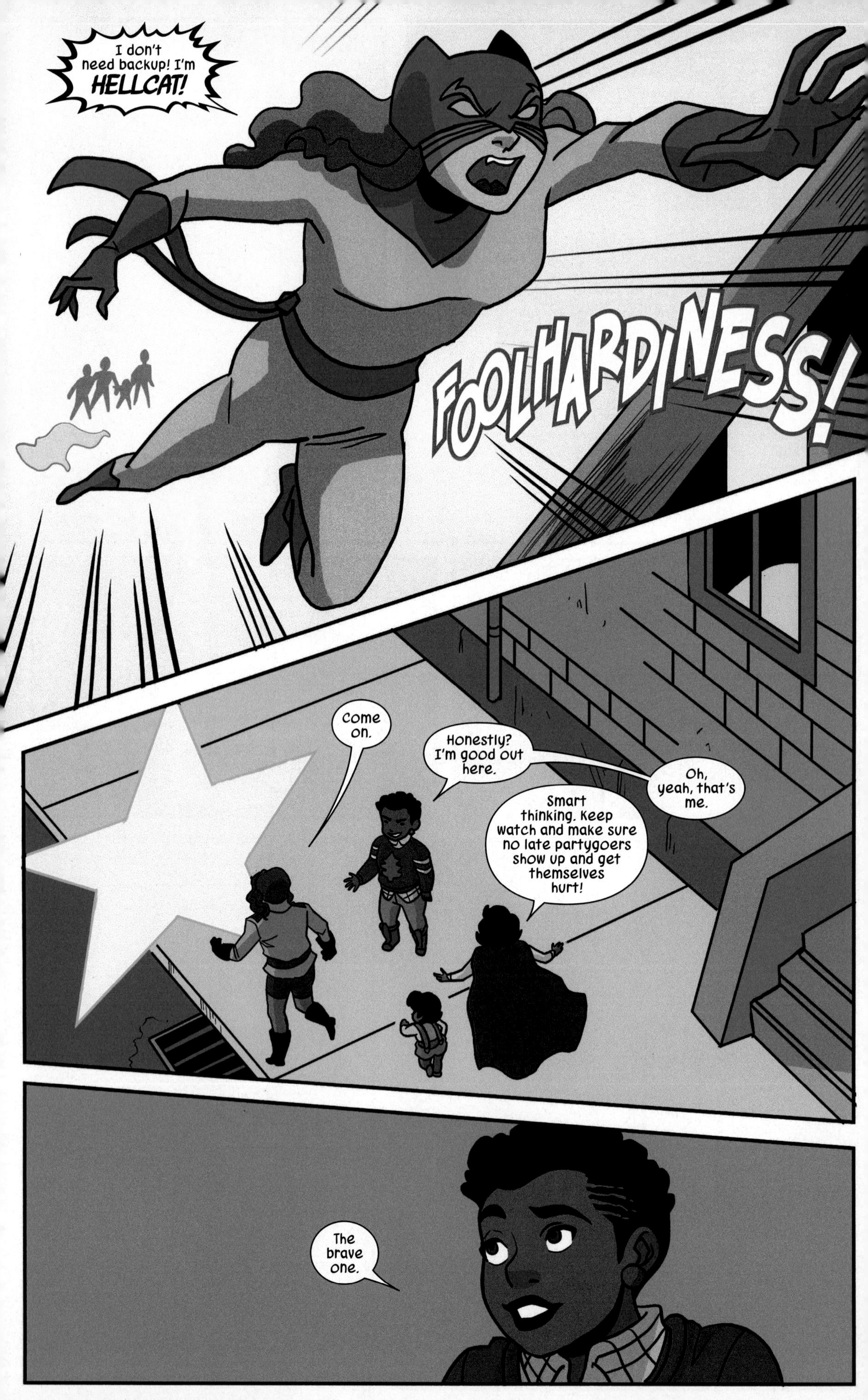

I don't need backup! I'm HELLCAT!
FOOLHARDINESS!
Come on.
Honestly? I'm good out here.
Oh, yeah, that's me.
Smart thinking. Keep watch and make sure no late partygoers show up and get themselves hurt!
The brave one.

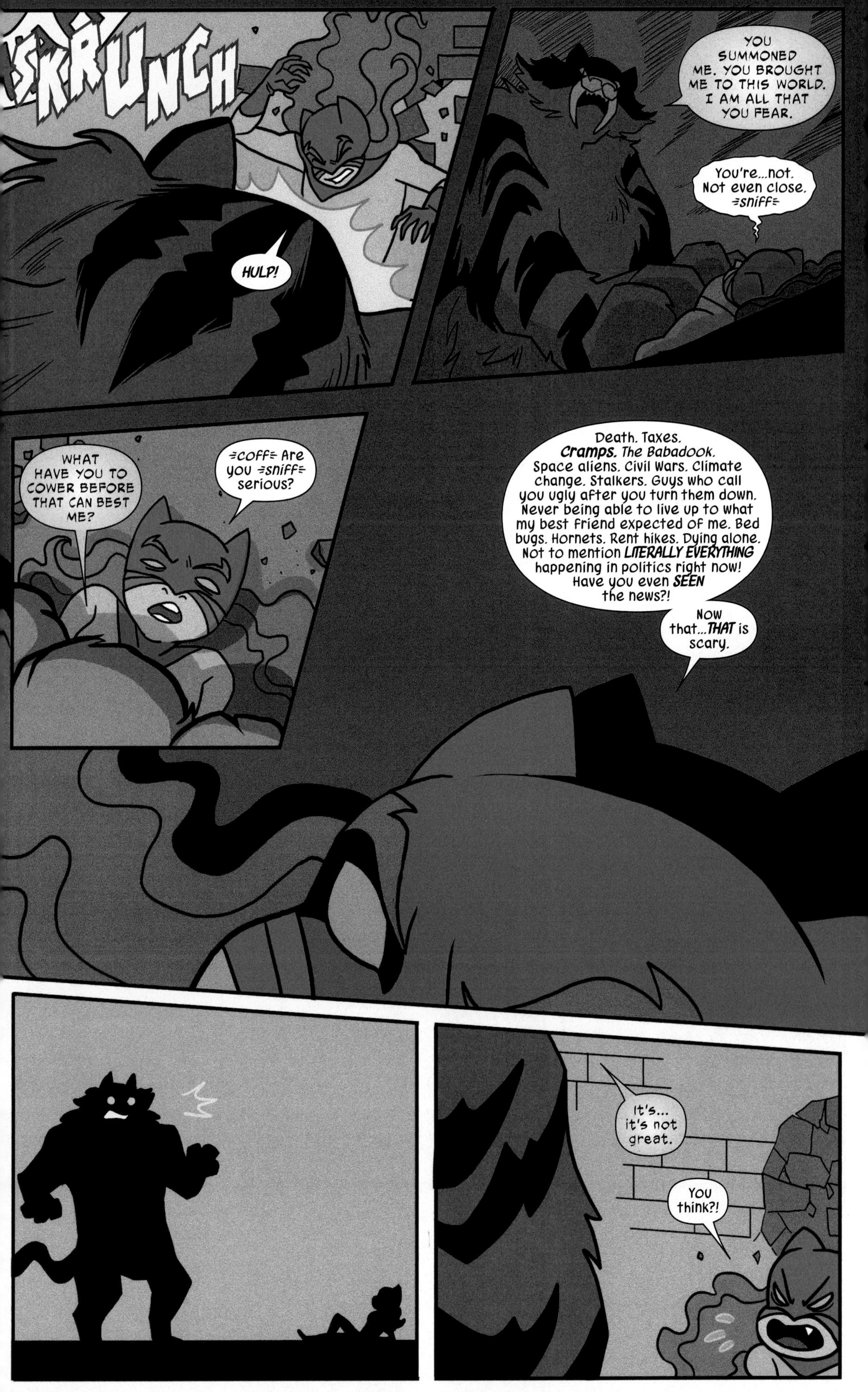
SKRUNCH
HULP!
YOU SUMMONED ME. YOU BROUGHT ME TO THIS WORLD. I AM ALL THAT YOU FEAR.
You're...not. Not even close. =sniff=
WHAT HAVE YOU TO COWER BEFORE THAT CAN BEST ME?
=COFF= Are you =sniff= serious?
Death. Taxes. Cramps. The Babadook. Space aliens. Civil Wars. Climate change. Stalkers. Guys who call you ugly after you turn them down. Never being able to live up to what my best friend expected of me. Bed bugs. Hornets. Rent hikes. Dying alone. Not to mention LITERALLY EVERYTHING happening in politics right now! Have you even SEEN the news?!
Now that...THAT is scary.
It's... it's not great.
You think?!

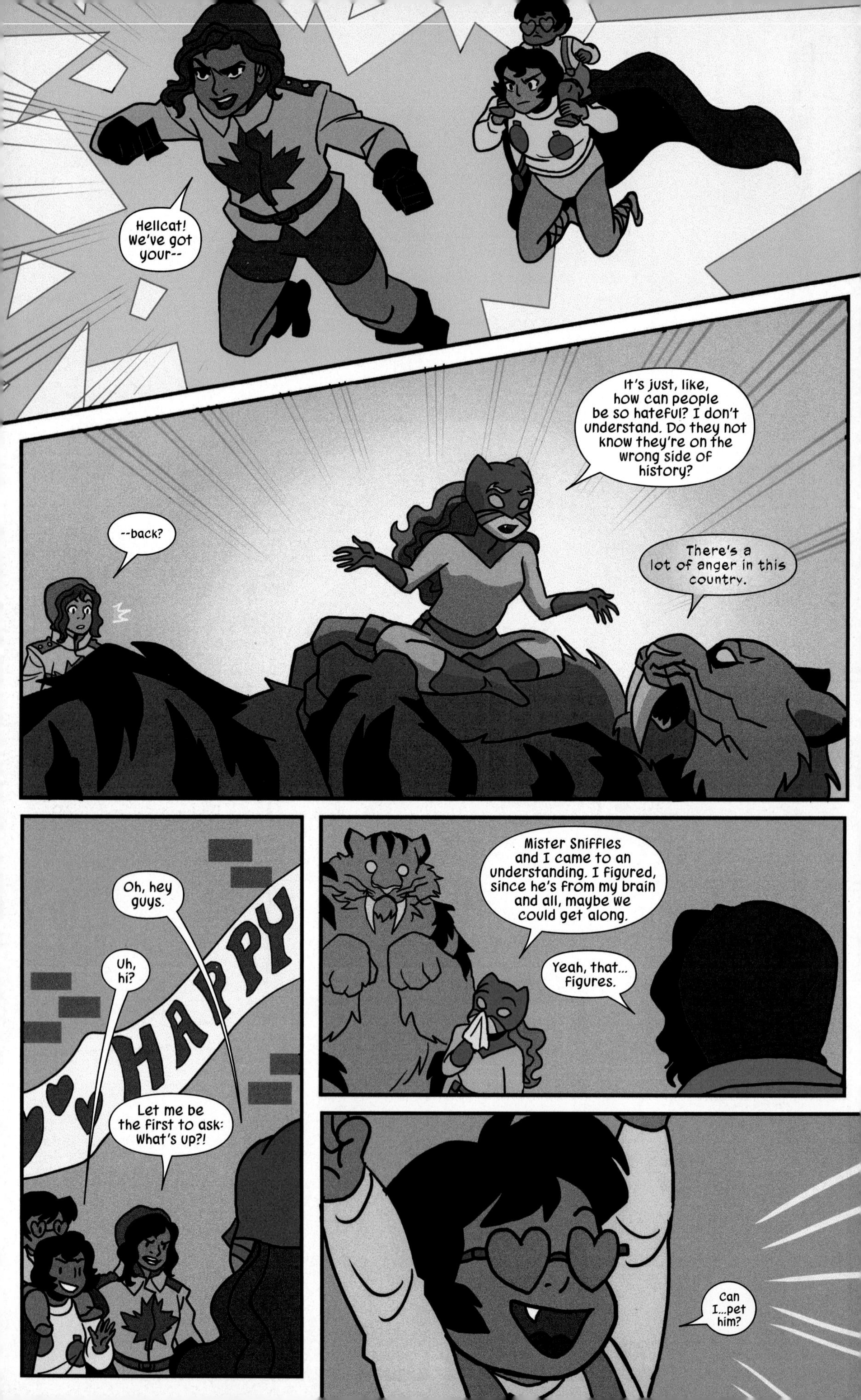
Hellcat! We've got your--
--back?
It's just, like, how can people be so hateful? I don't understand. Do they not know they're on the wrong side of history?
There's a lot of anger in this country.
Oh, hey guys.
Uh, hi?
Let me be the first to ask: What's up?!
HAPPY
Mister Sniffles and I came to an understanding. I figured, since he's from my brain and all, maybe we could get along.
Yeah, that... figures.
Can I...pet him?

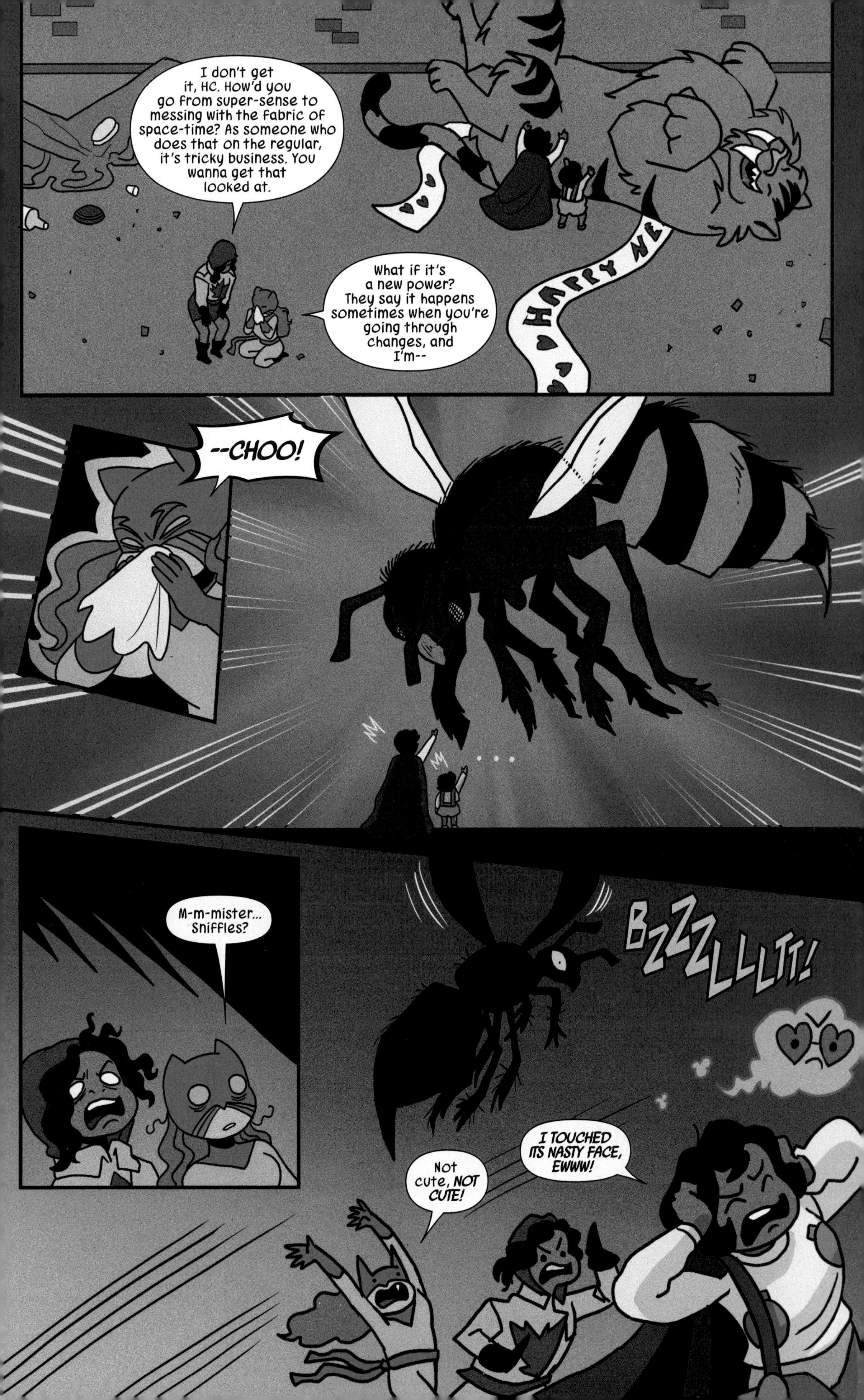
I don't get it, HC. How'd you go from super-sense to messing with the fabric of space-time? As someone who does that on the regular, it's tricky business. You wanna get that looked at.
What if it's a new power? They say it happens sometimes when you're going through changes, and I'm--
HAPPY NE
--CHOO!
M-m-mister... Sniffles?
BZZZLLLTT!
Not cute, NOT CUTE!
I TOUCHED ITS NASTY FACE, EWWW!

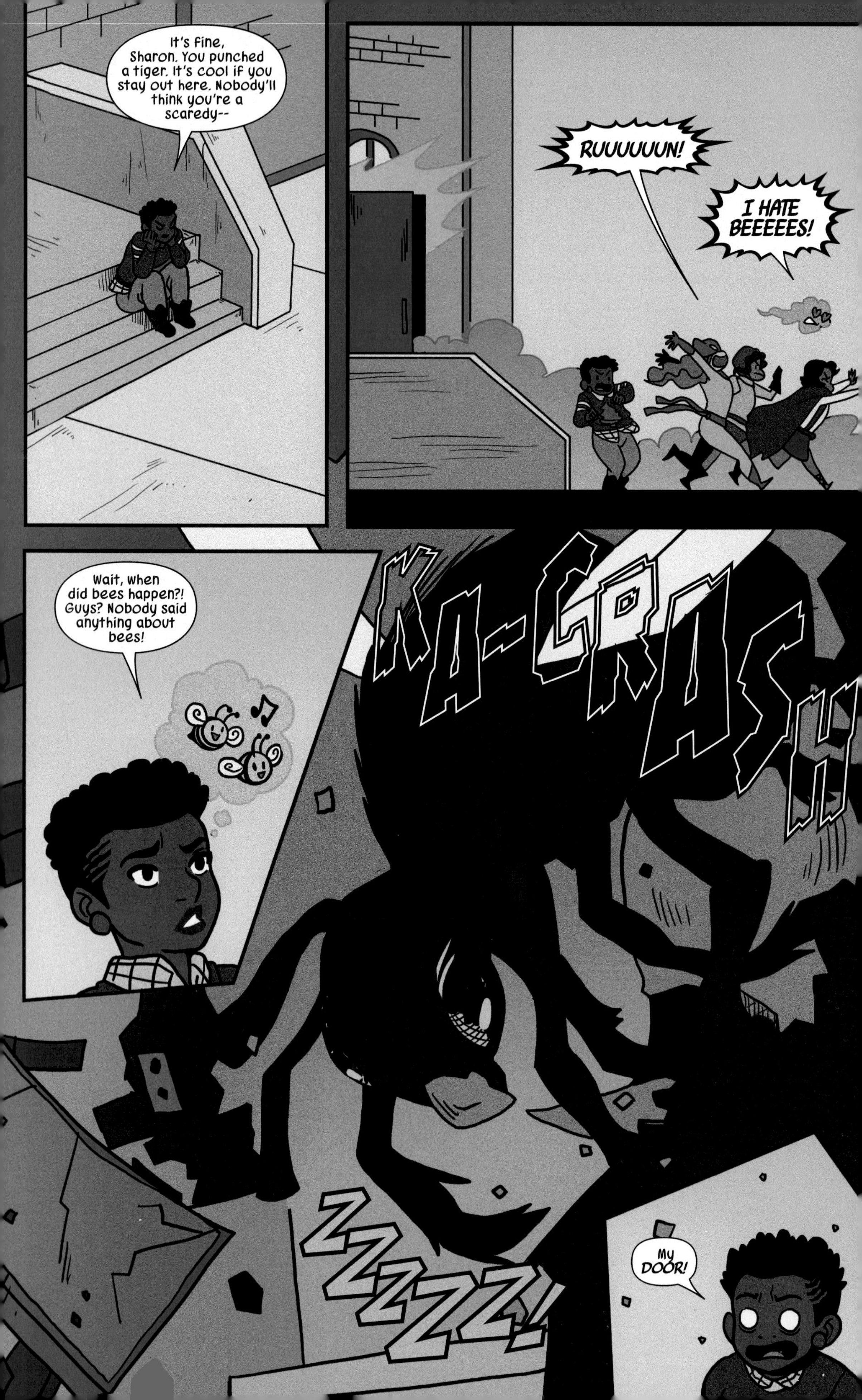
It's fine, Sharon. You punched a tiger. It's cool if you stay out here. Nobody'll think you're a scaredy--
RUUUUUUN!
I HATE BEEEEES!
Wait, when did bees happen?! Guys? Nobody said anything about bees!
KA-CRASH
ZZZZZ!
My DOOR!

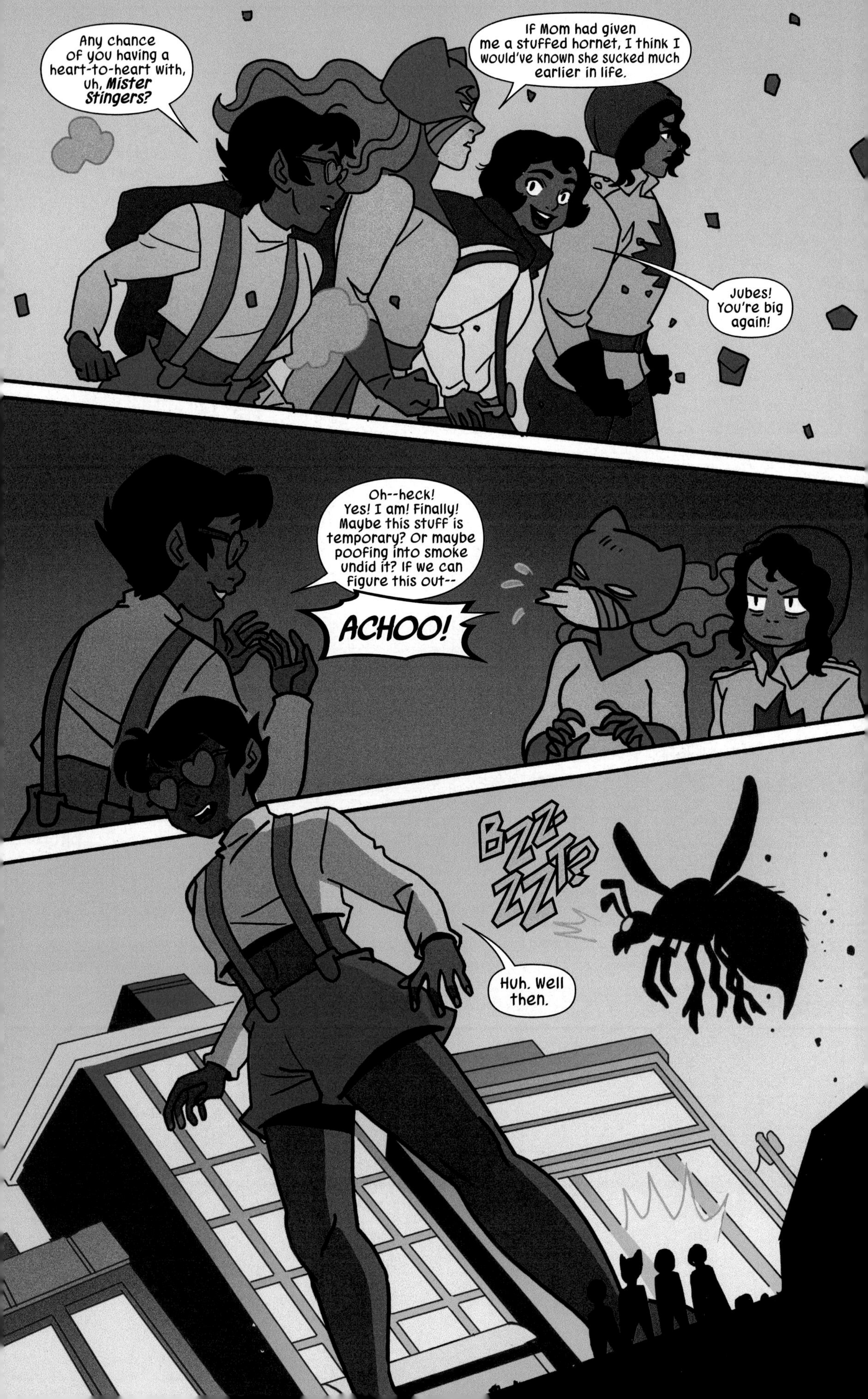

Any chance of you having a heart-to-heart with, uh, ***Mister Stingers?***
If Mom had given me a stuffed hornet, I think I would've known she sucked much earlier in life.
Jubes! You're big again!
Oh--heck! Yes! I am! Finally! Maybe this stuff is temporary? Or maybe poofing into smoke undid it? If we can figure this out--
ACHOO!
BZZ-ZZT?
Huh. Well then.

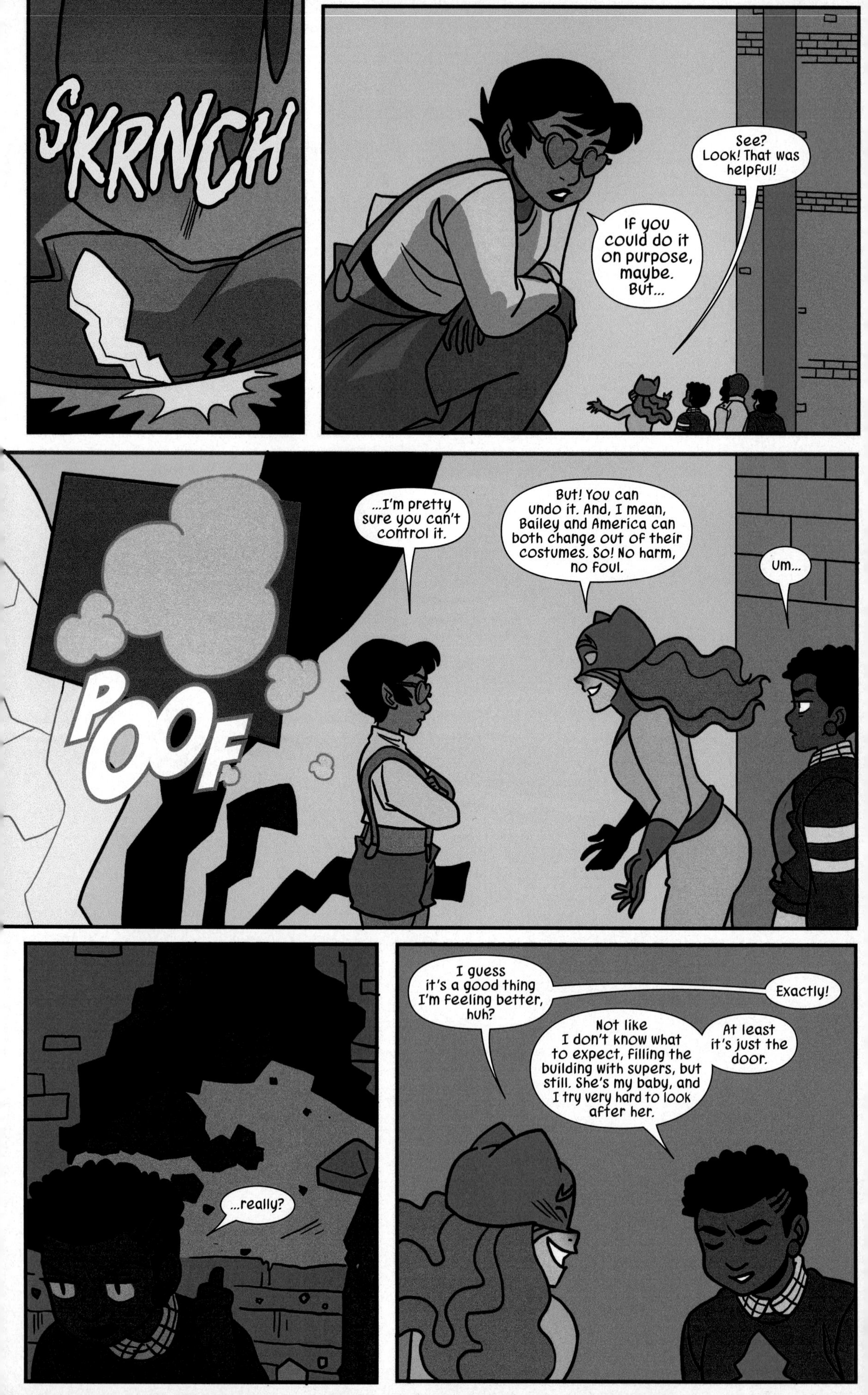
SKRNCH
If you could do it on purpose, maybe. But...
See? Look! That was helpful!
...I'm pretty sure you can't control it.
POOF
But! You can undo it. And, I mean, Bailey and America can both change out of their costumes. So! No harm, no foul.
Um...
...really?
I guess it's a good thing I'm feeling better, huh?
Exactly!
Not like I don't know what to expect, filling the building with supers, but still. She's my baby, and I try very hard to look after her.
At least it's just the door.

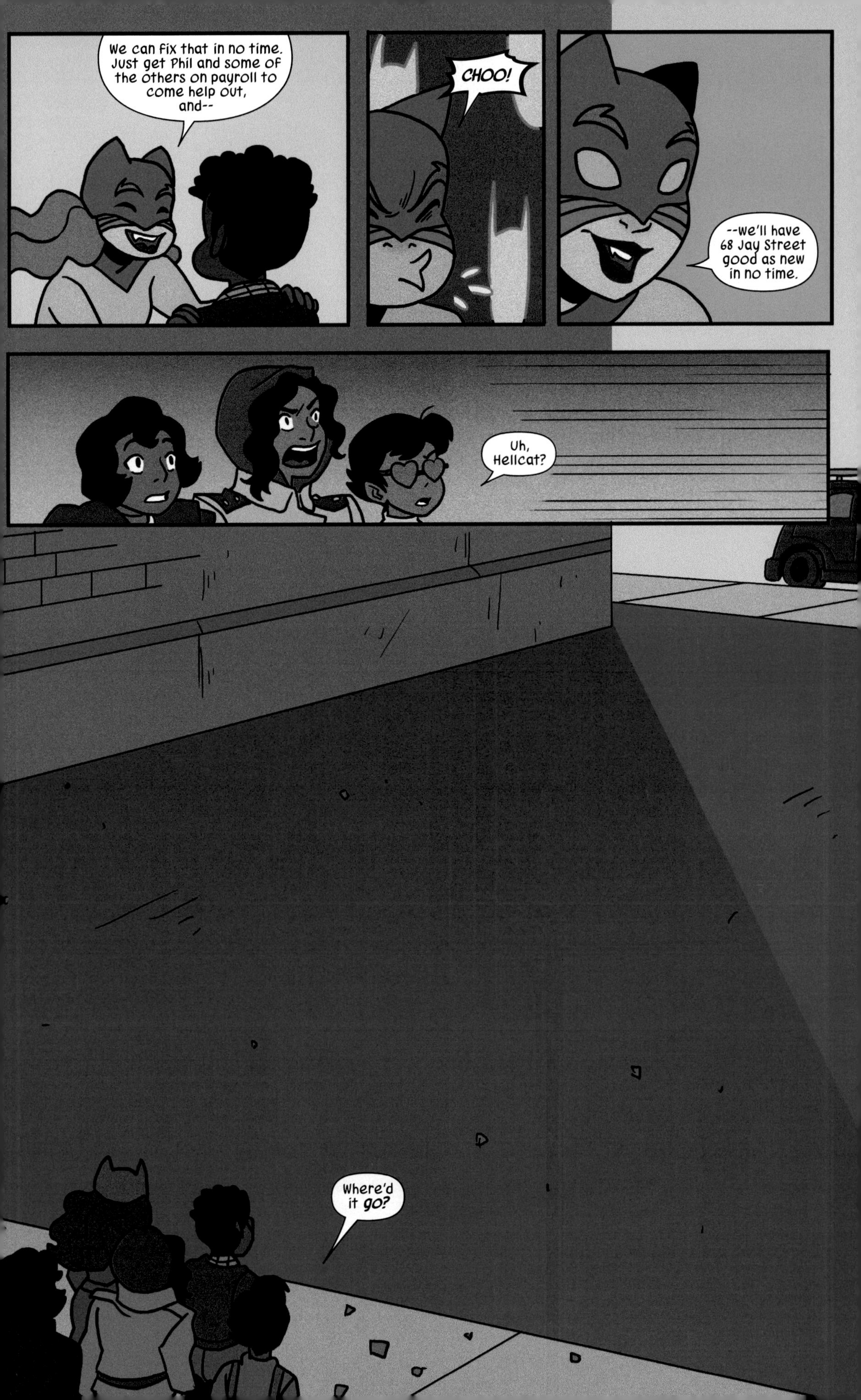
We can fix that in no time. Just get Phil and some of the others on payroll to come help out, and--
CHOO!
--we'll have 68 Jay Street good as new in no time.
Uh, Hellcat?
Where'd it go?

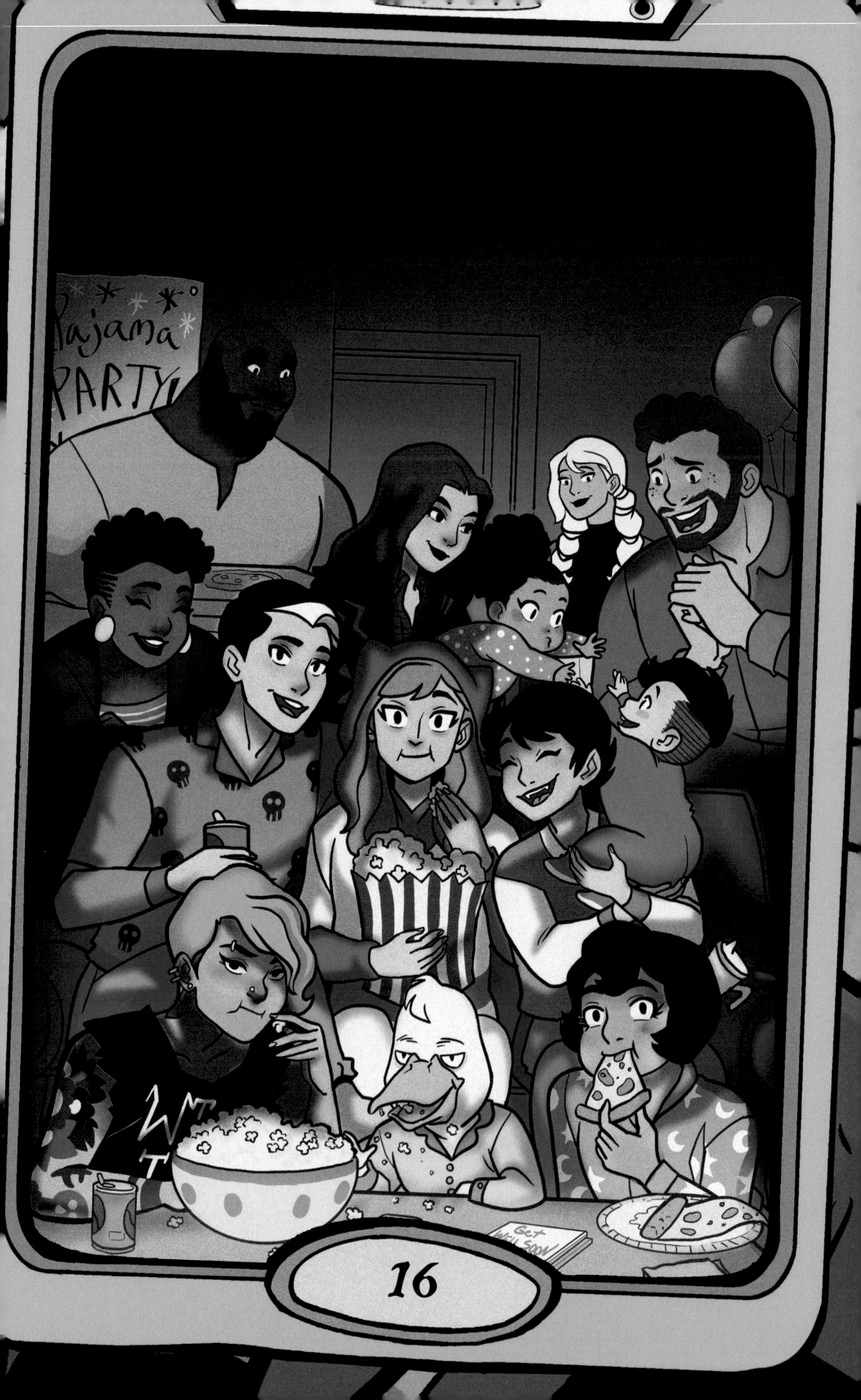
ajama
PARTY
WT
Get
WELL SOON
16

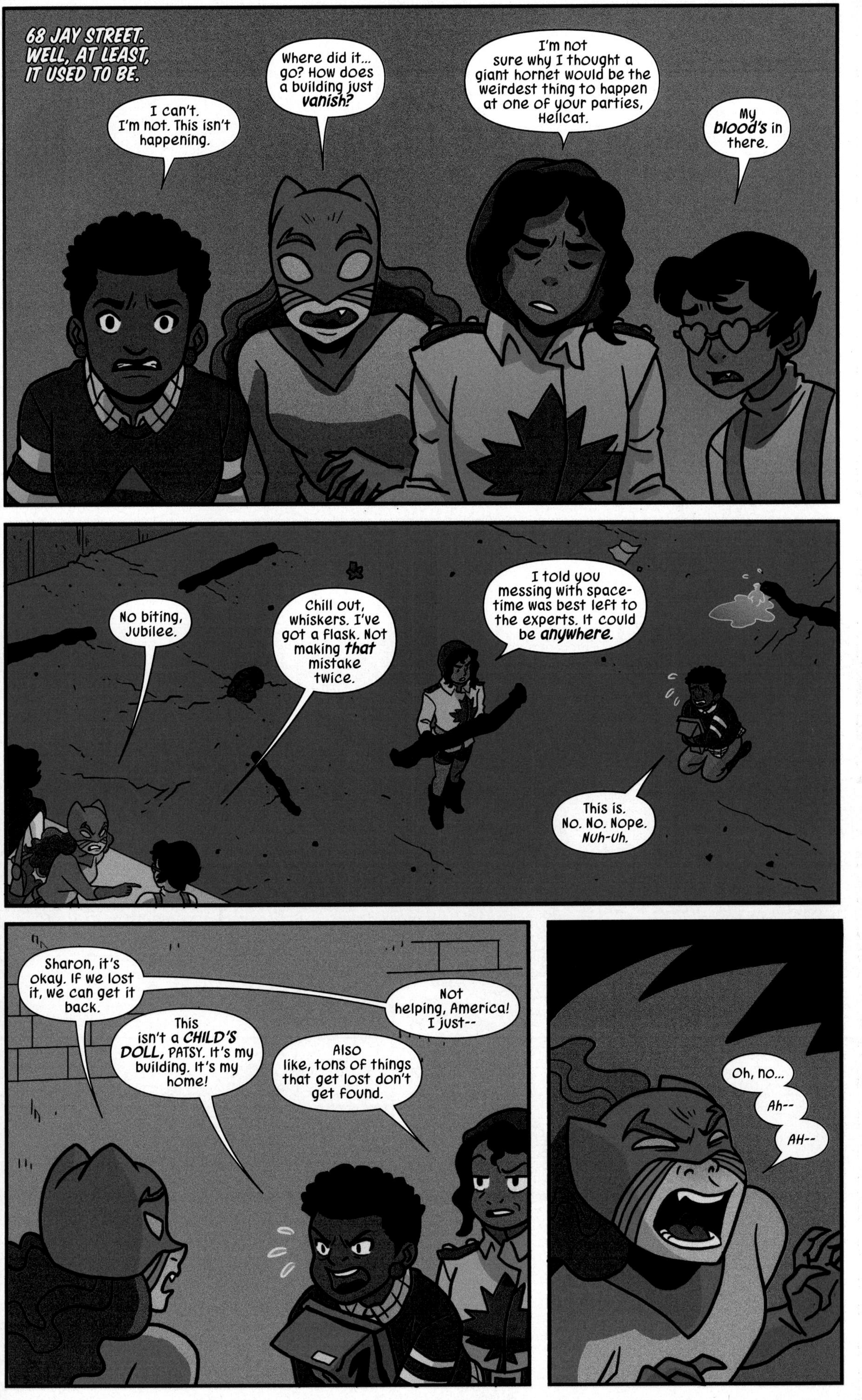
68 JAY STREET. WELL, AT LEAST, IT USED TO BE.
I can't. I'm not. This isn't happening.
Where did it... go? How does a building just vanish?
I'm not sure why I thought a giant hornet would be the weirdest thing to happen at one of your parties, Hellcat.
My blood's in there.
No biting, Jubilee.
Chill out, whiskers. I've got a flask. Not making that mistake twice.
I told you messing with space-time was best left to the experts. It could be anywhere.
This is. No. No. Nope. Nuh-uh.
Sharon, it's okay. If we lost it, we can get it back.
Not helping, America! I just--
This isn't a CHILD'S DOLL, PATSY. It's my building. It's my home!
Also like, tons of things that get lost don't get found.
Oh, no...
Ah--
AH--

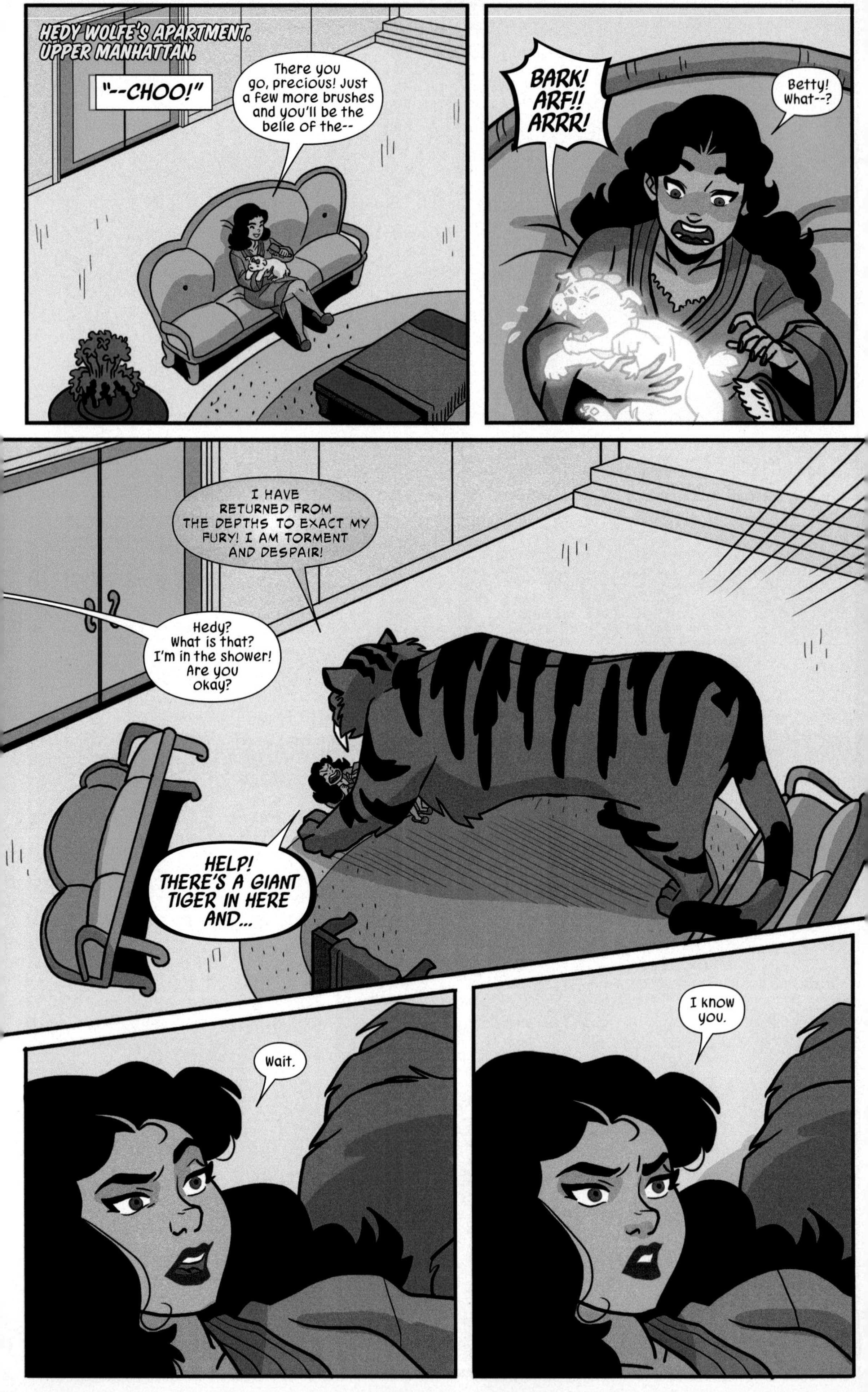
HEDY WOLFE'S APARTMENT. UPPER MANHATTAN.
"--CHOO!"
There you go, precious! Just a few more brushes and you'll be the belle of the--
BARK! ARF!! ARRR!
Betty! What--?
I HAVE RETURNED FROM THE DEPTHS TO EXACT MY FURY! I AM TORMENT AND DESPAIR!
Hedy? What is that? I'm in the shower! Are you okay?
HELP! THERE'S A GIANT TIGER IN HERE AND...
Wait.
I know you.

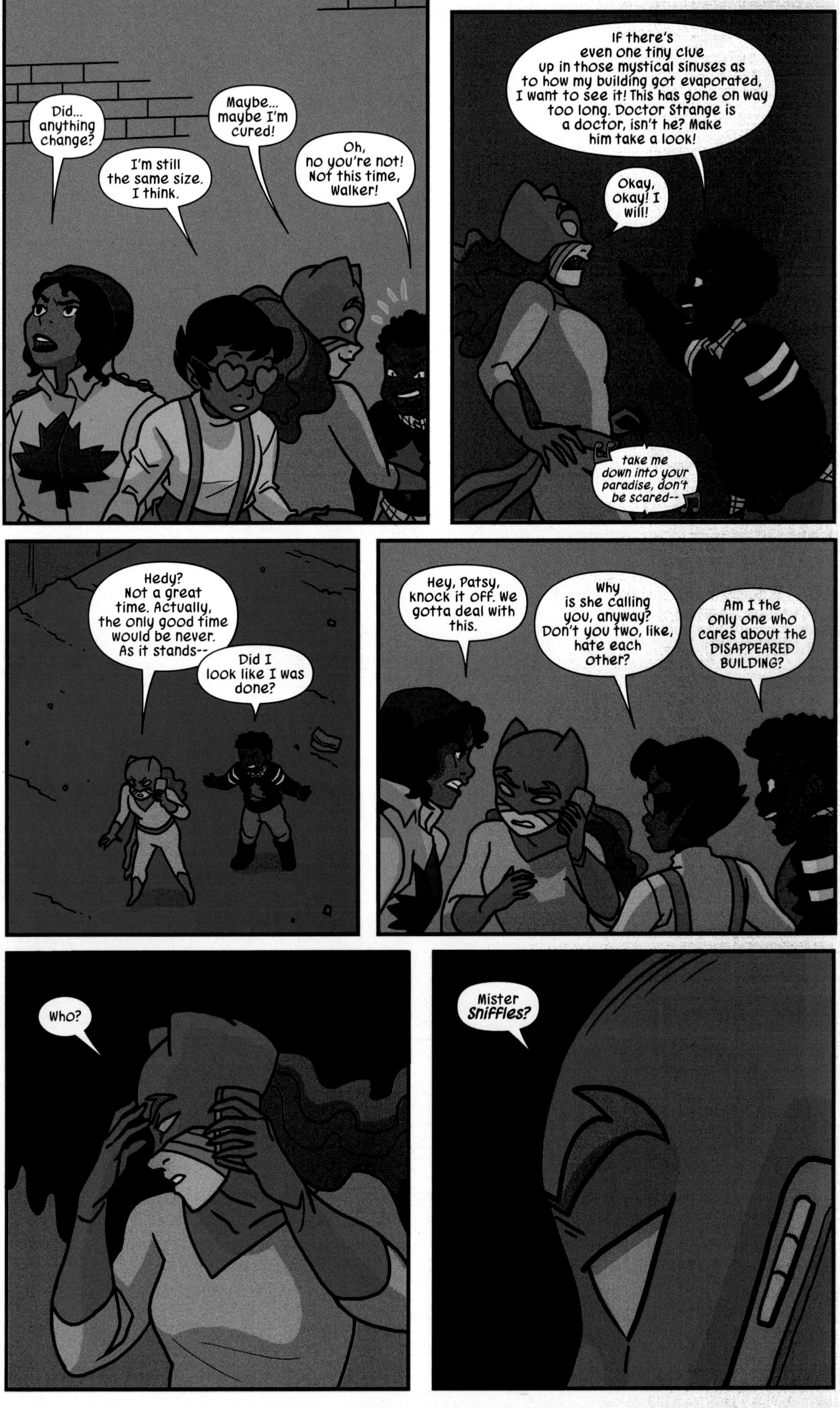
Did... anything change?
I'm still the same size. I think.
Maybe... maybe I'm cured!
Oh, no you're not! Not this time, Walker!
If there's even one tiny clue up in those mystical sinuses as to how my building got evaporated, I want to see it! This has gone on way too long. Doctor Strange is a doctor, isn't he? Make him take a look!
Okay, okay! I will!
take me down into your paradise, don't be scared--
Hedy? Not a great time. Actually, the only good time would be never. As it stands--
Did I look like I was done?
Hey, Patsy, knock it off. We gotta deal with this.
Why is she calling you, anyway? Don't you two, like, hate each other?
Am I the only one who cares about the DISAPPEARED BUILDING?
Who?
Mister *Sniffles?*

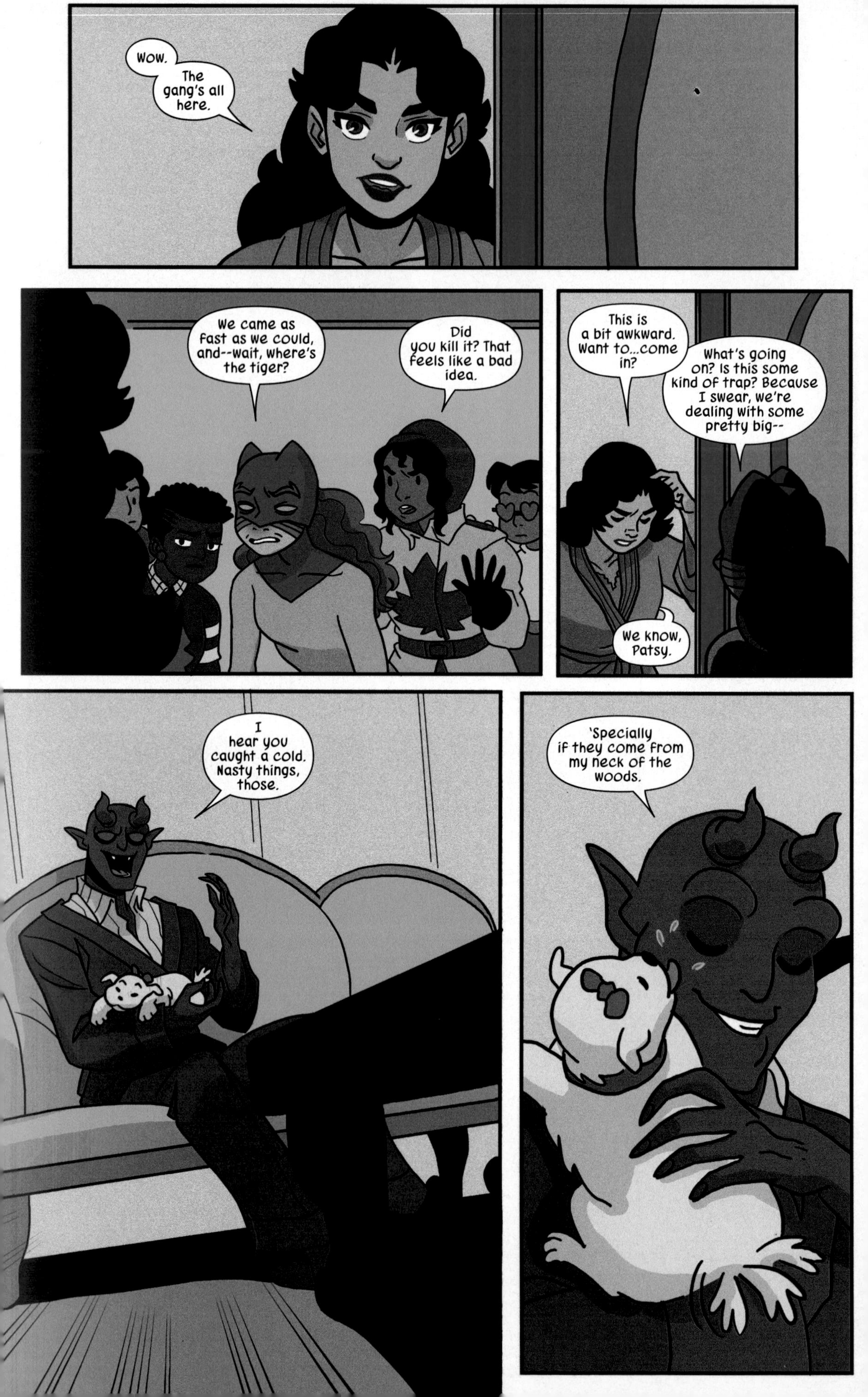
WOW.
The gang's all here.
We came as fast as we could, and--wait, where's the tiger?
Did you kill it? That feels like a bad idea.
This is a bit awkward. Want to...come in?
What's going on? Is this some kind of trap? Because I swear, we're dealing with some pretty big--
We know, Patsy.
I hear you caught a cold. Nasty things, those.
'Specially if they come from my neck of the woods.

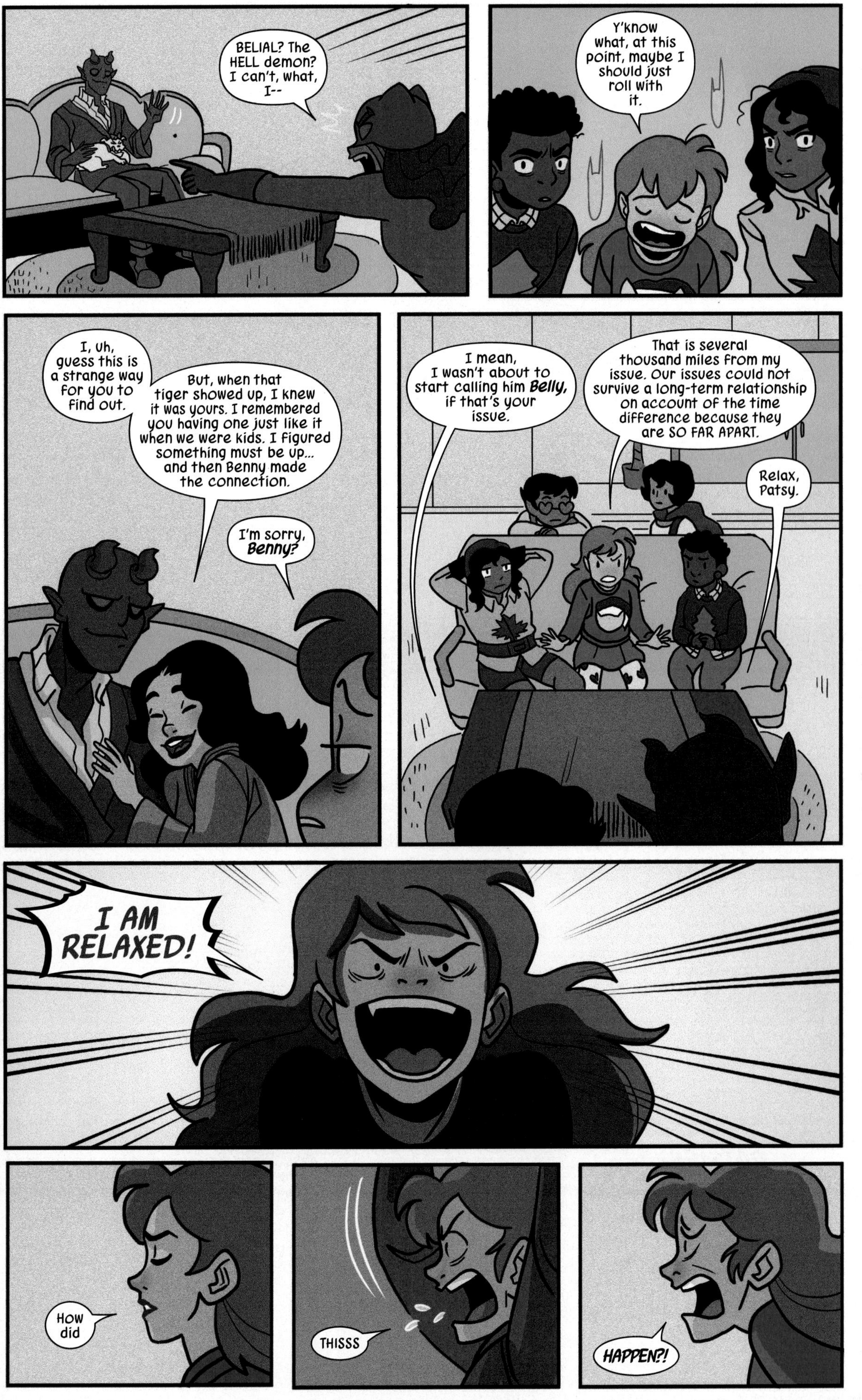

BELIAL? The HELL demon? I can't, what, I--
Y'know what, at this point, maybe I should just roll with it.
I, uh, guess this is a strange way for you to find out.
But, when that tiger showed up, I knew it was yours. I remembered you having one just like it when we were kids. I figured something must be up... and then Benny made the connection.
I'm sorry, Benny?
I mean, I wasn't about to start calling him Belly, if that's your issue.
That is several thousand miles from my issue. Our issues could not survive a long-term relationship on account of the time difference because they are SO FAR APART.
Relax, Patsy.
I AM RELAXED!
How did
THISSS
HAPPEN?!

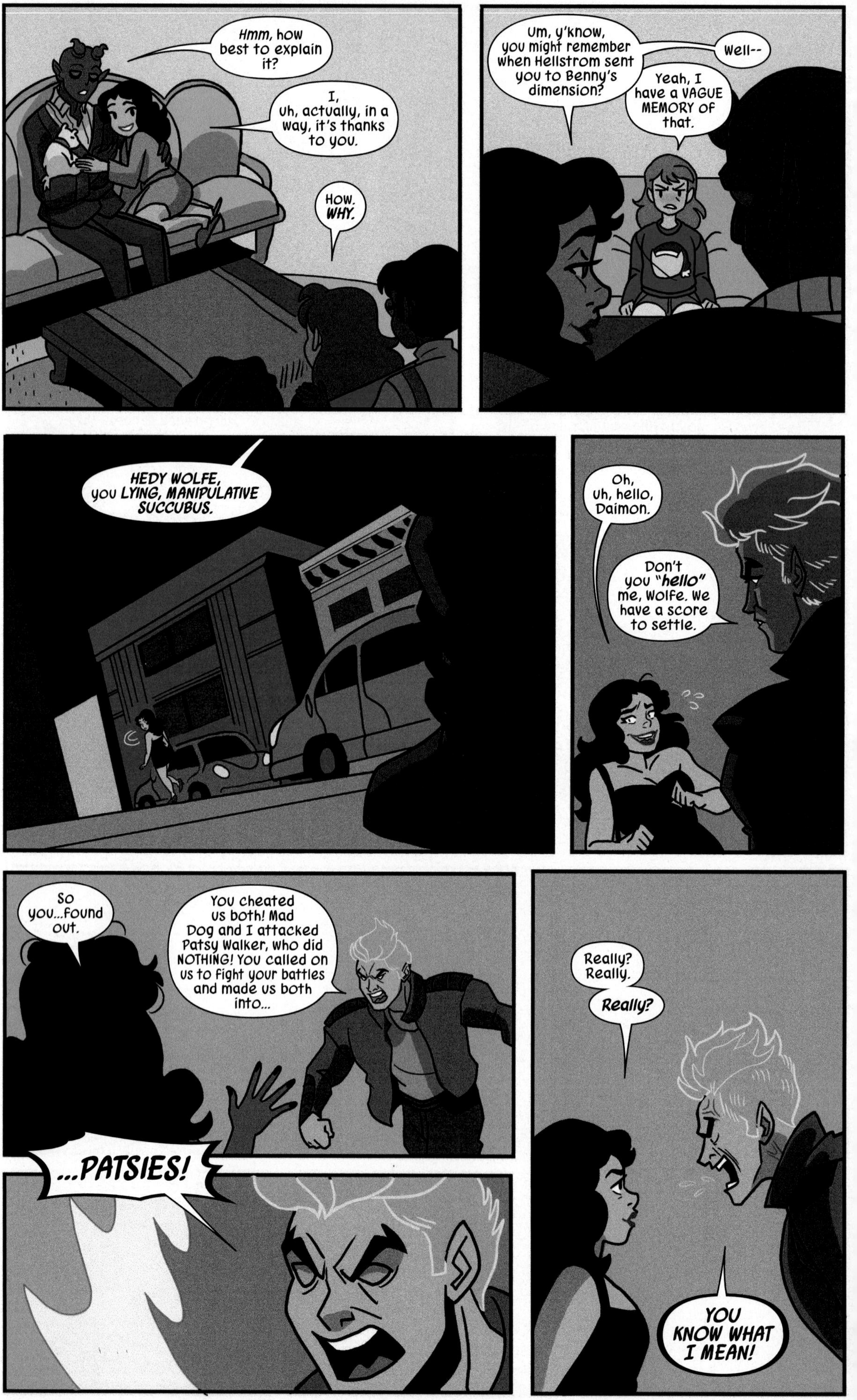
Hmm, how best to explain it?
I, uh, actually, in a way, it's thanks to you.
HOW. WHY.
Um, y'know, you might remember when Hellstrom sent you to Benny's dimension?
Well--
Yeah, I have a VAGUE MEMORY OF that.
HEDY WOLFE, you LYING, MANIPULATIVE SUCCUBUS.
Oh, uh, hello, Daimon.
Don't you "hello" me, Wolfe. We have a score to settle.
So you...found out.
You cheated us both! Mad Dog and I attacked Patsy Walker, who did NOTHING! You called on us to fight your battles and made us both into...
...PATSIES!
Really? Really.
Really?
YOU KNOW WHAT I MEAN!

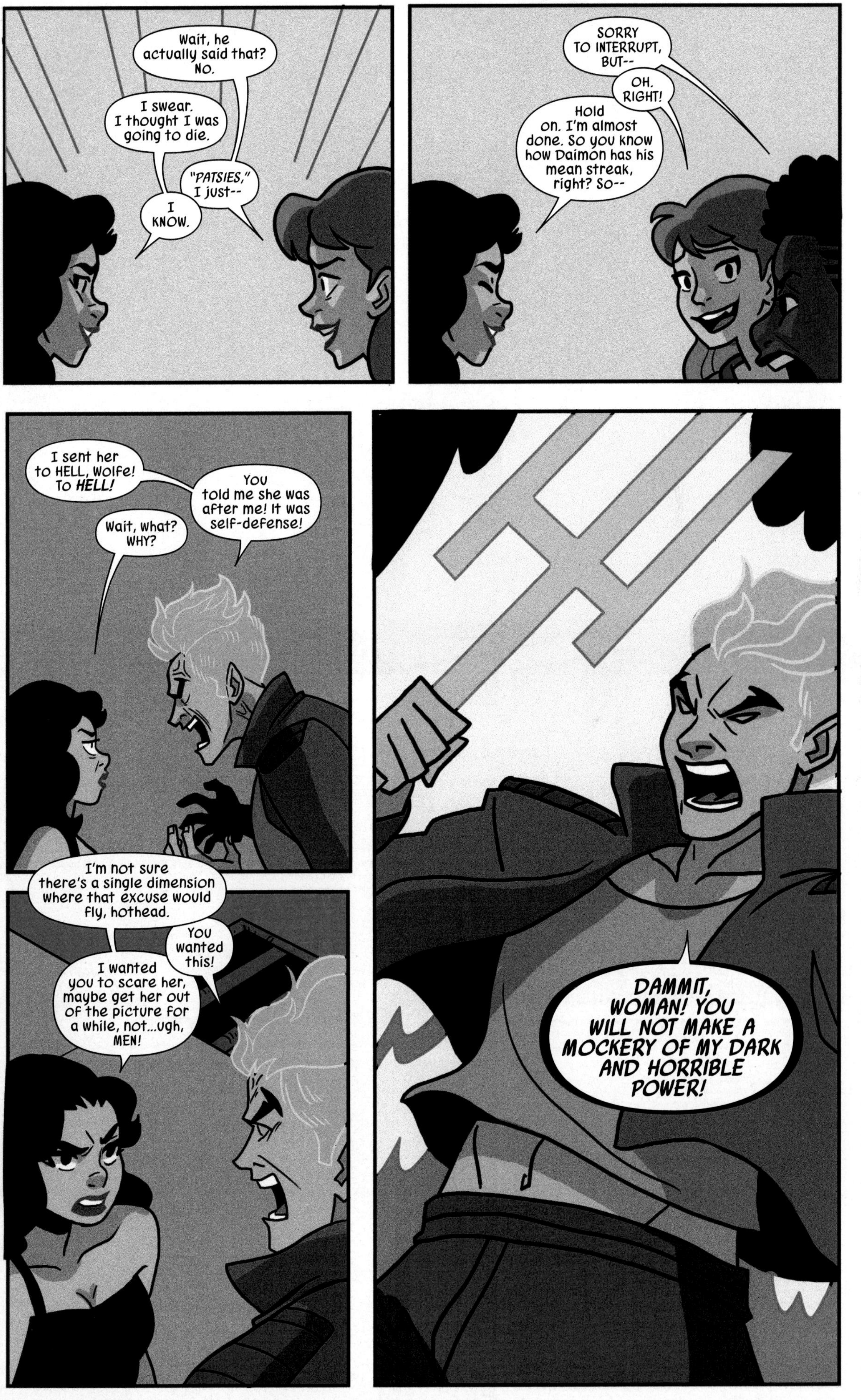
Wait, he actually said that? NO.
I swear. I thought I was going to die.
"PATSIES," I just--
I KNOW.
SORRY TO INTERRUPT, BUT--
OH. RIGHT!
Hold on. I'm almost done. So you know how Daimon has his mean streak, right? So--
I sent her to HELL, WOLFE! To HELL!
You told me she was after me! It was self-defense!
Wait, what? WHY?
I'm not sure there's a single dimension where that excuse would fly, hothead.
You wanted this!
I wanted you to scare her, maybe get her out of the picture for a while, not...ugh, MEN!
DAMMIT, WOMAN! YOU WILL NOT MAKE A MOCKERY OF MY DARK AND HORRIBLE POWER!

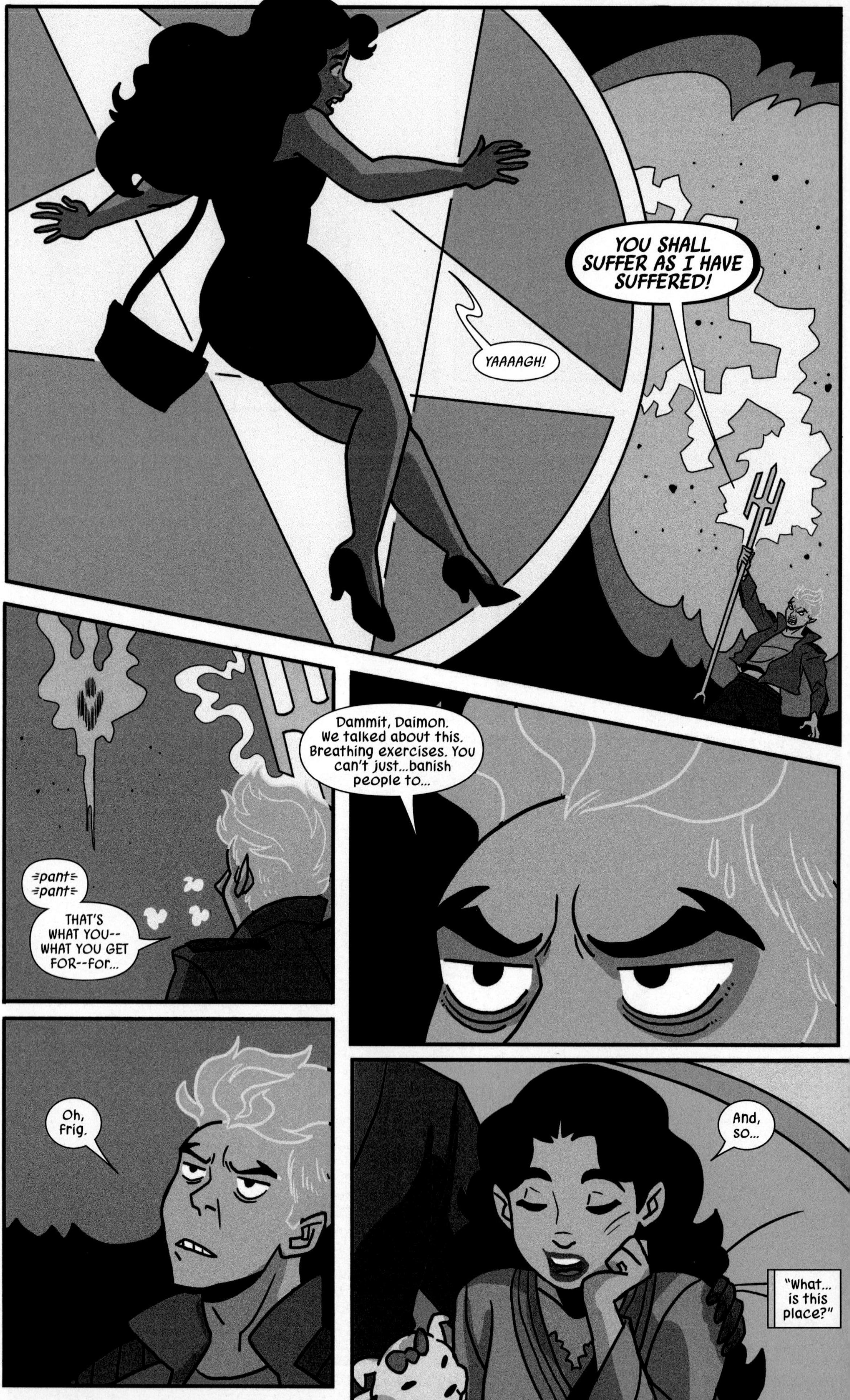
YOU SHALL SUFFER AS I HAVE SUFFERED!
YAAAAGH!
=pant=
=pant=
THAT'S WHAT YOU-- WHAT YOU GET FOR--for...
Dammit, Daimon. We talked about this. Breathing exercises. You can't just...banish people to...
Oh, frig.
And, so...
"What... is this place?"

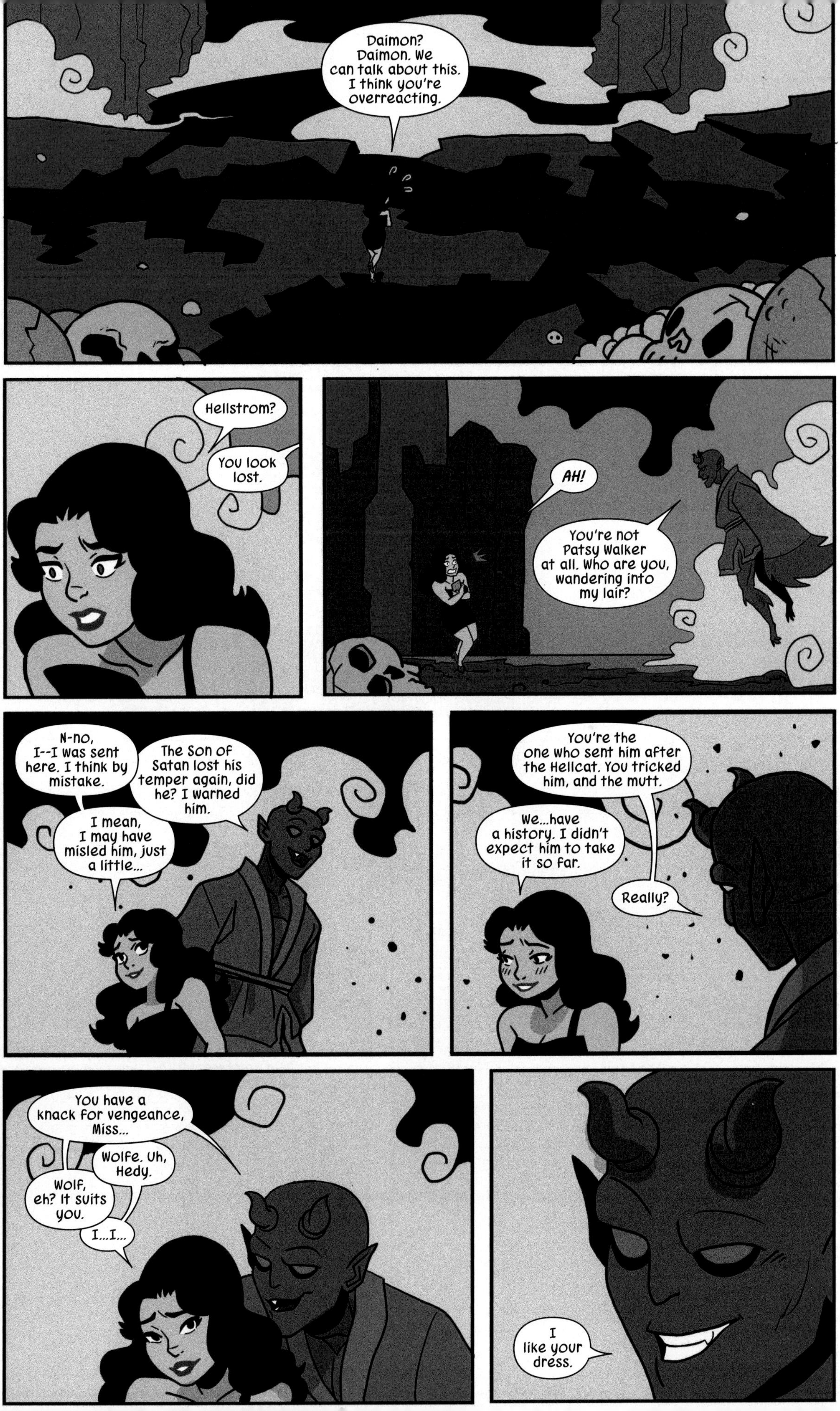

Daimon? Daimon. We can talk about this. I think you're overreacting.
Hellstrom?
You look lost.
AH!
You're not Patsy Walker at all. Who are you, wandering into my lair?
N-no, I--I was sent here. I think by mistake.
The Son of Satan lost his temper again, did he? I warned him.
I mean, I may have misled him, just a little...
You're the one who sent him after the Hellcat. You tricked him, and the mutt.
We...have a history. I didn't expect him to take it so far.
Really?
You have a knack for vengeance, Miss...
Wolfe. Uh, Hedy.
Wolf, eh? It suits you.
I...I...
I like your dress.

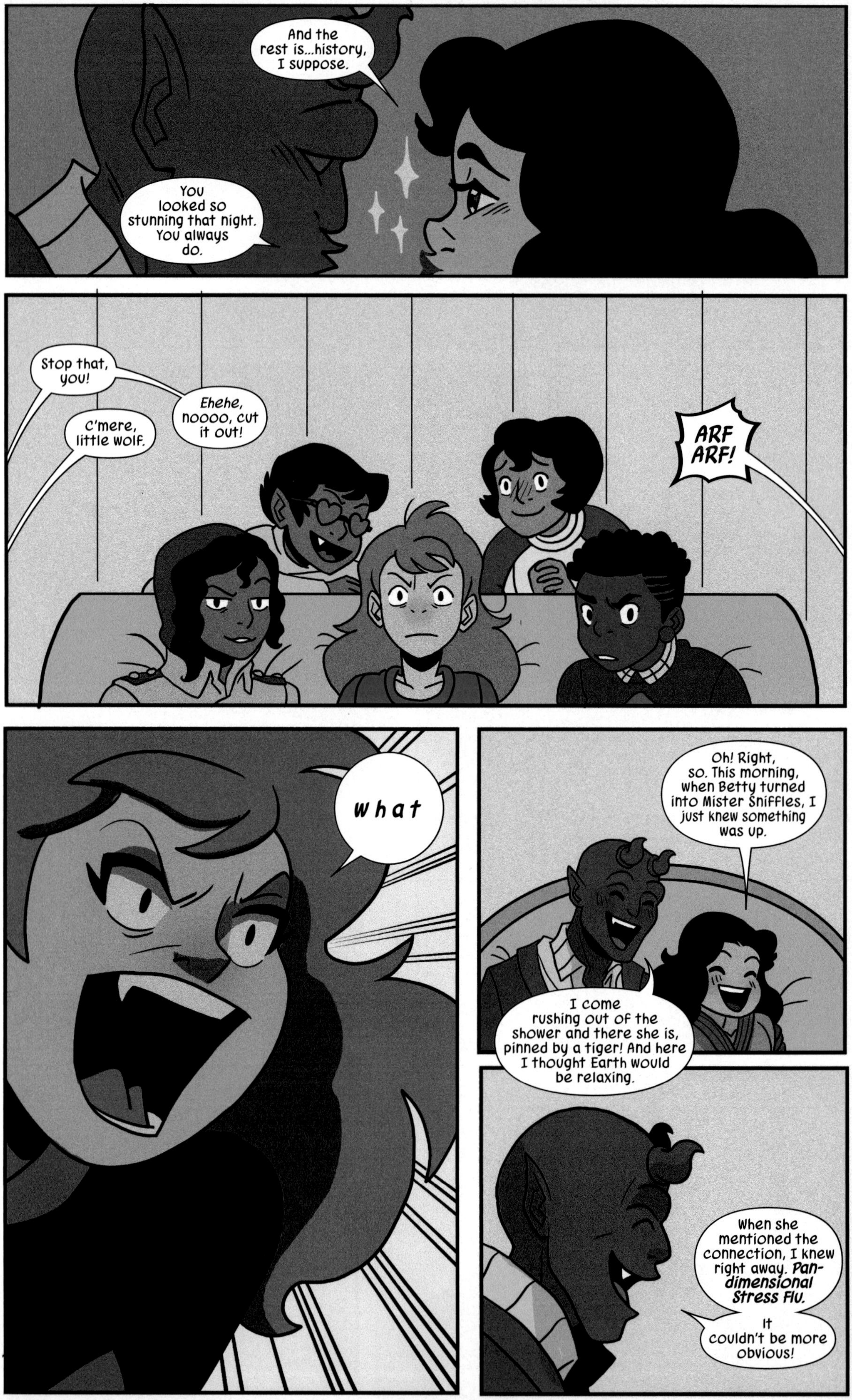

And the rest is...history, I suppose.
You looked so stunning that night. You always do.
Stop that, you!
C'mere, little wolf.
Ehehe, noooo, cut it out!
ARF ARF!
what
Oh! Right, so. This morning, when Betty turned into Mister Sniffles, I just knew something was up.
I come rushing out of the shower and there she is, pinned by a tiger! And here I thought Earth would be relaxing.
When she mentioned the connection, I knew right away. Pan-dimensional Stress Flu.
It couldn't be more obvious!

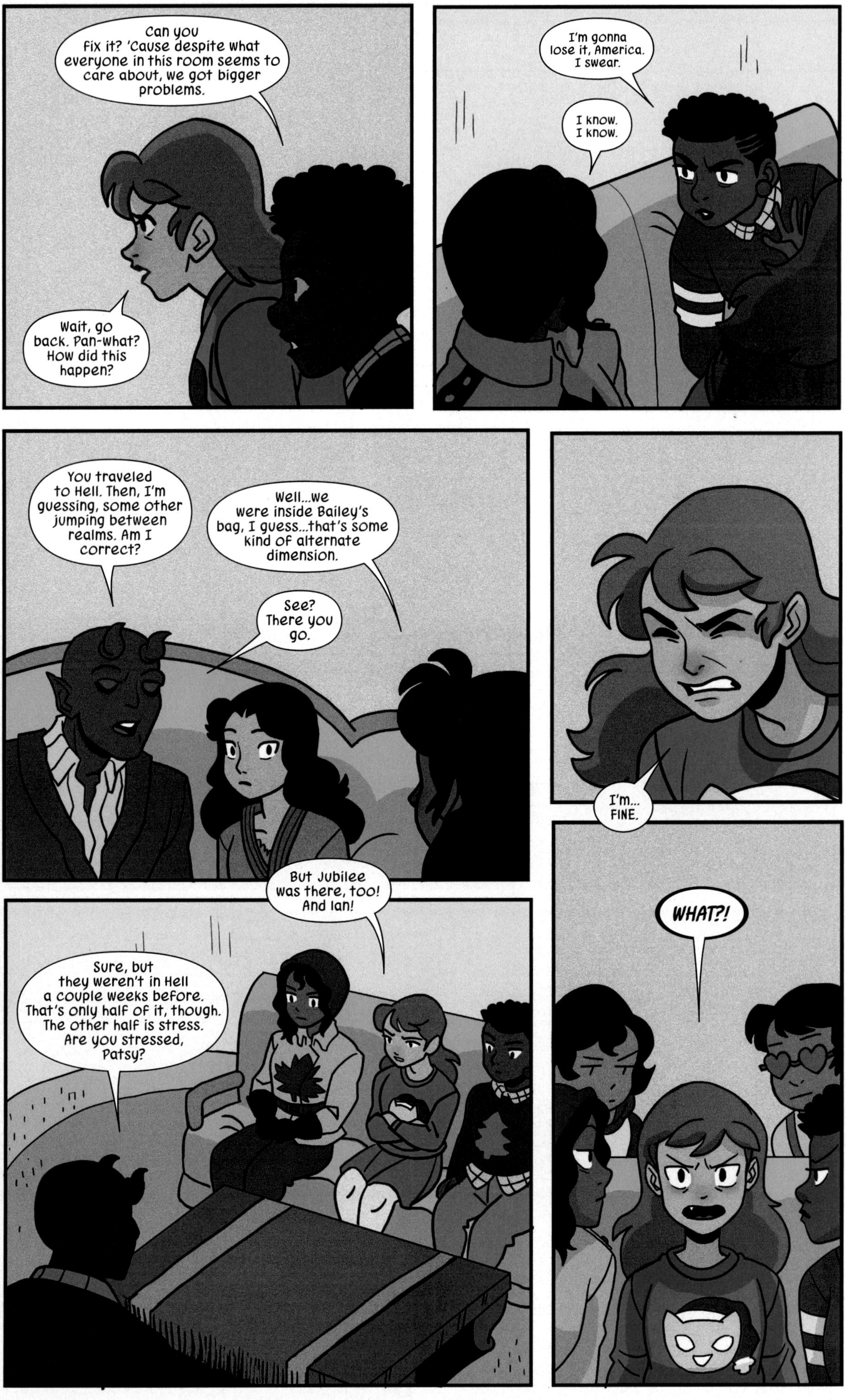
Can you fix it? 'Cause despite what everyone in this room seems to care about, we got bigger problems.
Wait, go back. Pan-what? How did this happen?
I'm gonna lose it, America. I swear.
I know. I know.
You traveled to Hell. Then, I'm guessing, some other jumping between realms. Am I correct?
Well...we were inside Bailey's bag, I guess...that's some kind of alternate dimension.
See? There you go.
I'm... FINE.
But Jubilee was there, too! And Ian!
Sure, but they weren't in Hell a couple weeks before. That's only half of it, though. The other half is stress. Are you stressed, Patsy?
WHAT?!

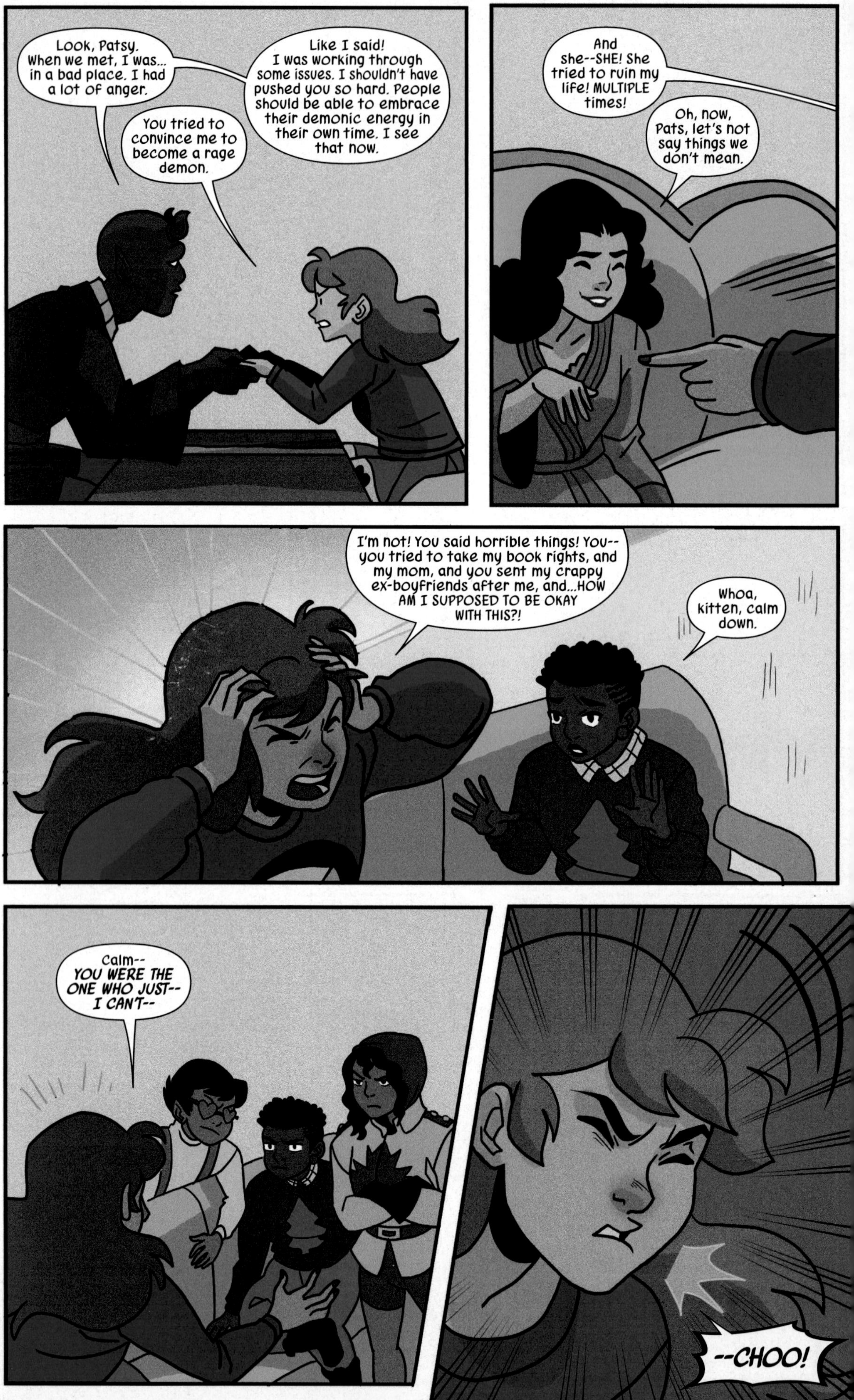
Look, Patsy. When we met, I was... in a bad place. I had a lot of anger.
You tried to convince me to become a rage demon.
Like I said! I was working through some issues. I shouldn't have pushed you so hard. People should be able to embrace their demonic energy in their own time. I see that now.
And she--SHE! She tried to ruin my life! MULTIPLE times!
Oh, now, Pats, let's not say things we don't mean.
I'm not! You said horrible things! You--you tried to take my book rights, and my mom, and you sent my crappy ex-boyfriends after me, and...HOW AM I SUPPOSED TO BE OKAY WITH THIS?!
Whoa, kitten, calm down.
Calm-- YOU WERE THE ONE WHO JUST-- I CAN'T--
--CHOO!

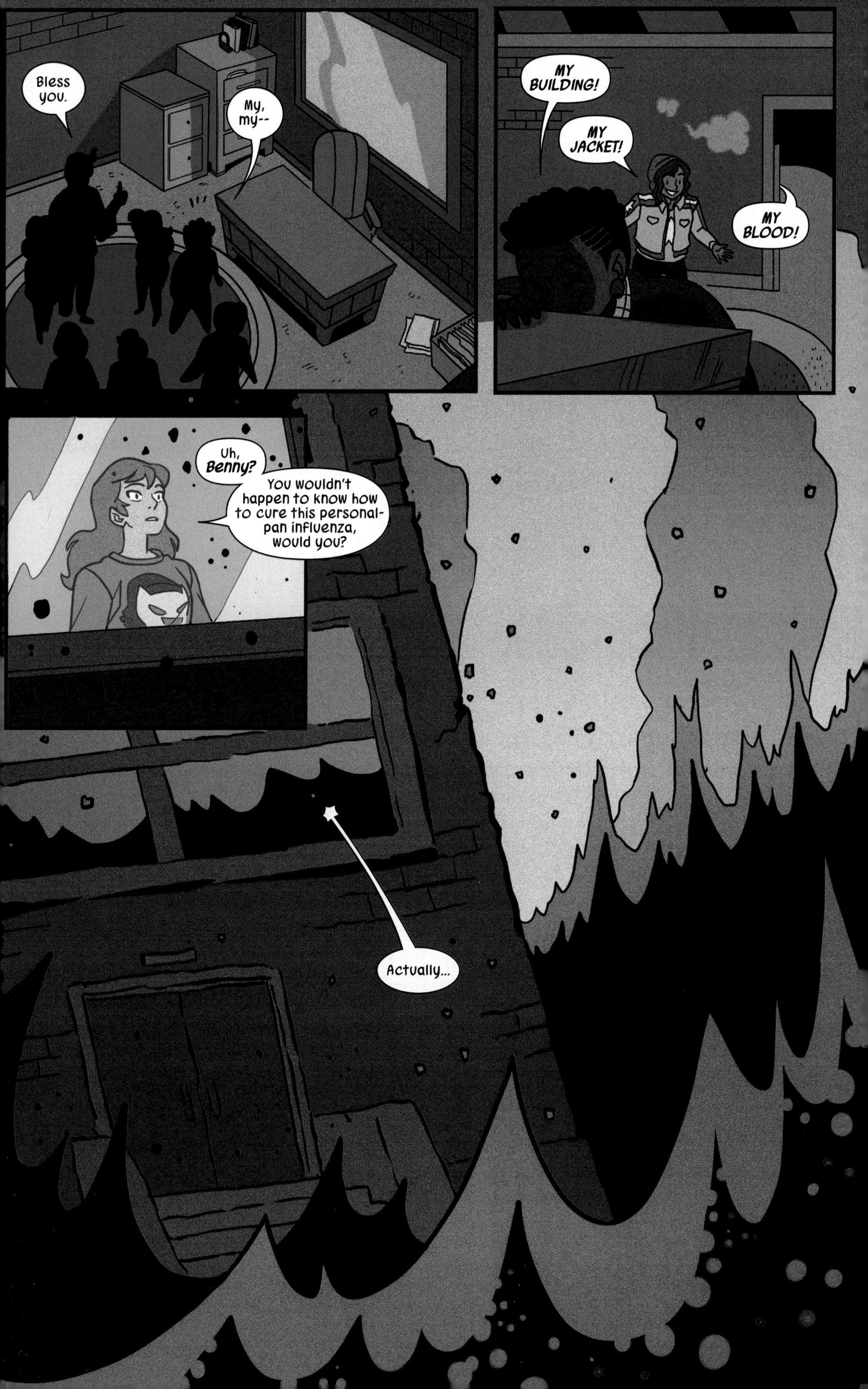
Bless you.
My, my--
MY BUILDING!
MY JACKET!
MY BLOOD!
Uh, Benny?
You wouldn't happen to know how to cure this personal-pan influenza, would you?
Actually...

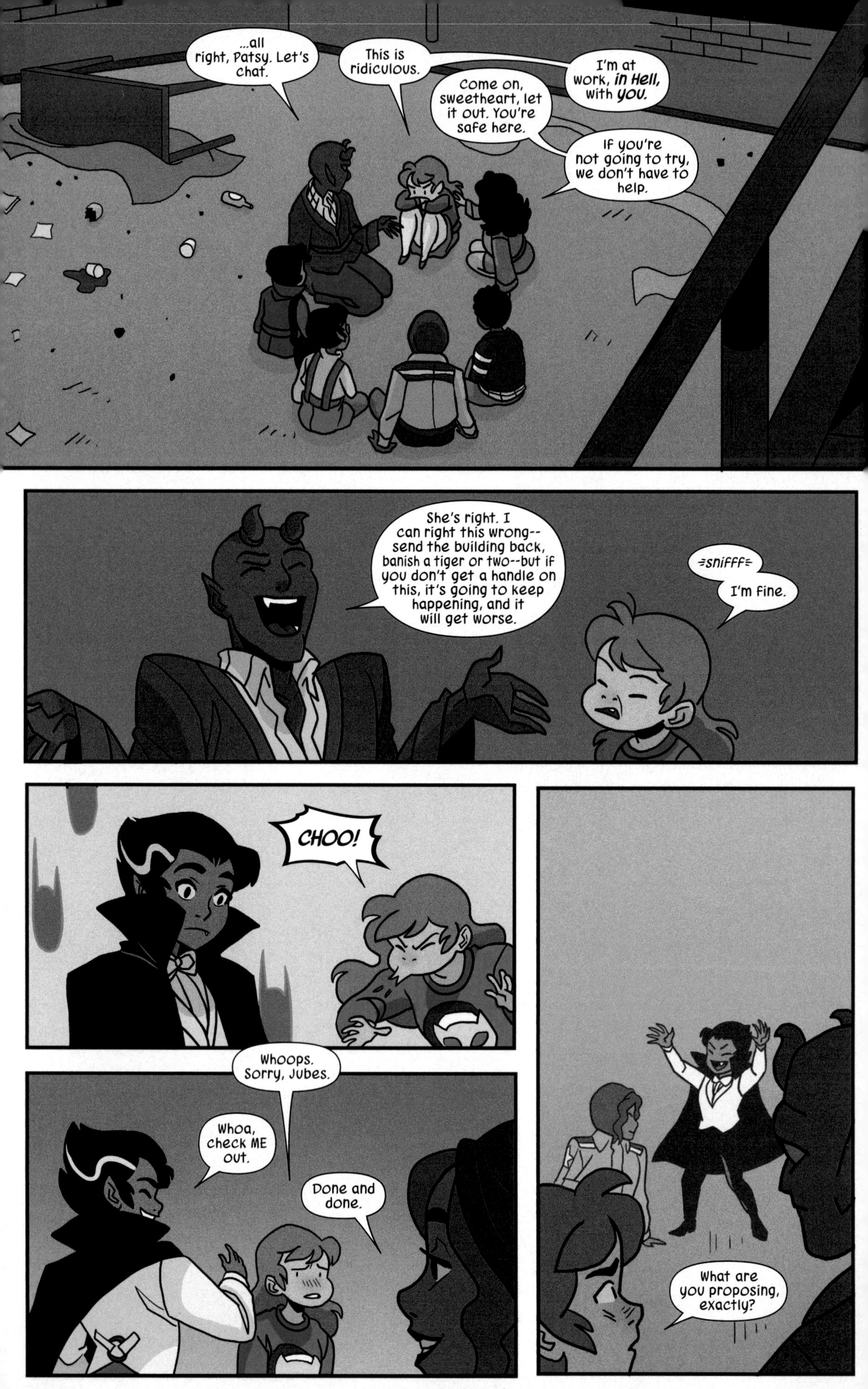
...all right, Patsy. Let's chat.
This is ridiculous.
I'm at work, *in Hell,* with *you.*
Come on, sweetheart, let it out. You're safe here.
If you're not going to try, we don't have to help.
She's right. I can right this wrong--send the building back, banish a tiger or two--but if you don't get a handle on this, it's going to keep happening, and it will get worse.
=sniFFF=
I'm fine.
CHOO!
Whoops. Sorry, Jubes.
Whoa, check ME out.
Done and done.
What are you proposing, exactly?

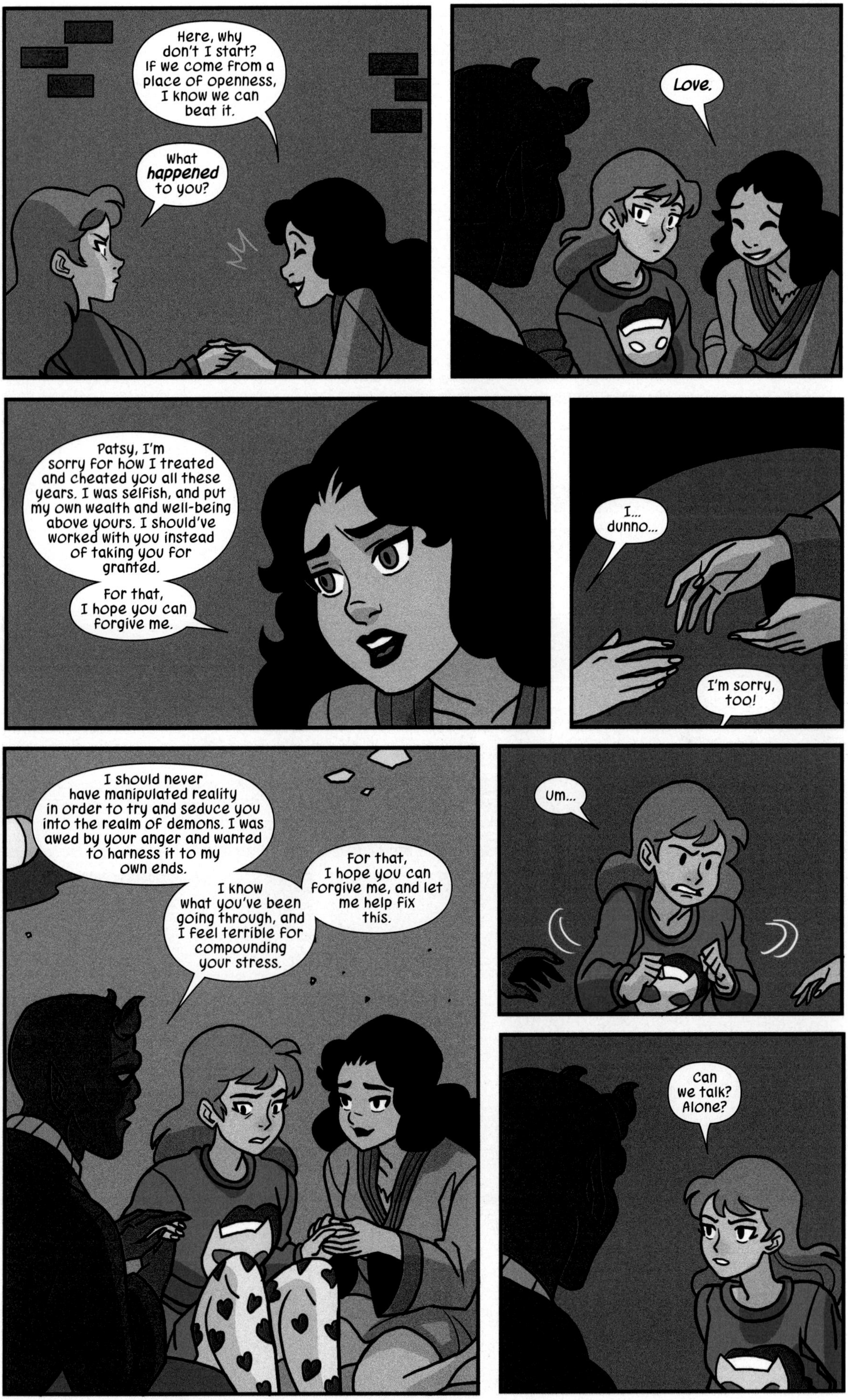
Here, why don't I start? If we come from a place of openness, I know we can beat it.
What happened to you?
Love.
Patsy, I'm sorry for how I treated and cheated you all these years. I was selfish, and put my own wealth and well-being above yours. I should've worked with you instead of taking you for granted.
For that, I hope you can forgive me.
I... dunno...
I'm sorry, too!
I should never have manipulated reality in order to try and seduce you into the realm of demons. I was awed by your anger and wanted to harness it to my own ends.
I know what you've been going through, and I feel terrible for compounding your stress.
For that, I hope you can forgive me, and let me help fix this.
Um...
Can we talk? Alone?

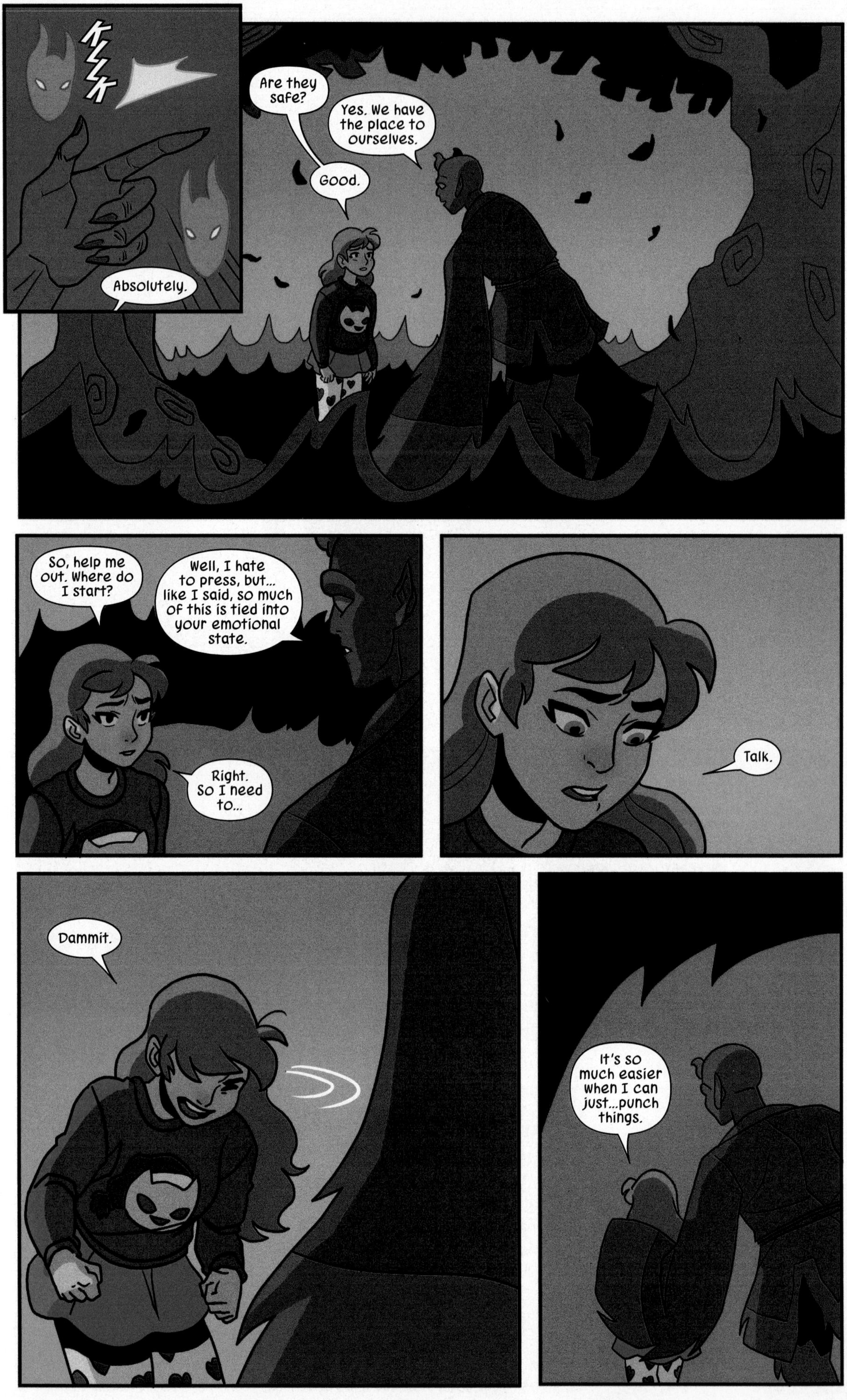
KLLK
Absolutely.
Are they safe?
Yes. We have the place to ourselves.
Good.
So, help me out. Where do I start?
Well, I hate to press, but... like I said, so much of this is tied into your emotional state.
Right. So I need to...
Talk.
Dammit.
It's so much easier when I can just...punch things.

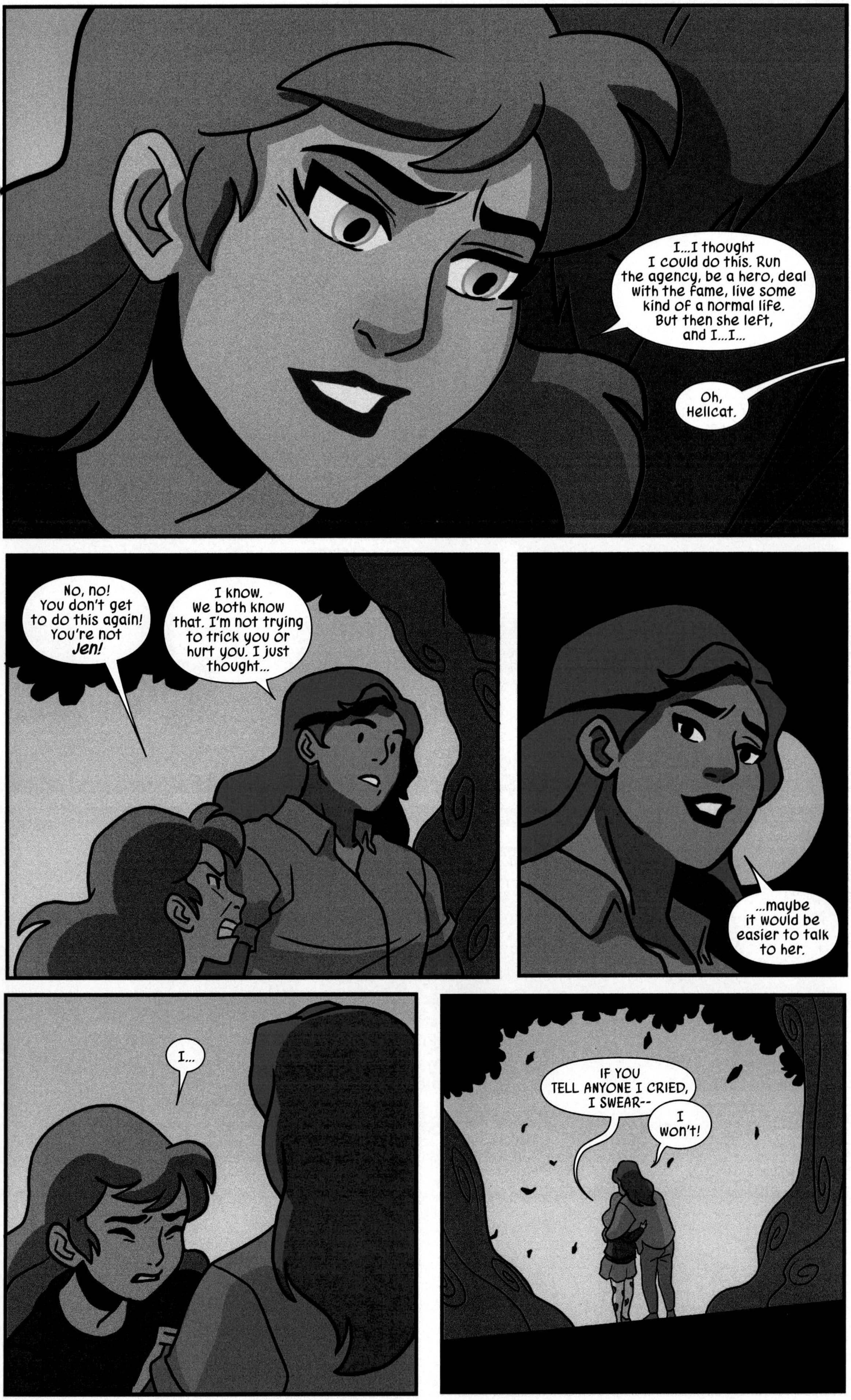
I...I thought I could do this. Run the agency, be a hero, deal with the fame, live some kind of a normal life. But then she left, and I...I...
Oh, Hellcat.
No, no! You don't get to do this again! You're not *Jen!*
I know. We both know that. I'm not trying to trick you or hurt you. I just thought...
...maybe it would be easier to talk to her.
I...
IF YOU TELL ANYONE I CRIED, I SWEAR--
I won't!

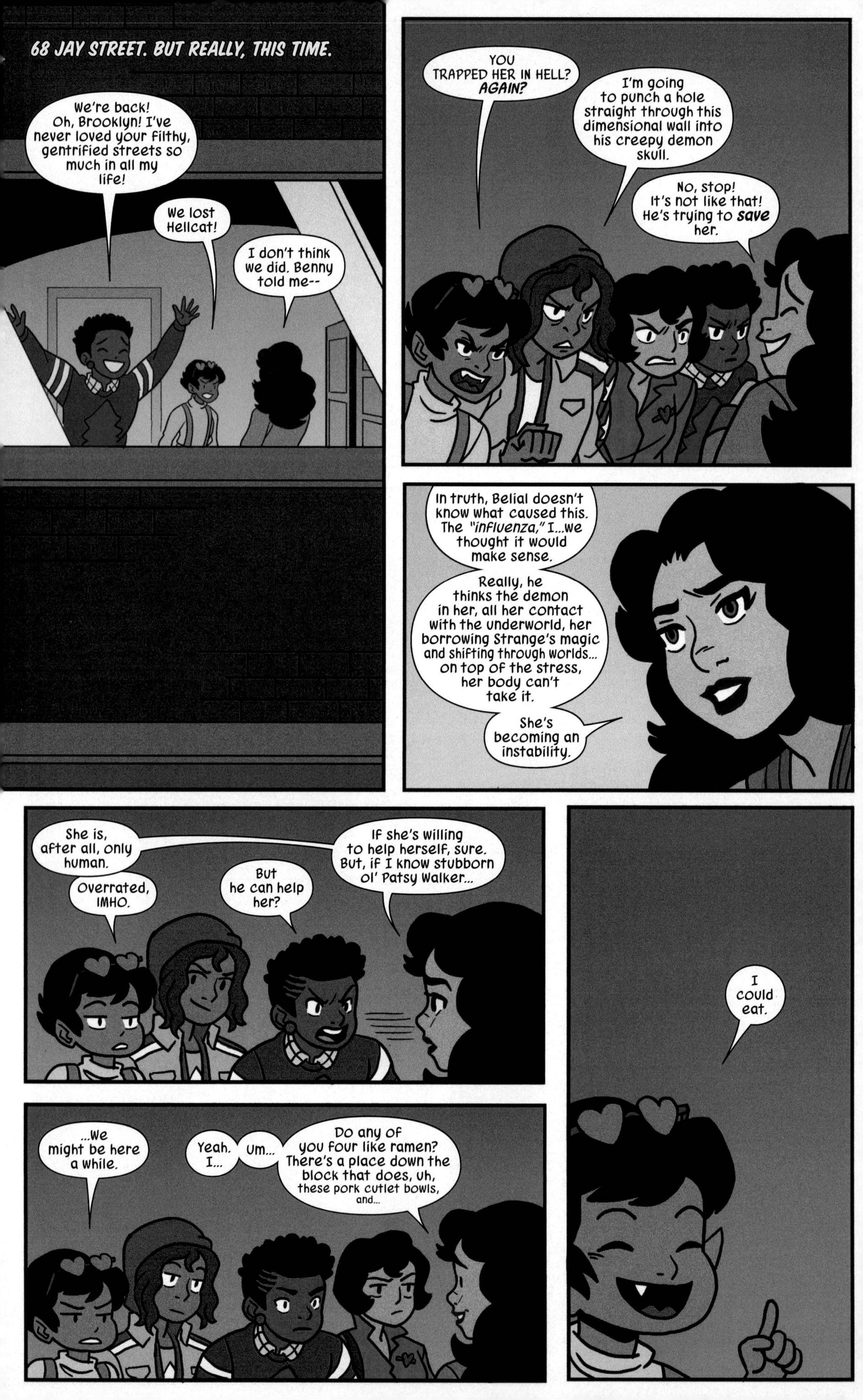
68 JAY STREET. BUT REALLY, THIS TIME.
We're back! Oh, Brooklyn! I've never loved your filthy, gentrified streets so much in all my life!
We lost Hellcat!
I don't think we did. Benny told me--
YOU TRAPPED HER IN HELL? AGAIN?
I'm going to punch a hole straight through this dimensional wall into his creepy demon skull.
No, stop! It's not like that! He's trying to save her.
In truth, Belial doesn't know what caused this. The "influenza," I...we thought it would make sense.
Really, he thinks the demon in her, all her contact with the underworld, her borrowing Strange's magic and shifting through worlds... on top of the stress, her body can't take it.
She's becoming an instability.
She is, after all, only human.
If she's willing to help herself, sure. But, if I know stubborn ol' Patsy Walker...
Overrated, IMHO.
But he can help her?
...We might be here a while.
Yeah. I...
Um...
Do any of you four like ramen? There's a place down the block that does, uh, these pork cutlet bowls, and...
I could eat.

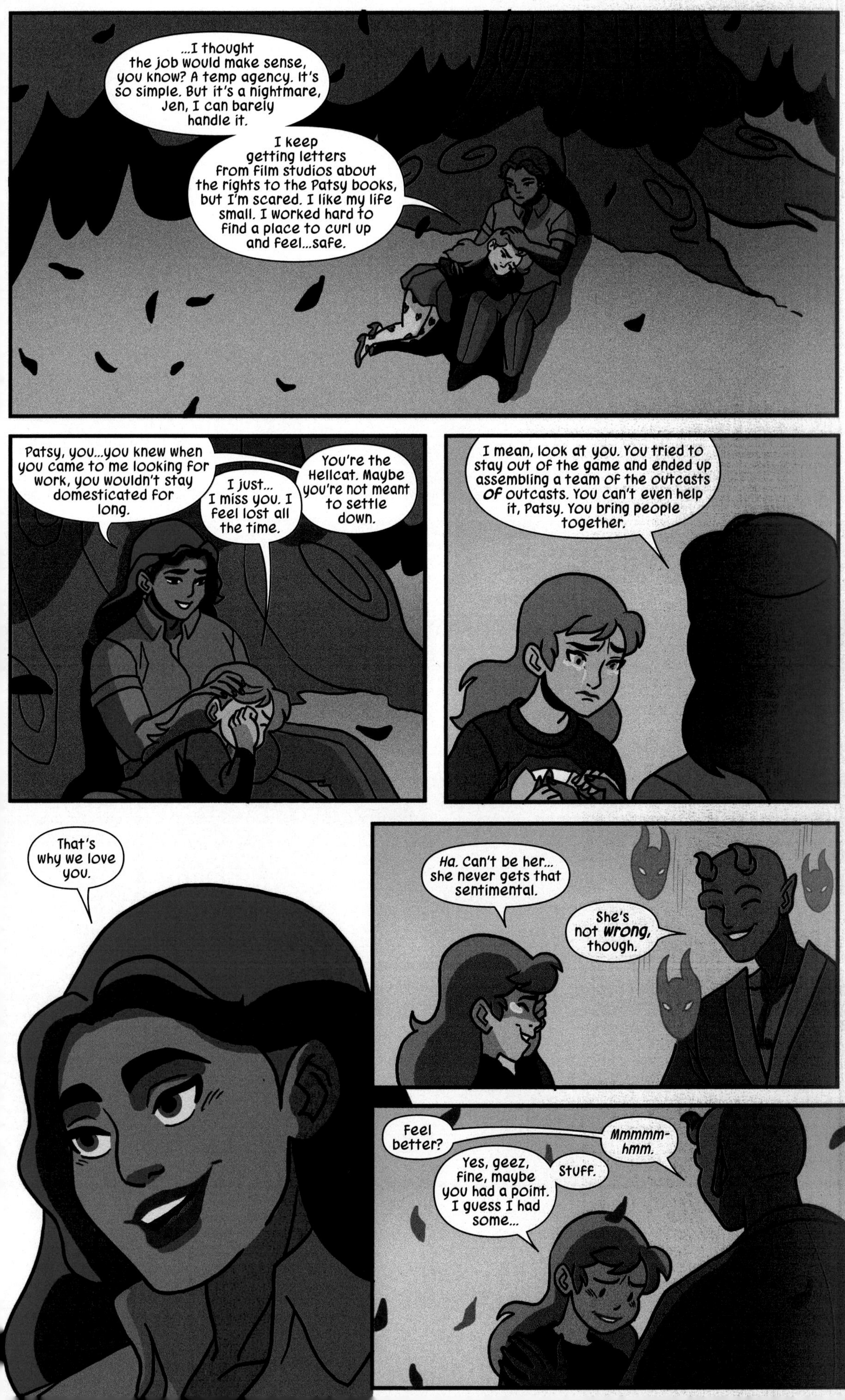

...I thought the job would make sense, you know? A temp agency. It's so simple. But it's a nightmare, Jen, I can barely handle it.
I keep getting letters from film studios about the rights to the Patsy books, but I'm scared. I like my life small. I worked hard to find a place to curl up and feel...safe.
Patsy, you...you knew when you came to me looking for work, you wouldn't stay domesticated for long.
I just... I miss you. I feel lost all the time.
You're the Hellcat. Maybe you're not meant to settle down.
I mean, look at you. You tried to stay out of the game and ended up assembling a team of the outcasts *of* outcasts. You can't even help it, Patsy. You bring people together.
That's why we love you.
Ha. Can't be her... she never gets that sentimental.
She's not ***wrong,*** though.
Feel better?
Mmmmm-hmm.
Yes, geez, fine, maybe you had a point. I guess I had some...
Stuff.

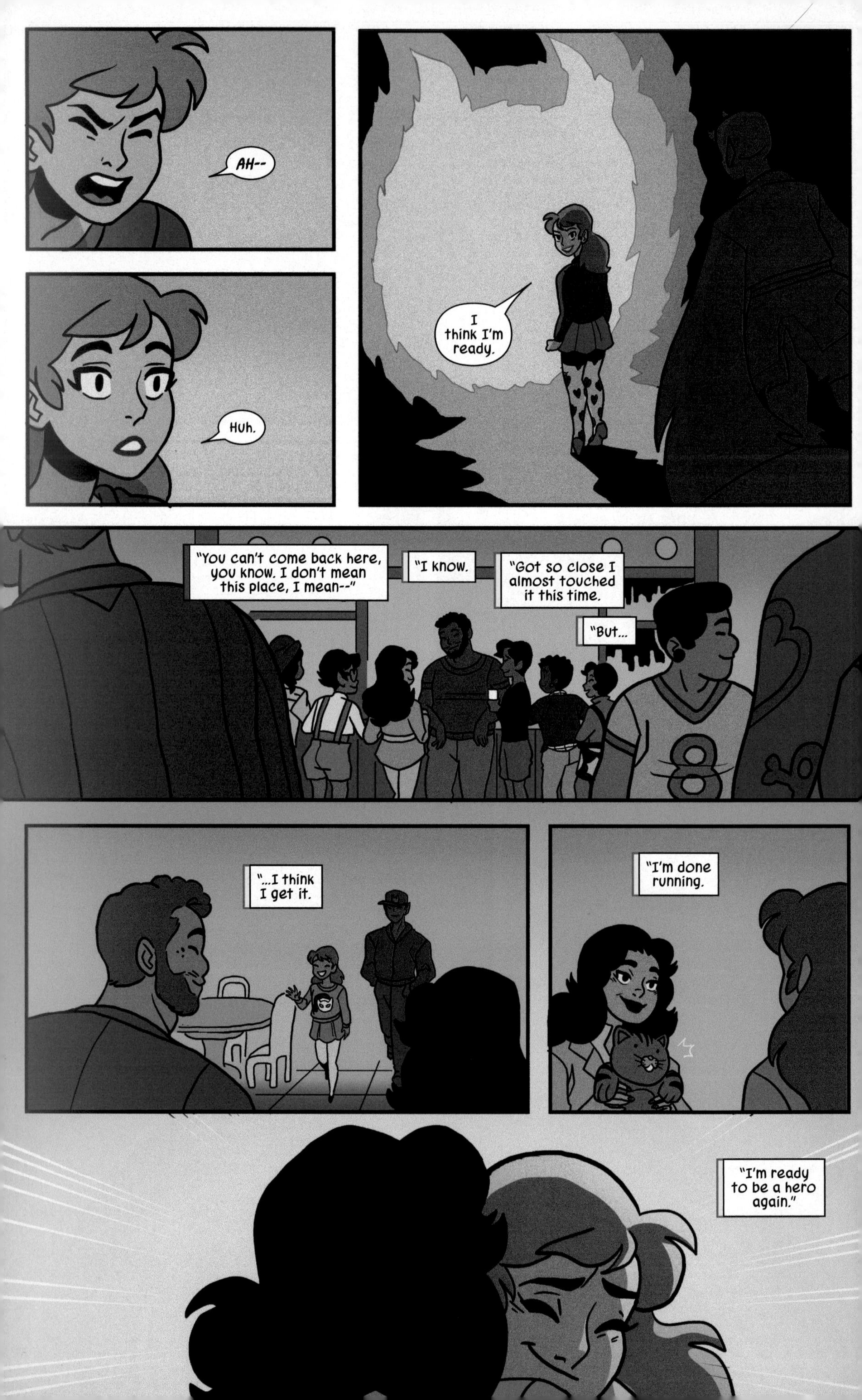
AH--
Huh.
I think I'm ready.
"You can't come back here, you know. I don't mean this place, I mean--"
"I know.
"Got so close I almost touched it this time.
"But...
"...I think I get it.
"I'm done running.
"I'm ready to be a hero again."

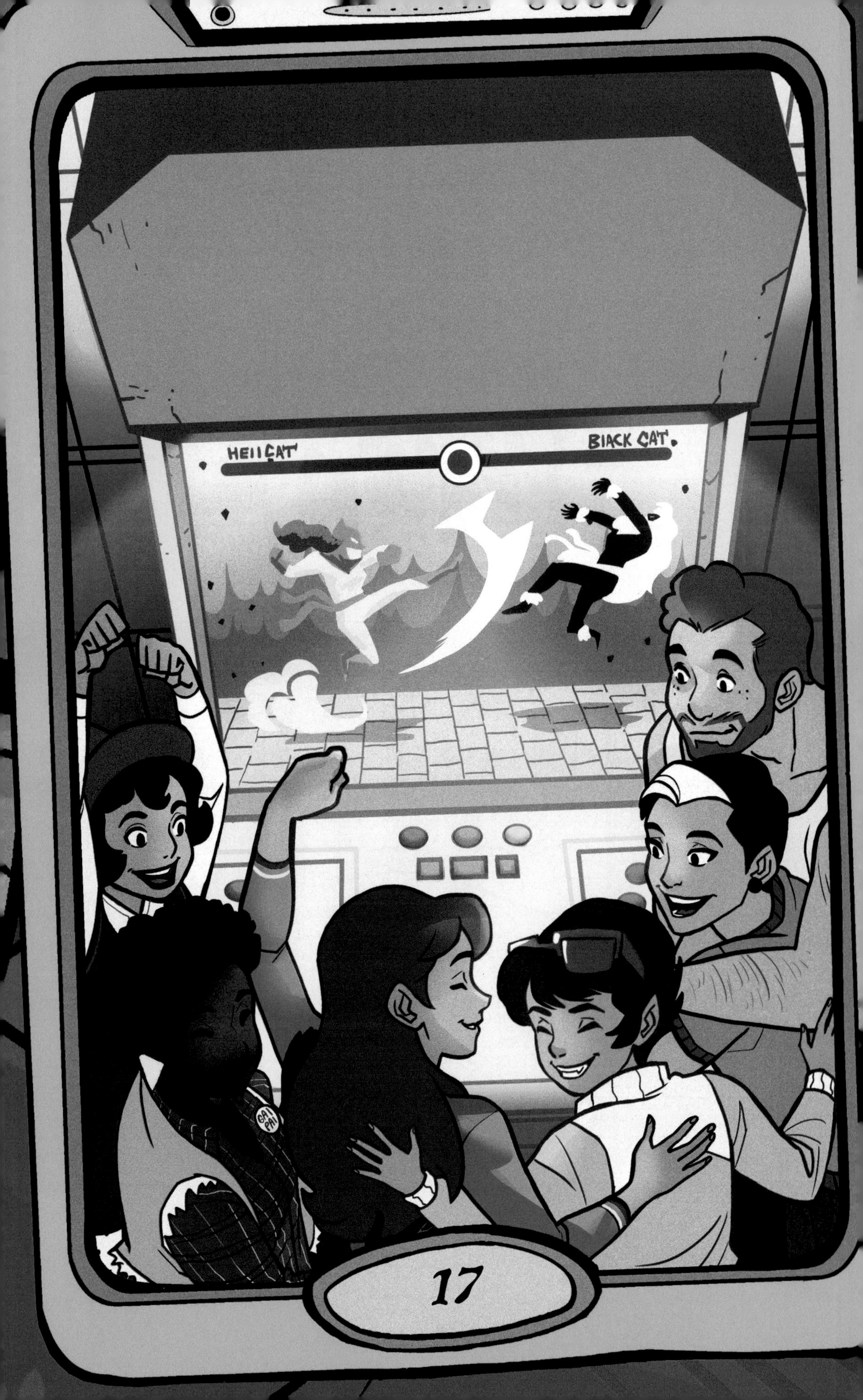
HELLCAT
BLACK CAT
GAL PAL
17

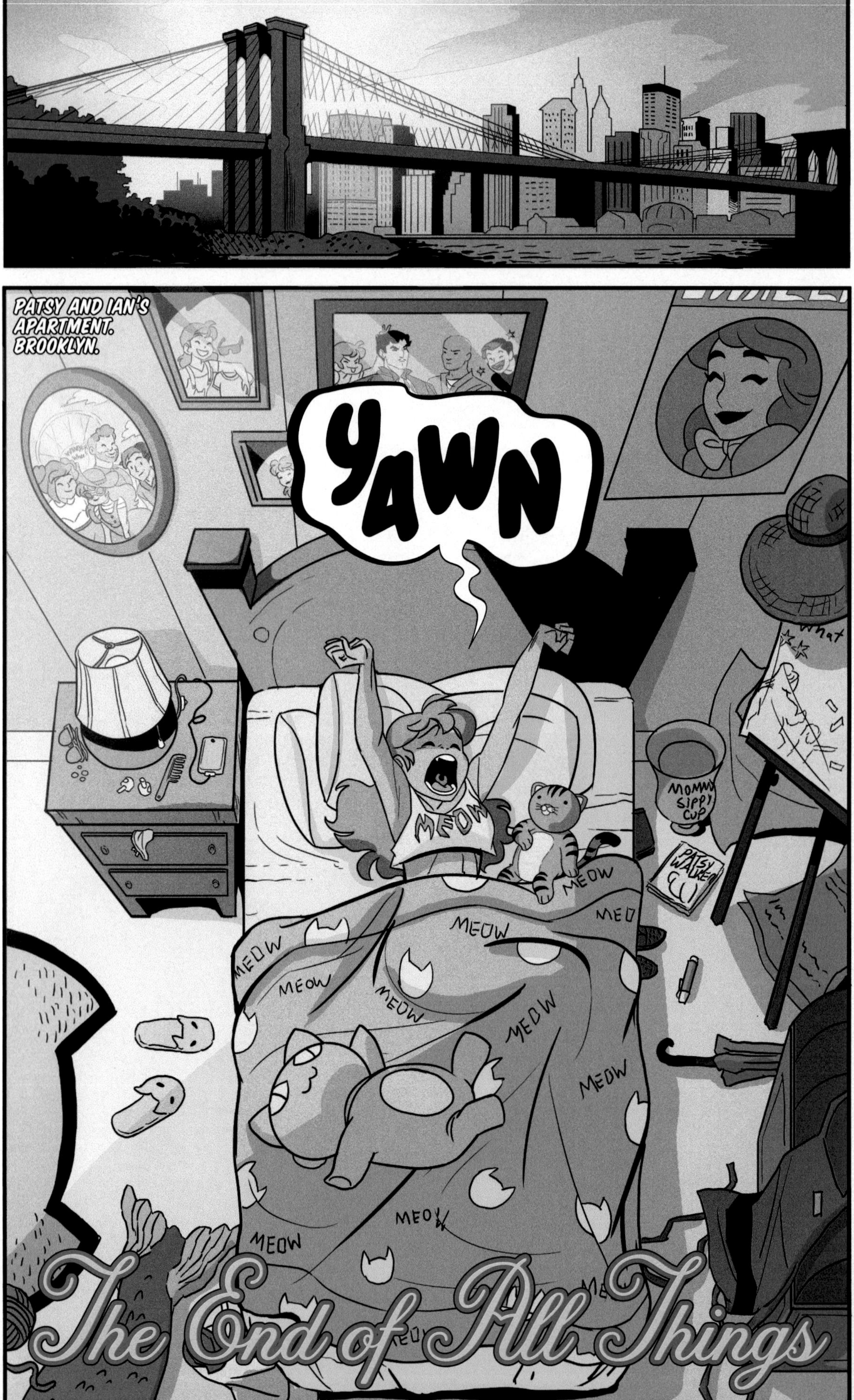
PATSY AND IAN'S APARTMENT. BROOKLYN.
YAWN
MEOW
MOMMY SIPPY CUP
PATSY WALKER
The End of All Things

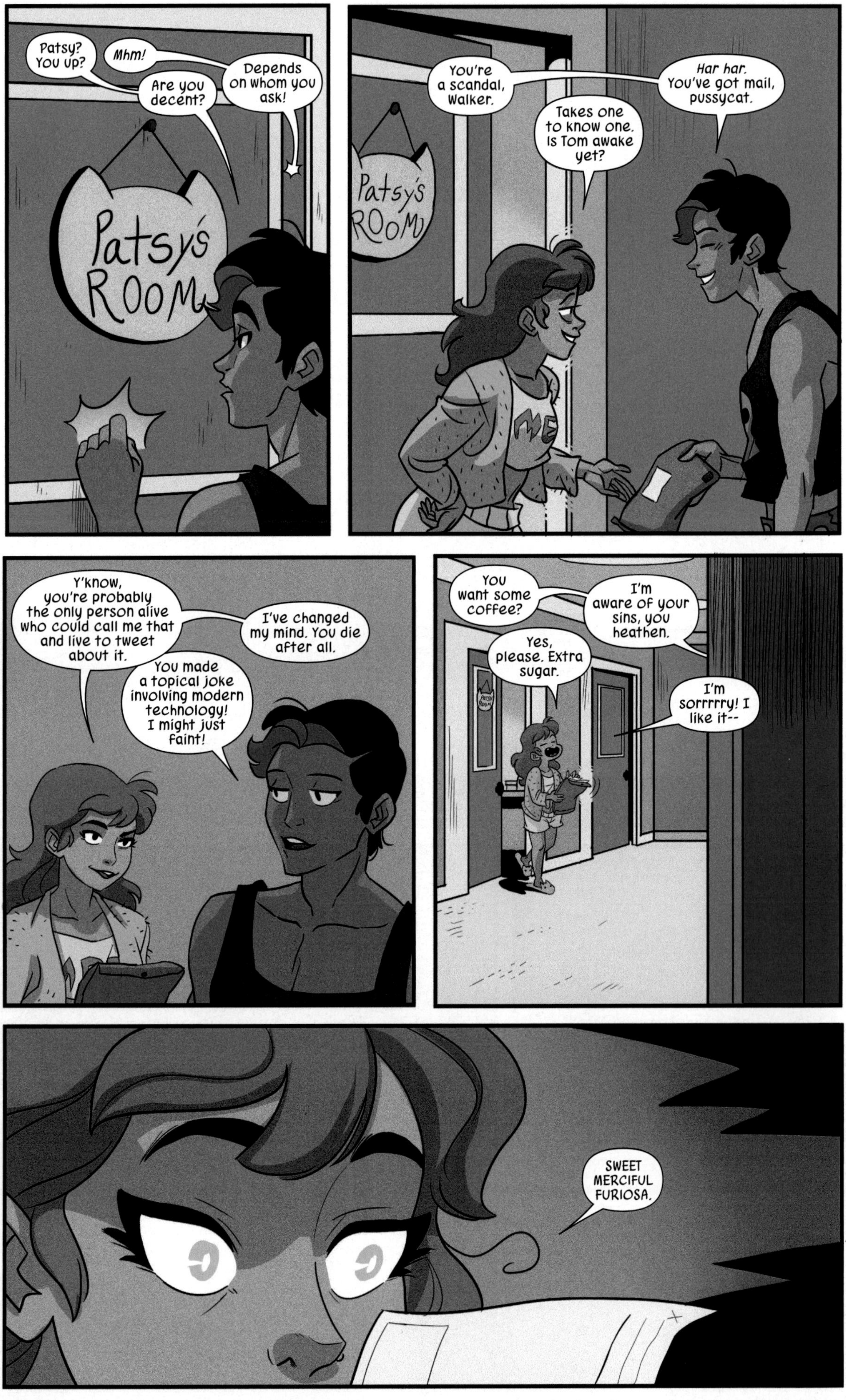

Patsy? You up?
Mhm!
Are you decent?
Depends on whom you ask!
Patsy's ROOM
You're a scandal, Walker.
Har har. You've got mail, pussycat.
Takes one to know one. Is Tom awake yet?
Y'know, you're probably the only person alive who could call me that and live to tweet about it.
You made a topical joke involving modern technology! I might just faint!
I've changed my mind. You die after all.
You want some coffee?
I'm aware of your sins, you heathen.
Yes, please. Extra sugar.
I'm sorrrrry! I like it--
SWEET MERCIFUL FURIOSA.

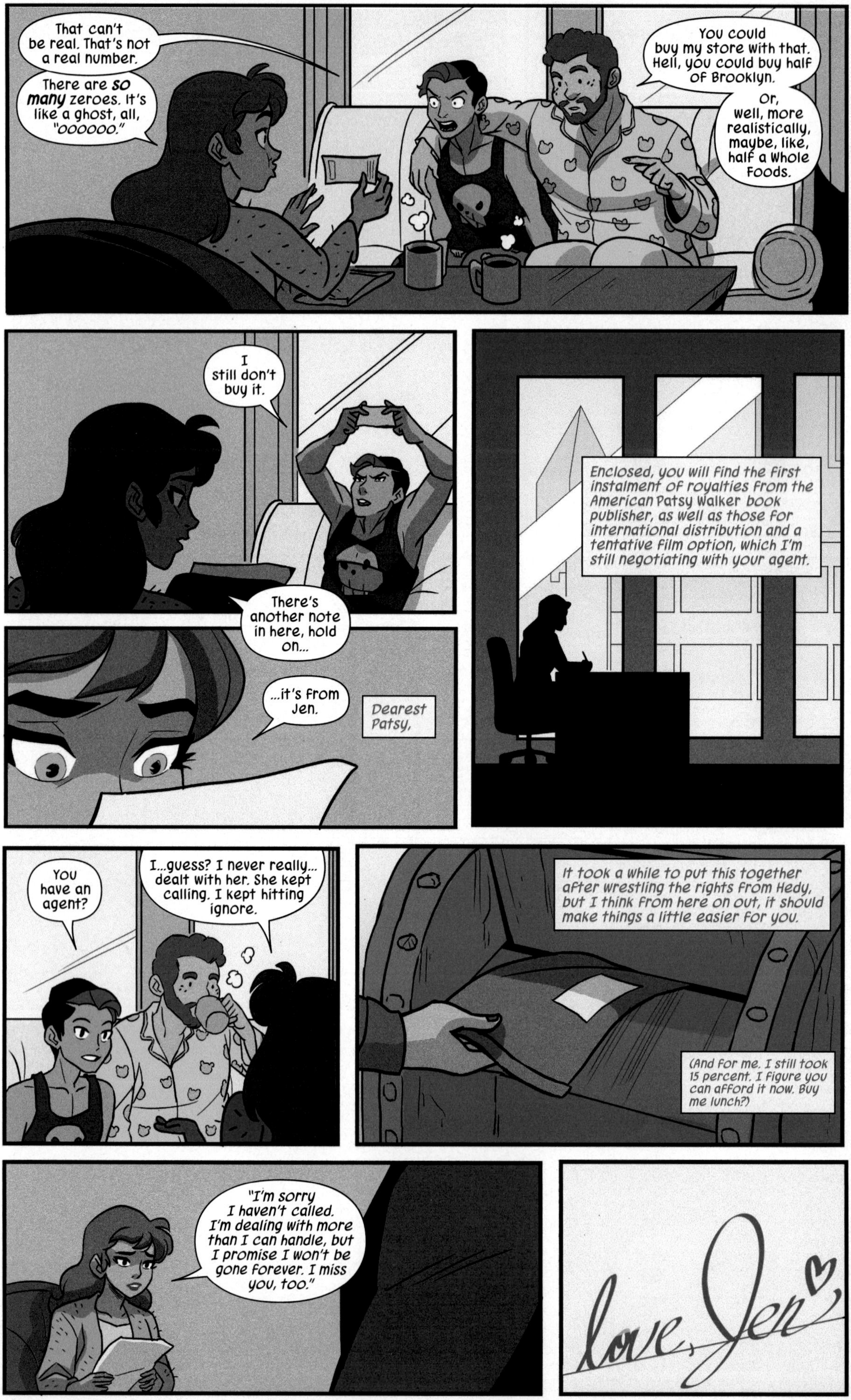

That can't be real. That's not a real number.
There are **so many** zeroes. It's like a ghost, all, "oooooo."
You could buy my store with that. Hell, you could buy half of Brooklyn.
Or, well, more realistically, maybe, like, half a Whole Foods.
I still don't buy it.
There's another note in here, hold on...
...it's from Jen.
Dearest Patsy,
Enclosed, you will find the first instalment of royalties from the American Patsy Walker book publisher, as well as those for international distribution and a tentative film option, which I'm still negotiating with your agent.
You have an agent?
I...guess? I never really... dealt with her. She kept calling. I kept hitting ignore.
It took a while to put this together after wrestling the rights from Hedy, but I think from here on out, it should make things a little easier for you.
(And for me. I still took 15 percent. I figure you can afford it now. Buy me lunch?)
"I'm sorry I haven't called. I'm dealing with more than I can handle, but I promise I won't be gone forever. I miss you, too."
love, Jen

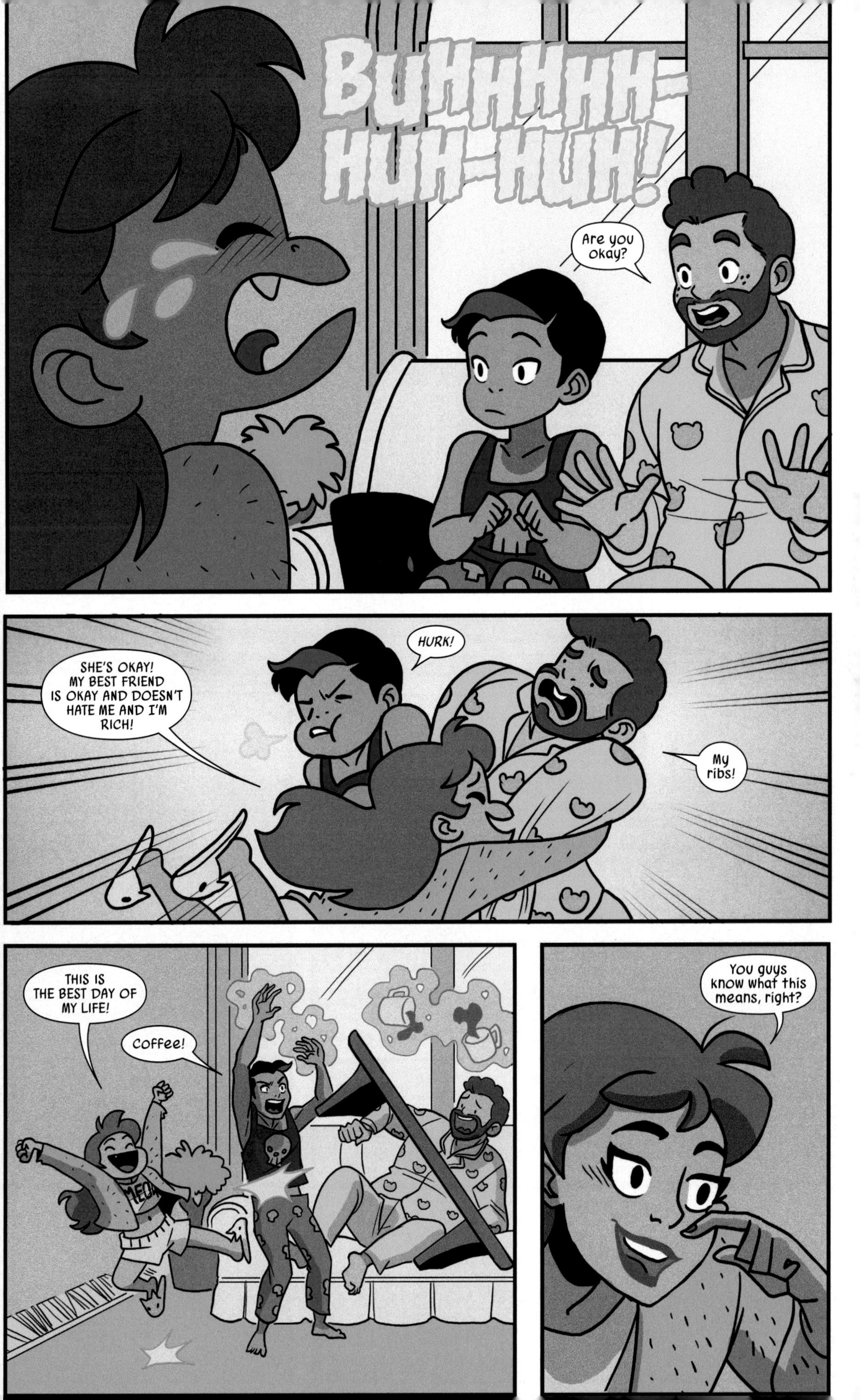
BUHHHHH-HUH-HUH!
Are you okay?
SHE'S OKAY! MY BEST FRIEND IS OKAY AND DOESN'T HATE ME AND I'M RICH!
HURK!
My ribs!
THIS IS THE BEST DAY OF MY LIFE!
Coffee!
You guys know what this means, right?

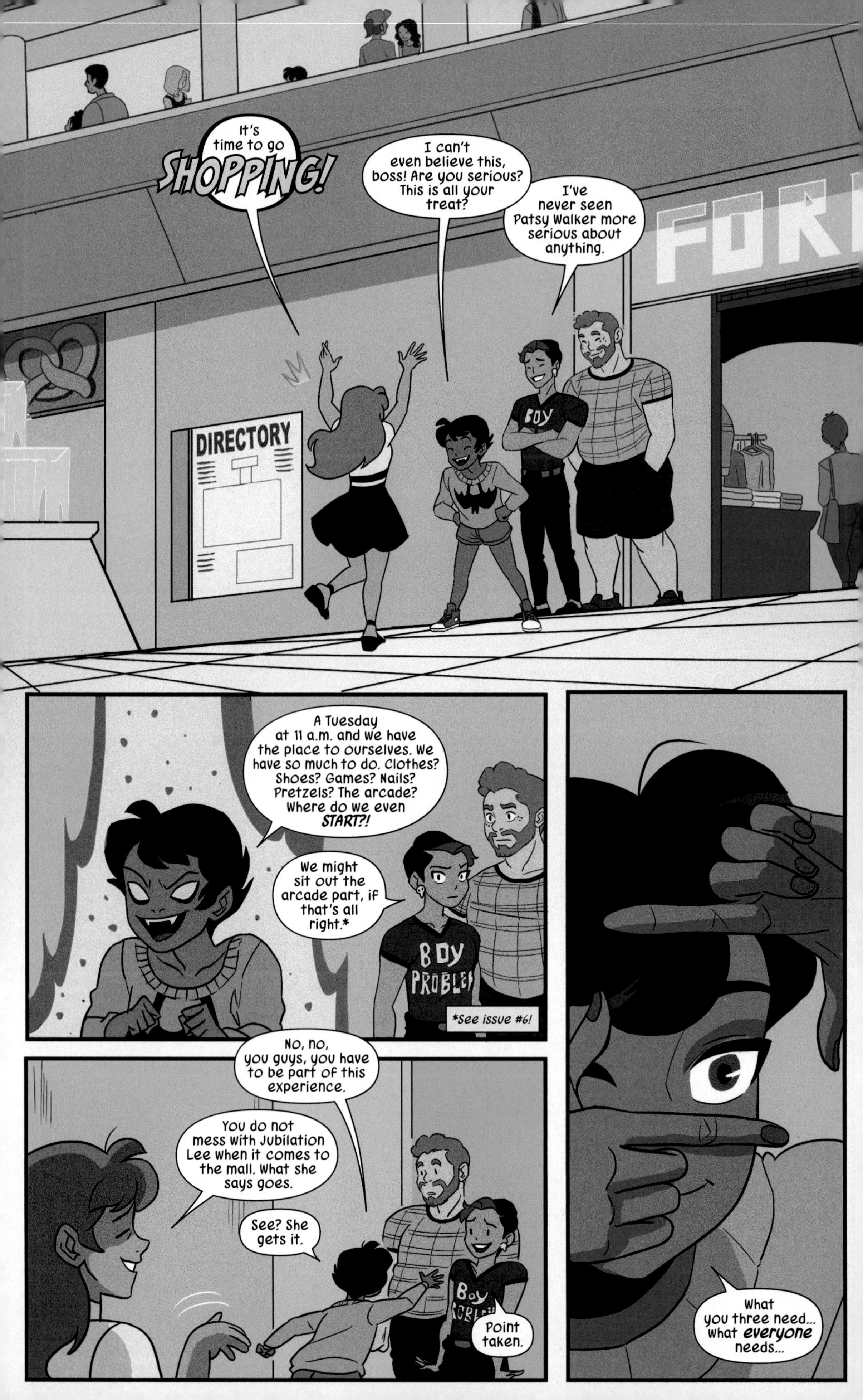
It's time to go SHOPPING!
I can't even believe this, boss! Are you serious? This is all your treat?
I've never seen Patsy Walker more serious about anything.
FOR
DIRECTORY
A Tuesday at 11 a.m. and we have the place to ourselves. We have so much to do. Clothes? Shoes? Games? Nails? Pretzels? The arcade? Where do we even START?!
We might sit out the arcade part, if that's all right.*
BOY PROBLE
*See issue #6!
No, no, you guys, you have to be part of this experience.
You do not mess with Jubilation Lee when it comes to the mall. What she says goes.
See? She gets it.
Point taken.
What you three need... what everyone needs...

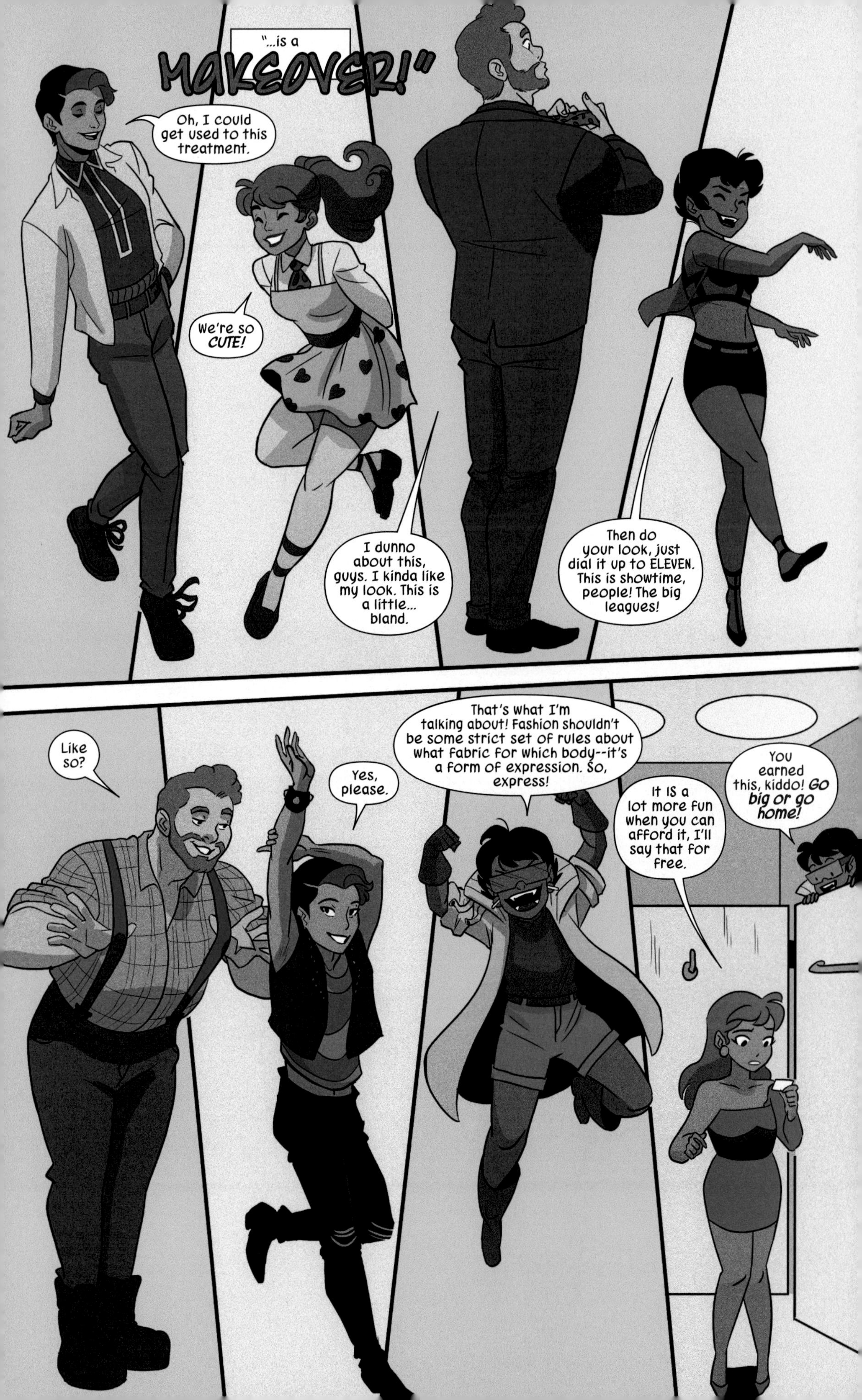
"...is a
MAKEOVER!"
Oh, I could get used to this treatment.
We're so CUTE!
I dunno about this, guys. I kinda like my look. This is a little... bland.
Then do your look, just dial it up to ELEVEN. This is showtime, people! The big leagues!
Like so?
Yes, please.
That's what I'm talking about! Fashion shouldn't be some strict set of rules about what fabric for which body--it's a form of expression. So, express!
It IS a lot more fun when you can afford it, I'll say that for free.
You earned this, kiddo! Go big or go home!

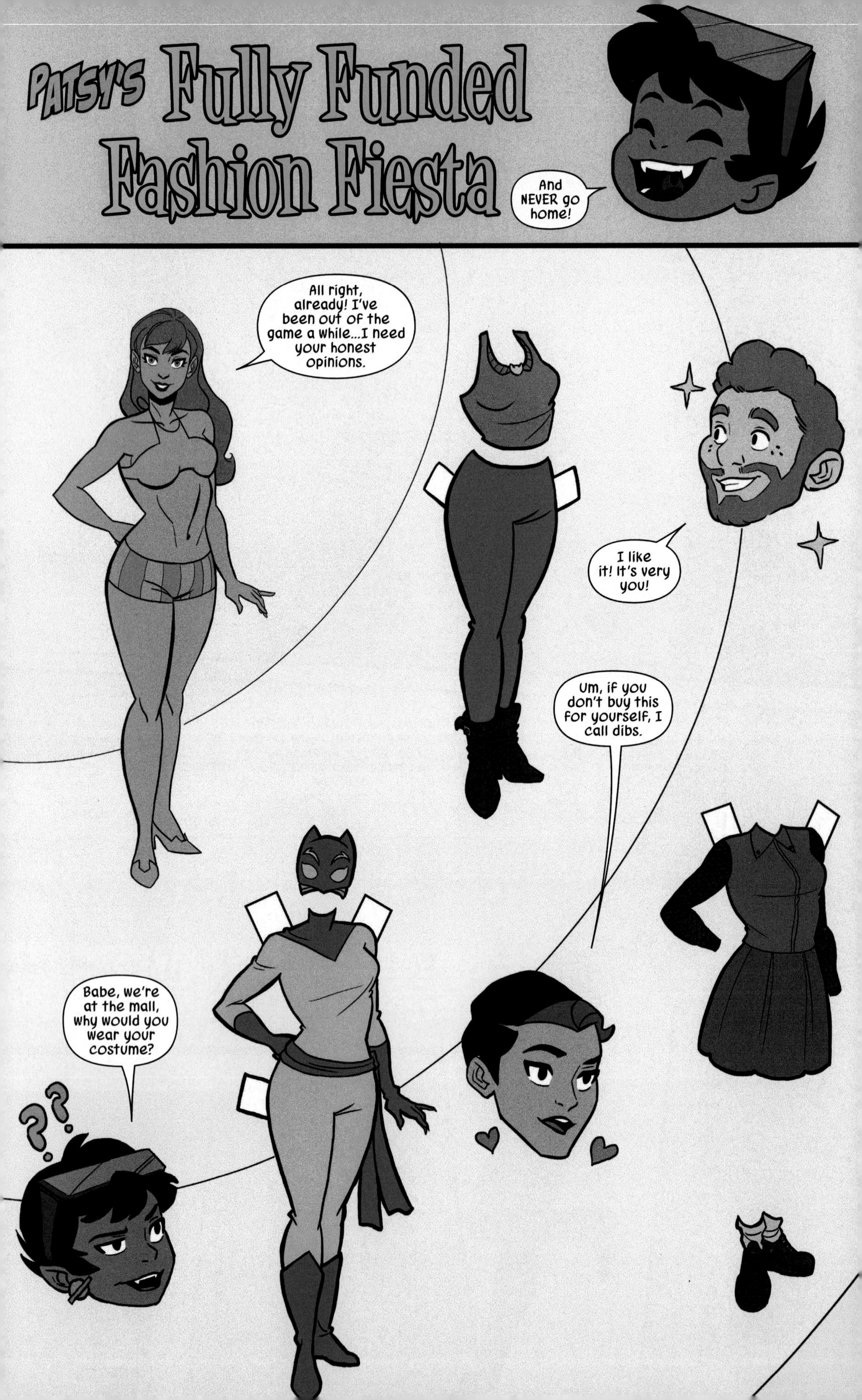
PATSY'S Fully Funded Fashion Fiesta
And NEVER go home!
All right, already! I've been out of the game a while...I need your honest opinions.
I like it! It's very you!
Um, if you don't buy this for yourself, I call dibs.
Babe, we're at the mall, why would you wear your costume?
??

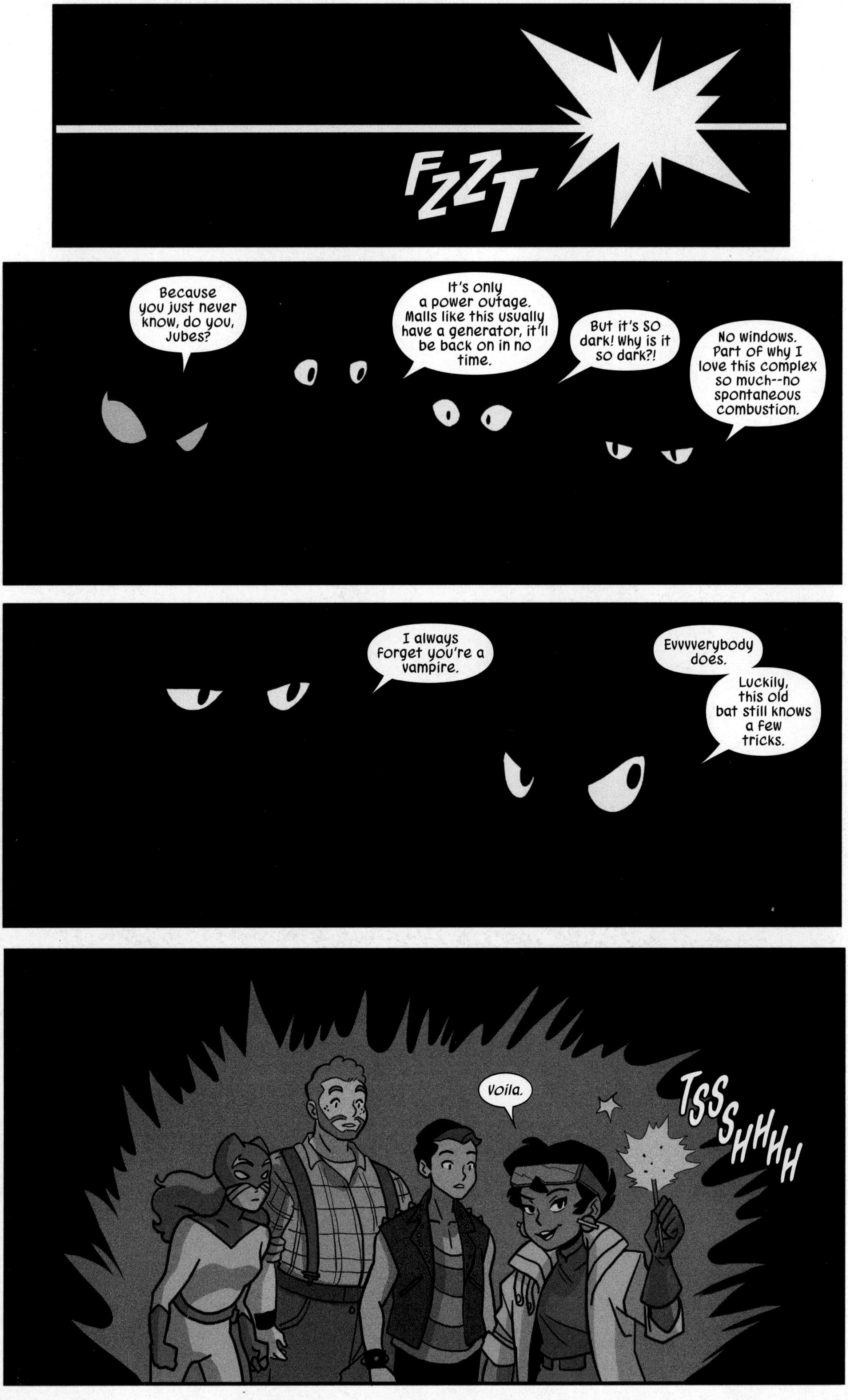
FZZT
Because you just never know, do you, Jubes?
It's only a power outage. Malls like this usually have a generator, it'll be back on in no time.
But it's SO dark! Why is it so dark?!
No windows. Part of why I love this complex so much--no spontaneous combustion.
I always forget you're a vampire.
Evvvverybody does.
Luckily, this old bat still knows a few tricks.
Voila.
TSSSHHHH

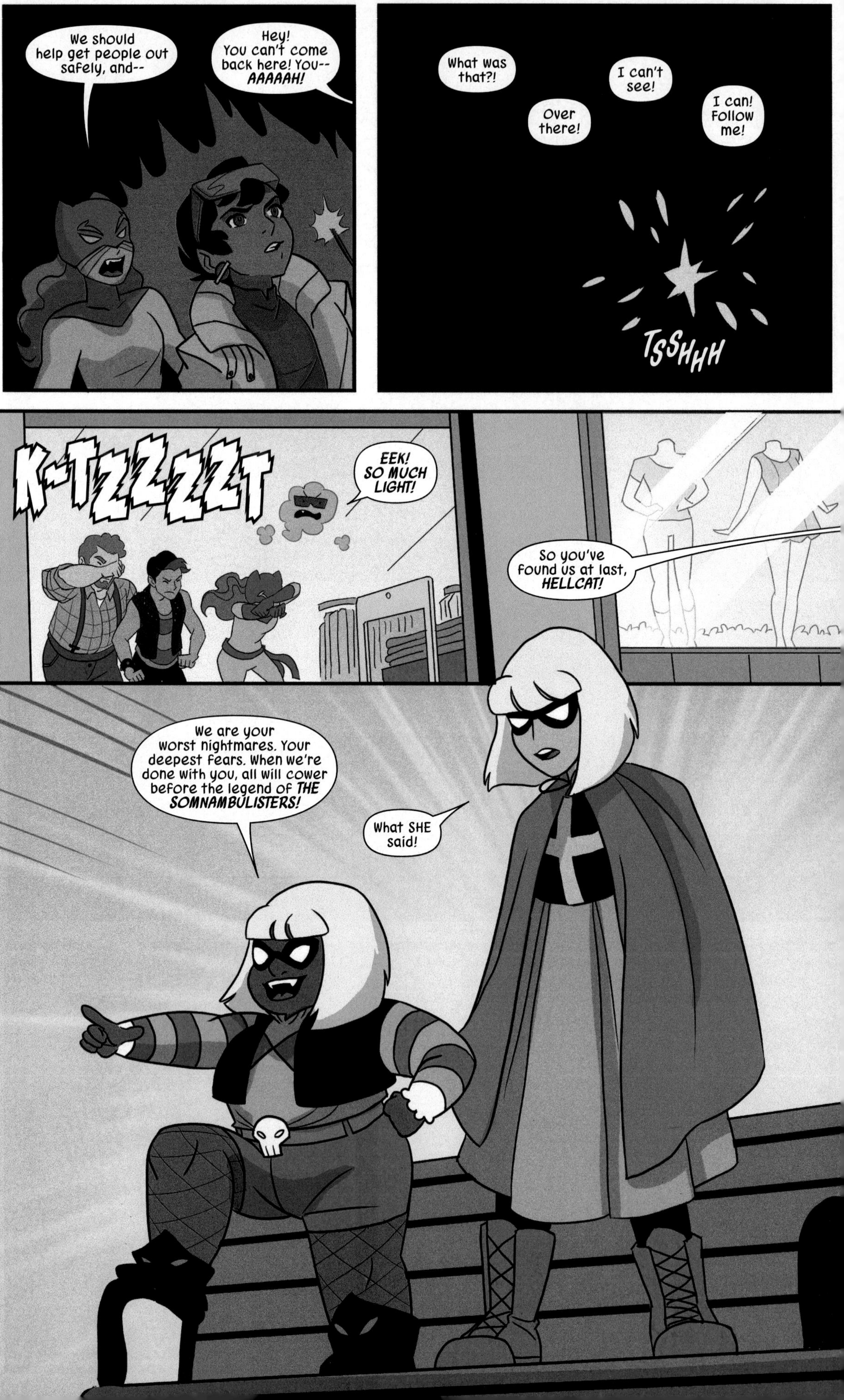
We should help get people out safely, and--
Hey! You can't come back here! You-- AAAAAH!
What was that?!
Over there!
I can't see!
I can! Follow me!
TSSHHH
K-TZZZZZT
EEK! SO MUCH LIGHT!
So you've found us at last, HELLCAT!
We are your worst nightmares. Your deepest fears. When we're done with you, all will cower before the legend of THE SOMNAMBULISTERS!
What SHE said!

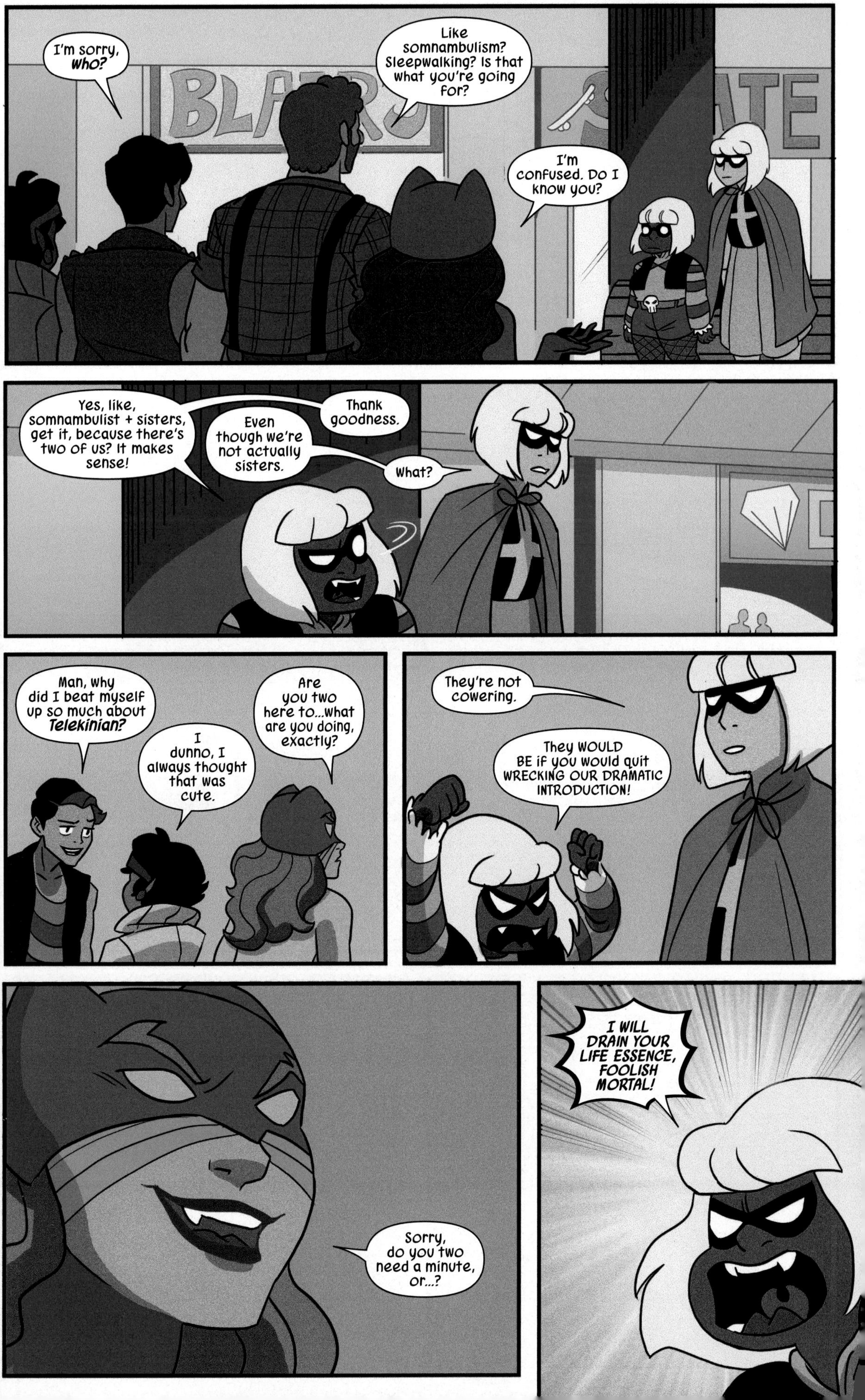
I'm sorry, **who?**
Like somnambulism? Sleepwalking? Is that what you're going for?
I'm confused. Do I know you?
Yes, like, somnambulist + sisters, get it, because there's two of us? It makes sense!
Thank goodness.
Even though we're not actually sisters.
What?
Man, why did I beat myself up so much about ***Telekinian?***
I dunno, I always thought that was cute.
Are you two here to...what are you doing, exactly?
They're not cowering.
They WOULD BE if you would quit WRECKING OUR DRAMATIC INTRODUCTION!
Sorry, do you two need a minute, or...?
I WILL DRAIN YOUR LIFE ESSENCE, FOOLISH MORTAL!

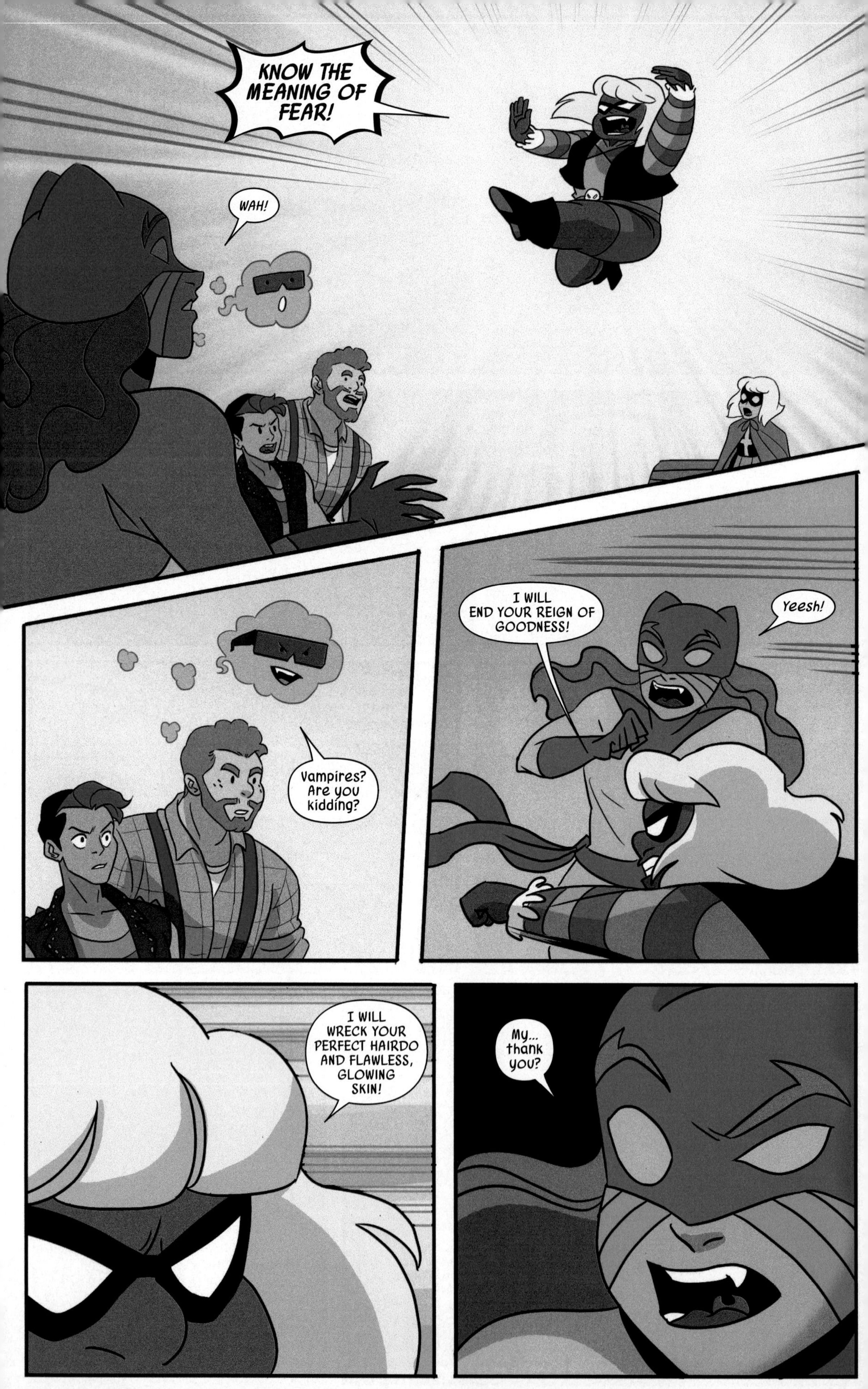
KNOW THE MEANING OF FEAR!
WAH!
Vampires? Are you kidding?
I WILL END YOUR REIGN OF GOODNESS!
Yeesh!
I WILL WRECK YOUR PERFECT HAIRDO AND FLAWLESS, GLOWING SKIN!
My... thank you?

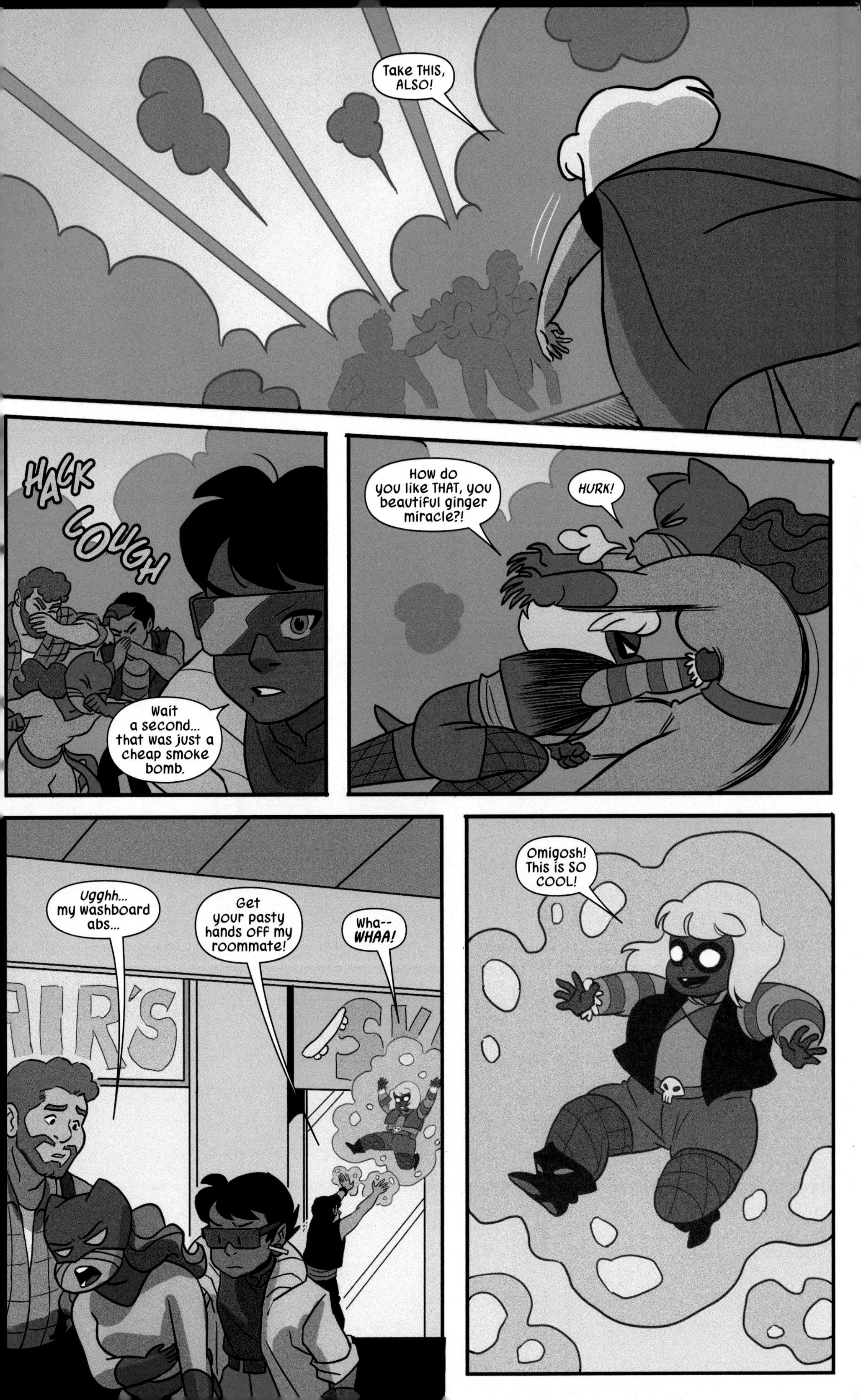
Take THIS, ALSO!
HACK
COUGH
Wait a second... that was just a cheap smoke bomb.
HOW do you like THAT, you beautiful ginger miracle?!
HURK!
Ugghh... my washboard abs...
Get your pasty hands off my roommate!
Wha-- WHAA!
Omigosh! This is SO COOL!

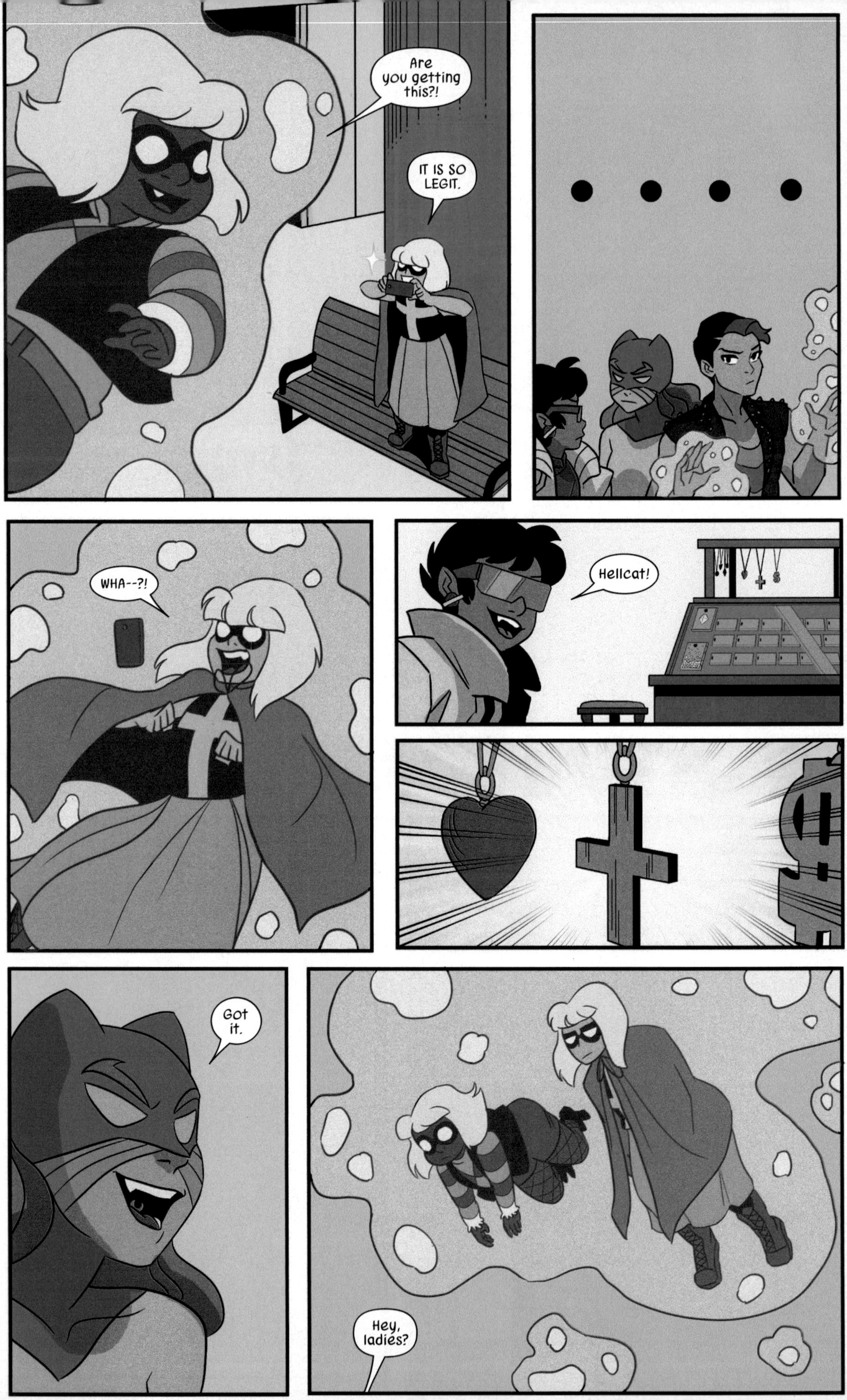
Are you getting this?!
IT IS SO LEGIT.
WHA--?!
Hellcat!
Got it.
Hey, ladies?

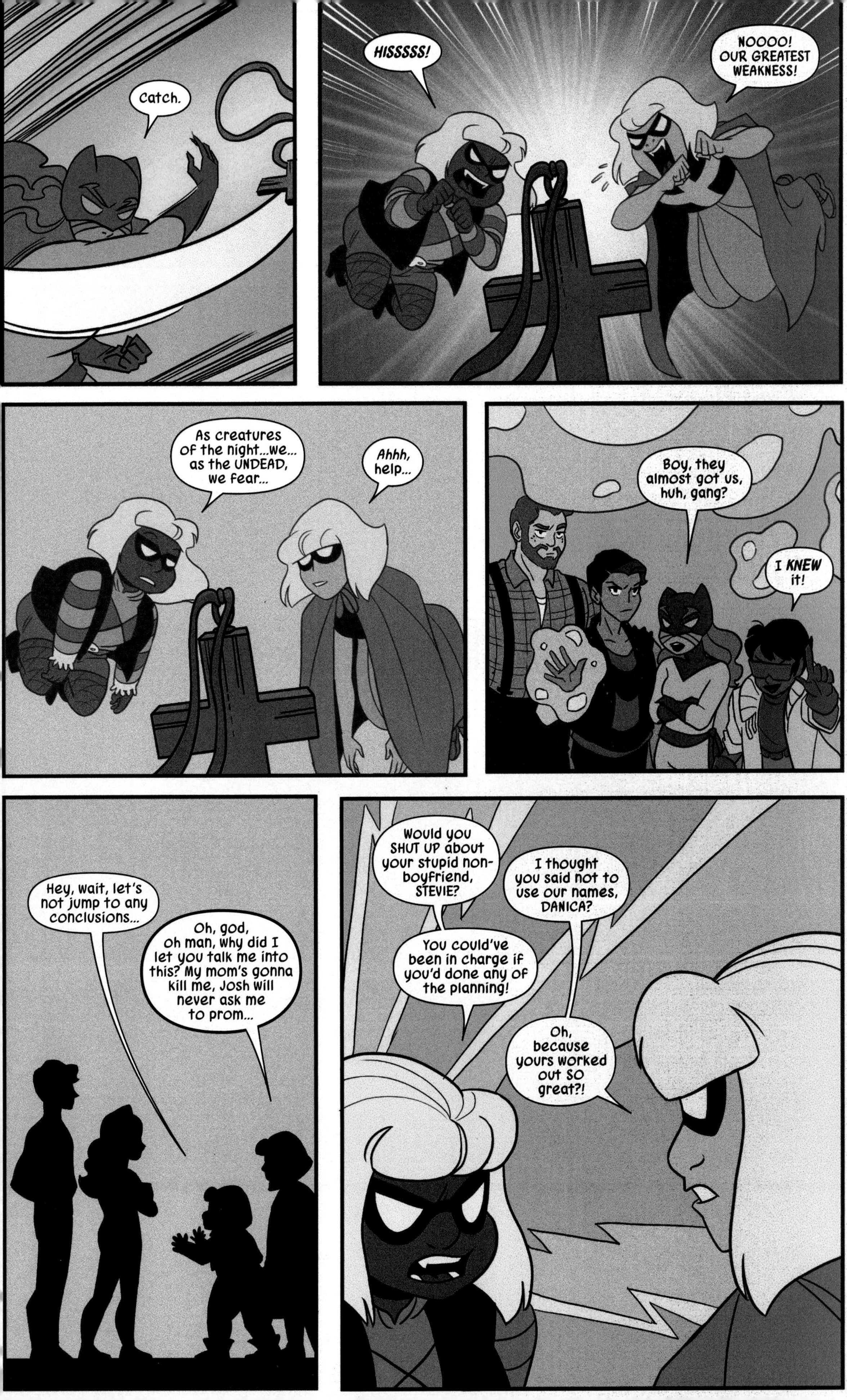

Catch.
HISSSSS!
NOOOO! OUR GREATEST WEAKNESS!
As creatures of the night...we... as the UNDEAD, we fear...
Ahhh, help...
Boy, they almost got us, huh, gang?
I KNEW it!
Hey, wait, let's not jump to any conclusions...
Oh, god, oh man, why did I let you talk me into this? My mom's gonna kill me, Josh will never ask me to prom...
Would you SHUT UP about your stupid non-boyfriend, STEVIE?
I thought you said not to use our names, DANICA?
You could've been in charge if you'd done any of the planning!
Oh, because yours worked out SO great?!

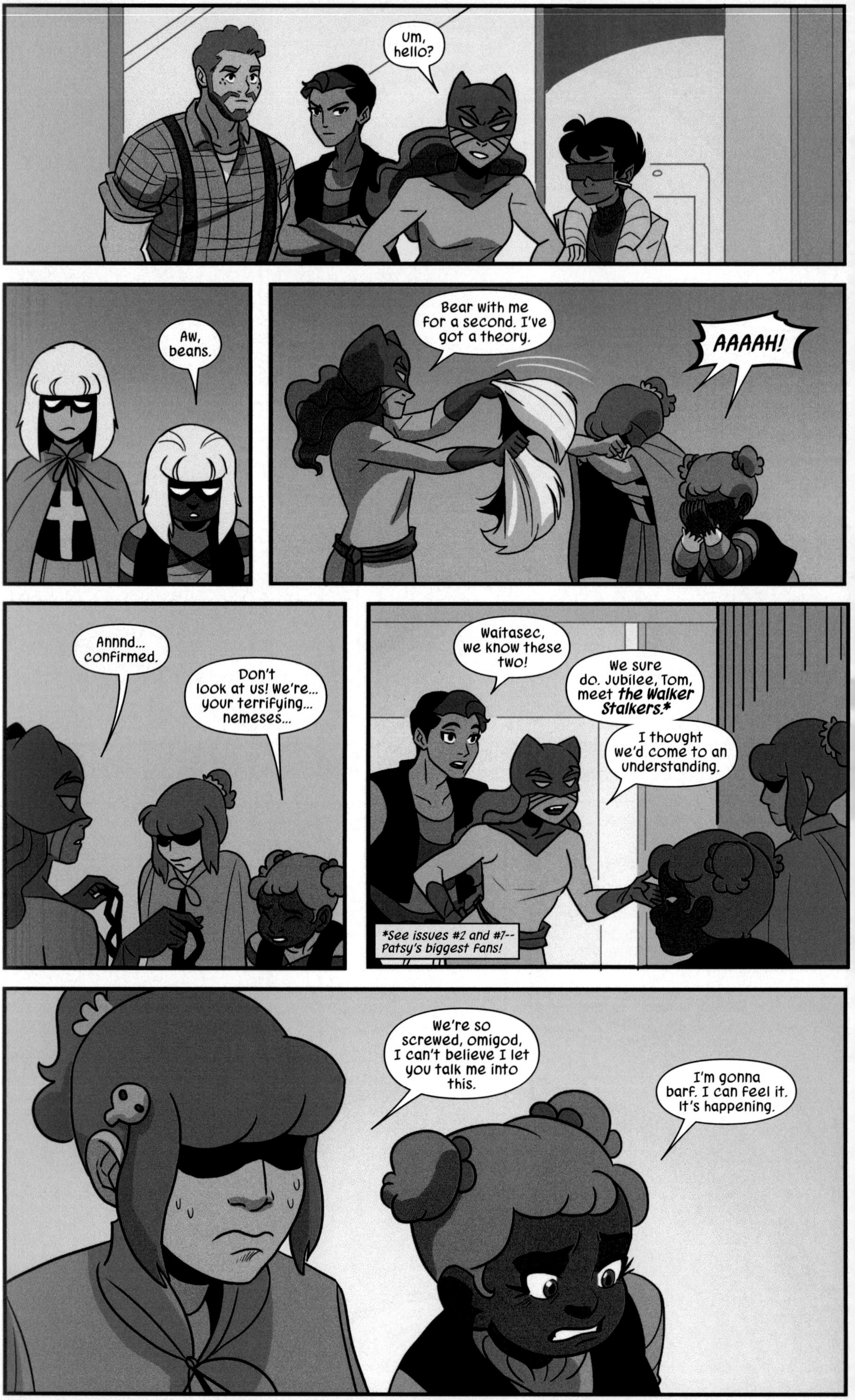

Um, hello?
Aw, beans.
Bear with me for a second. I've got a theory.
AAAAH!
Annnd... confirmed.
Don't look at us! We're... your terrifying... nemeses...
Waitasec, we know these two!
We sure do. Jubilee, Tom, meet ***the Walker Stalkers.****
I thought we'd come to an understanding.
*See issues #2 and #7-- Patsy's biggest fans!
We're so screwed, omigod, I can't believe I let you talk me into this.
I'm gonna barf. I can feel it. It's happening.

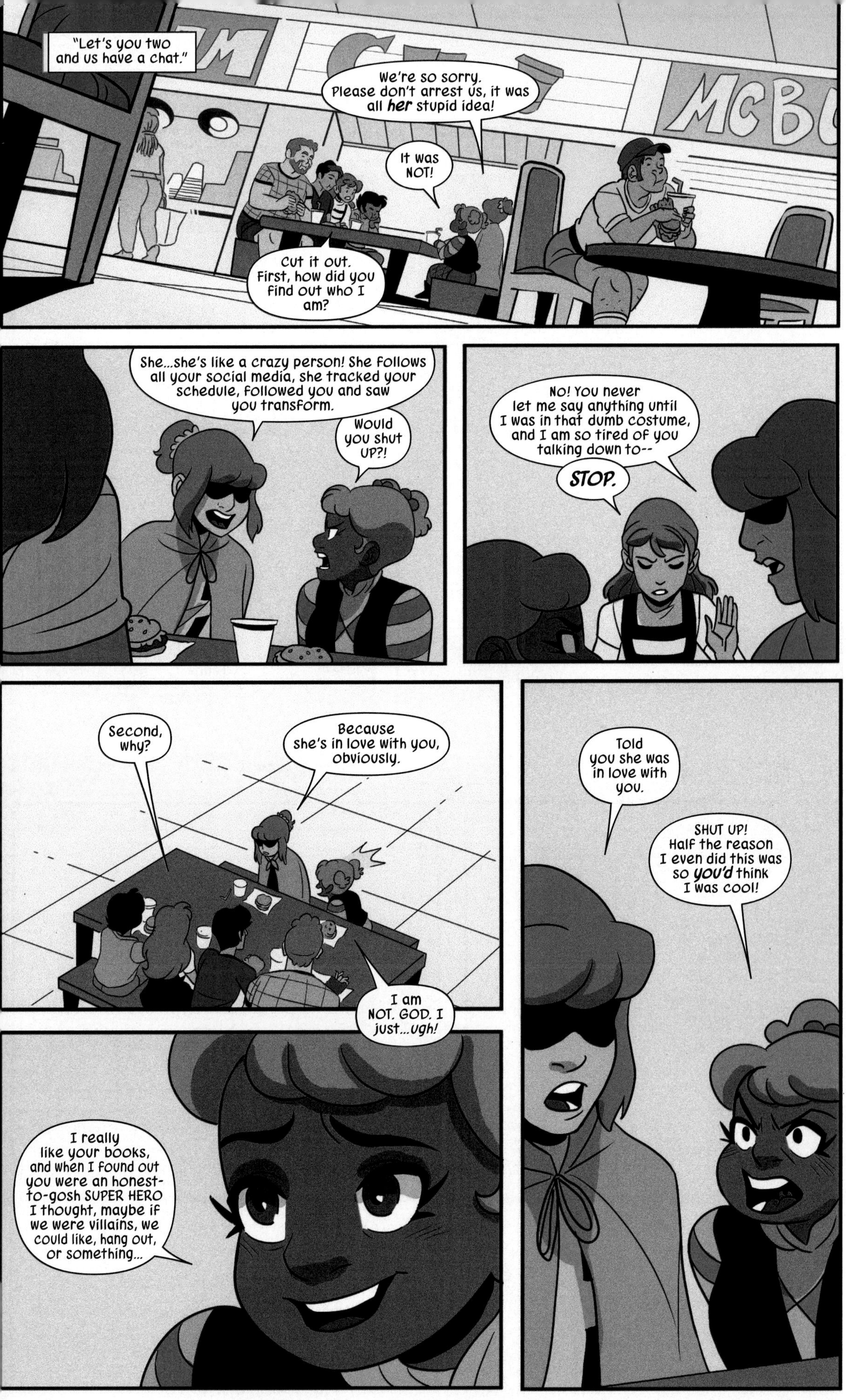
"Let's you two and us have a chat."
We're so sorry. Please don't arrest us, it was all **her** stupid idea!
It was NOT!
Cut it out. First, how did you find out who I am?
She...she's like a crazy person! She follows all your social media, she tracked your schedule, followed you and saw you transform.
Would you shut up?!
No! You never let me say anything until I was in that dumb costume, and I am so tired of you talking down to--
STOP.
Second, why?
Because she's in love with you, obviously.
I am NOT. GOD. I just...ugh!
I really like your books, and when I found out you were an honest-to-gosh SUPER HERO I thought, maybe if we were villains, we could like, hang out, or something...
Told you she was in love with you.
SHUT UP! Half the reason I even did this was so *you'd* think I was cool!

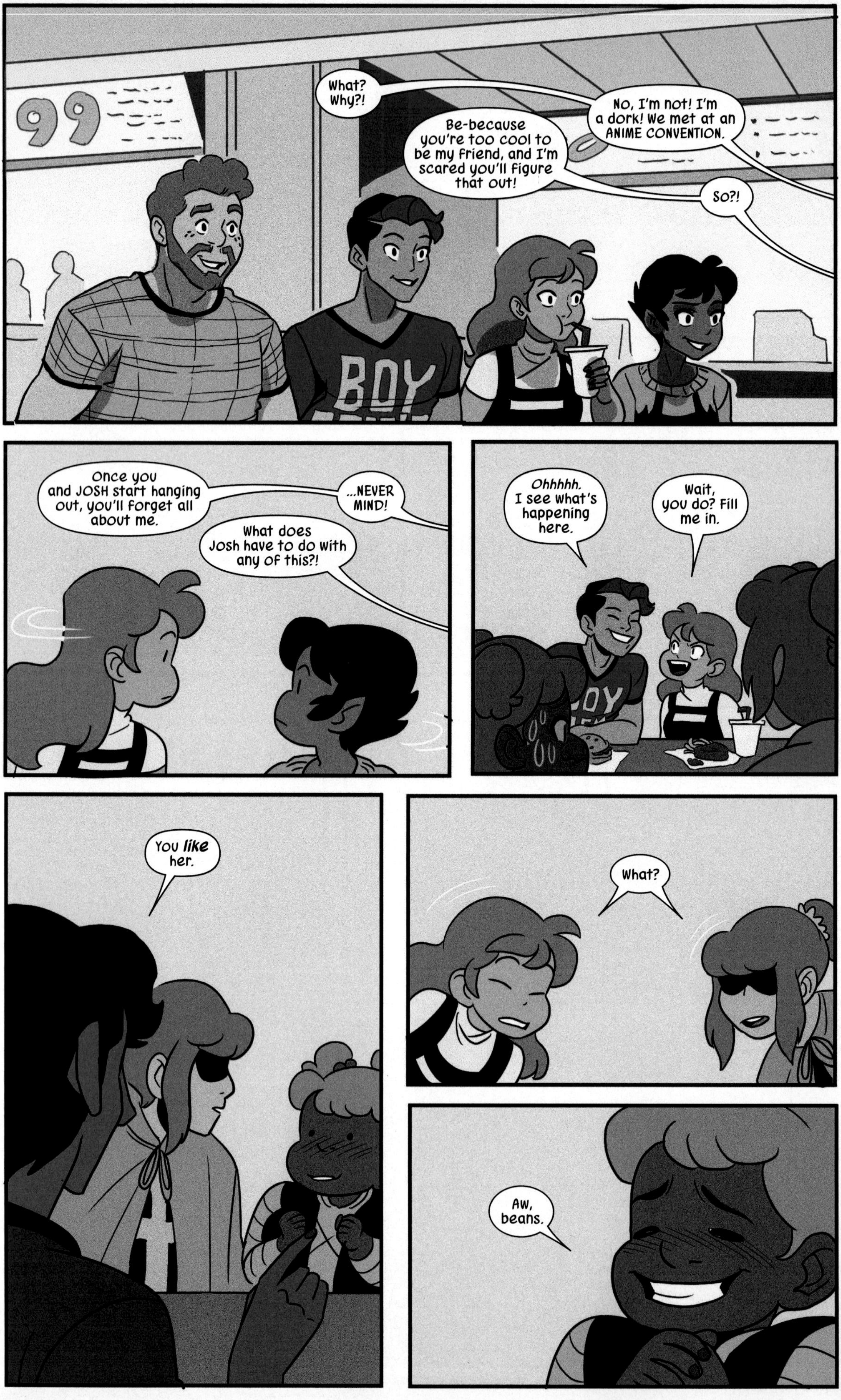
What? Why?!
No, I'm not! I'm a dork! We met at an ANIME CONVENTION.
Be-because you're too cool to be my friend, and I'm scared you'll figure that out!
So?!
Once you and JOSH start hanging out, you'll forget all about me.
...NEVER MIND!
What does Josh have to do with any of this?!
Ohhhhh. I see what's happening here.
Wait, you do? Fill me in.
You *like* her.
What?
Aw, beans.

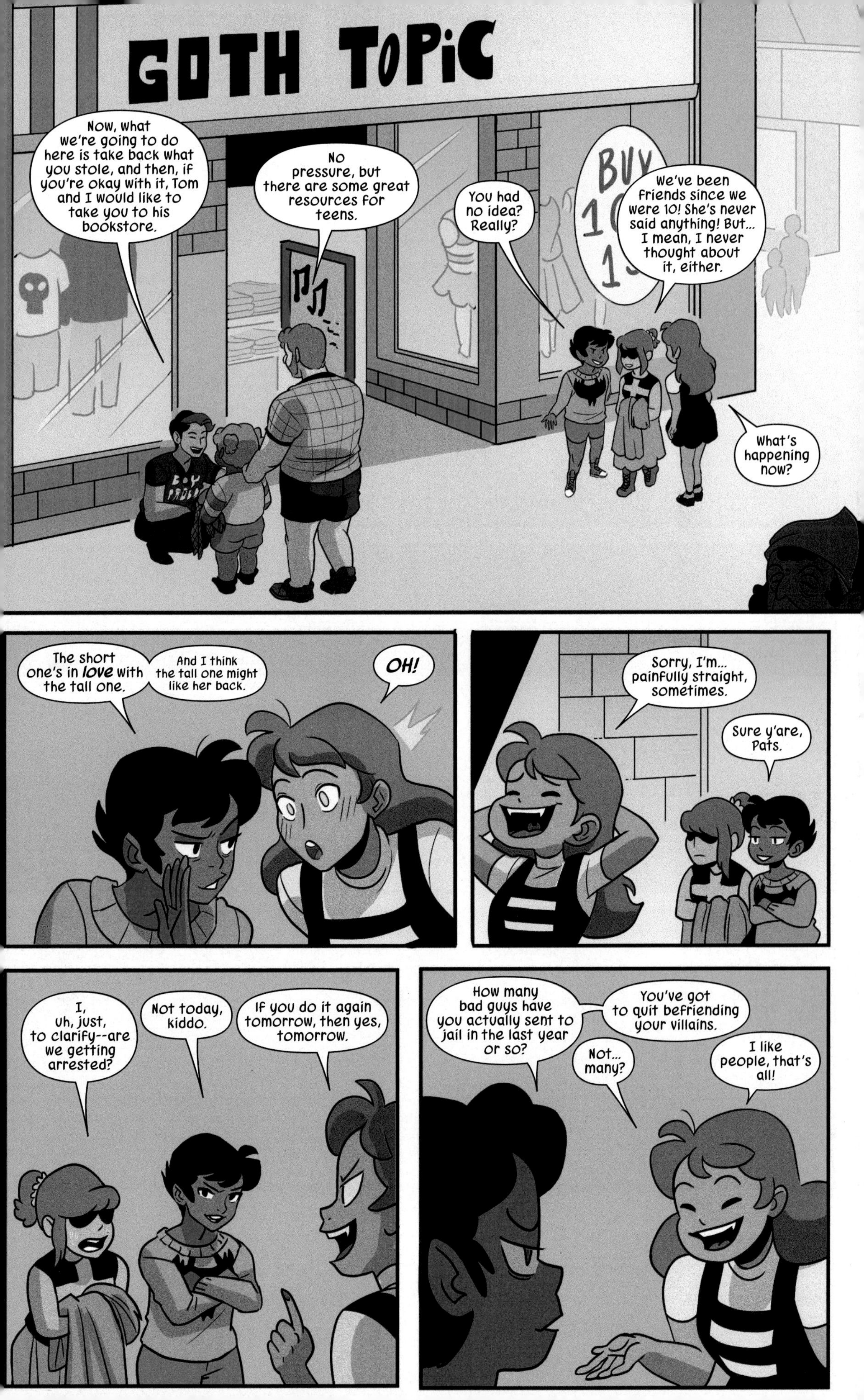
GOTH TOPIC
Now, what we're going to do here is take back what you stole, and then, if you're okay with it, Tom and I would like to take you to his bookstore.
No pressure, but there are some great resources for teens.
You had no idea? Really?
We've been friends since we were 10! She's never said anything! But... I mean, I never thought about it, either.
What's happening now?
The short one's in *love* with the tall one.
And I think the tall one might like her back.
OH!
Sorry, I'm... painfully straight, sometimes.
Sure y'are, Pats.
I, uh, just, to clarify--are we getting arrested?
Not today, kiddo.
If you do it again tomorrow, then yes, tomorrow.
How many bad guys have you actually sent to jail in the last year or so?
You've got to quit befriending your villains.
Not... many?
I like people, that's all!

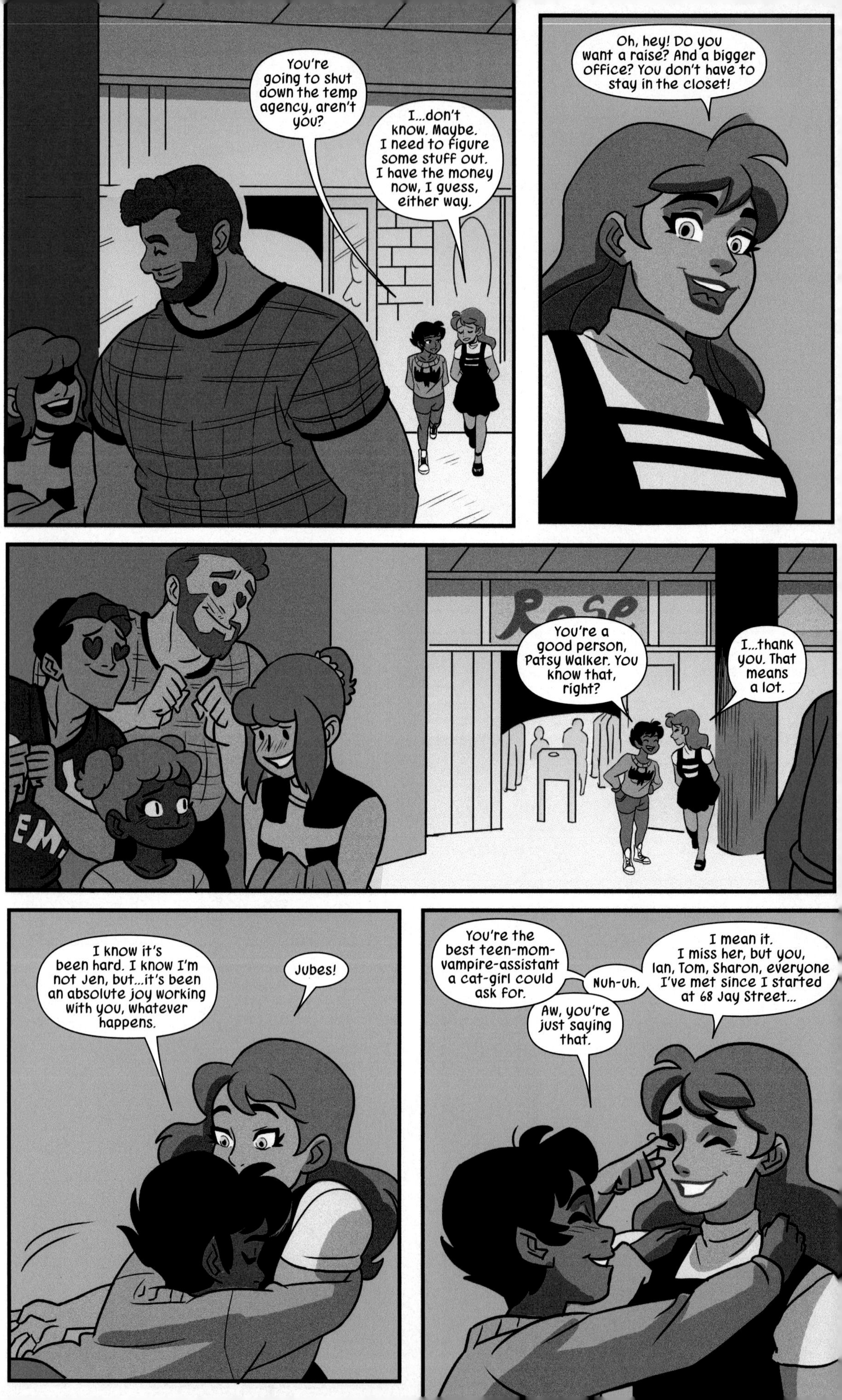

You're going to shut down the temp agency, aren't you?
I...don't know. Maybe. I need to figure some stuff out. I have the money now, I guess, either way.
Oh, hey! Do you want a raise? And a bigger office? You don't have to stay in the closet!
You're a good person, Patsy Walker. You know that, right?
I...thank you. That means a lot.
I know it's been hard. I know I'm not Jen, but...it's been an absolute joy working with you, whatever happens.
Jubes!
You're the best teen-mom-vampire-assistant a cat-girl could ask for.
Nuh-uh.
Aw, you're just saying that.
I mean it. I miss her, but you, Ian, Tom, Sharon, everyone I've met since I started at 68 Jay Street...

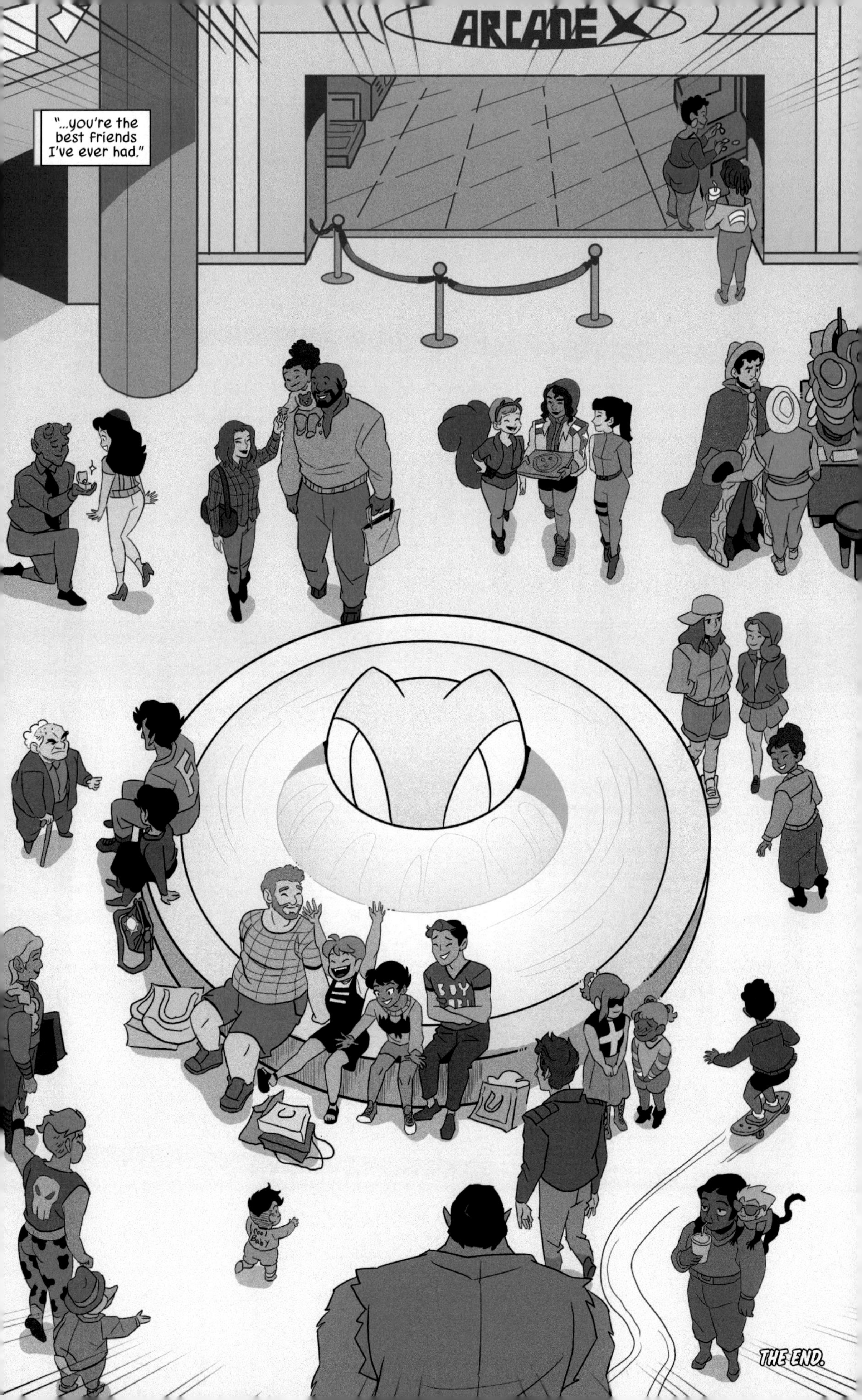
ARCADE X
"...you're the best friends I've ever had."
BOY
Cool Baby
THE END.

COVER SKETCH GALLERY

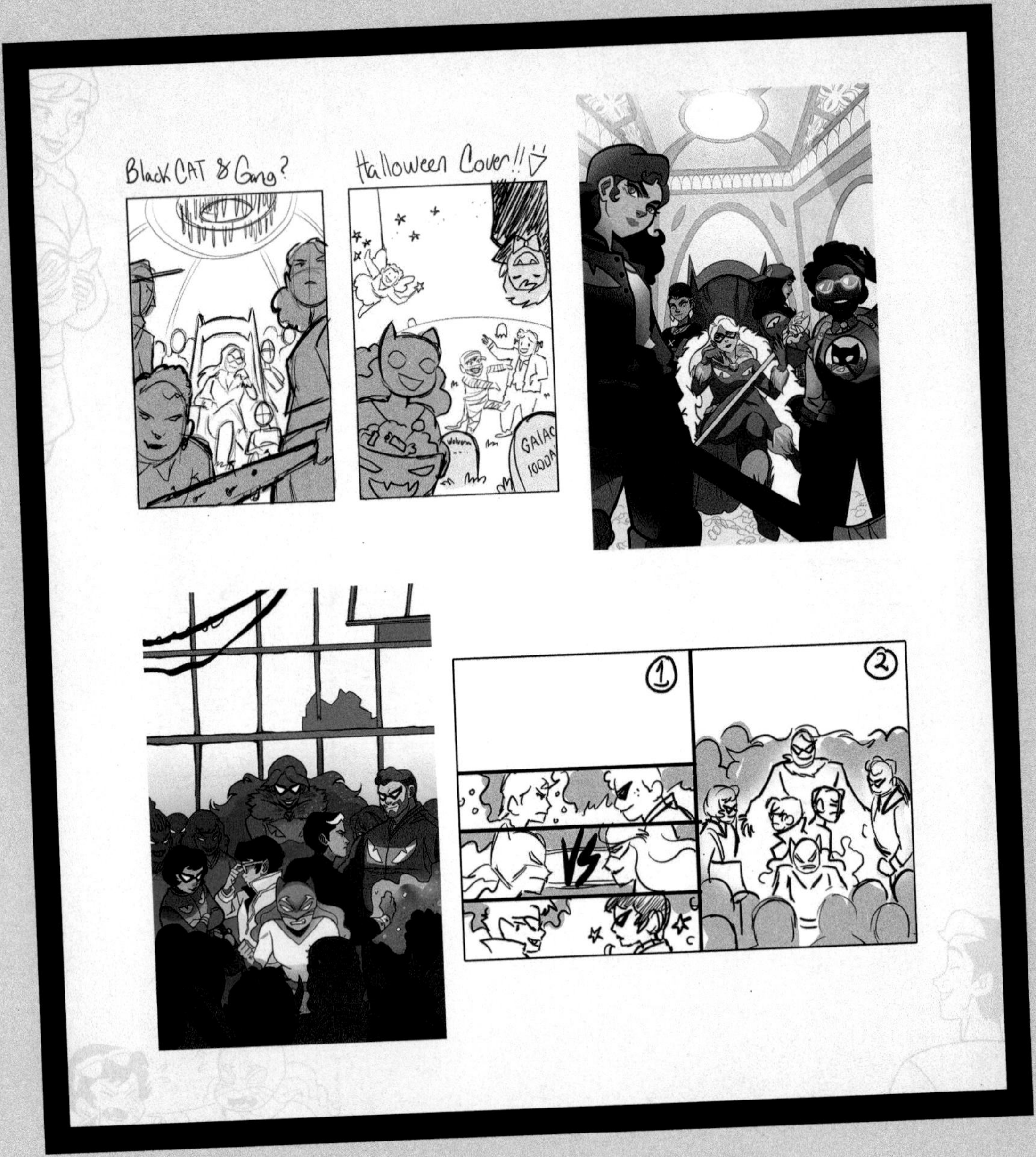
Black CAT & Gang?
Halloween Cover!!
1
VS
2

#13 & 14 SKETCHES BY **Brittney L. Williams**

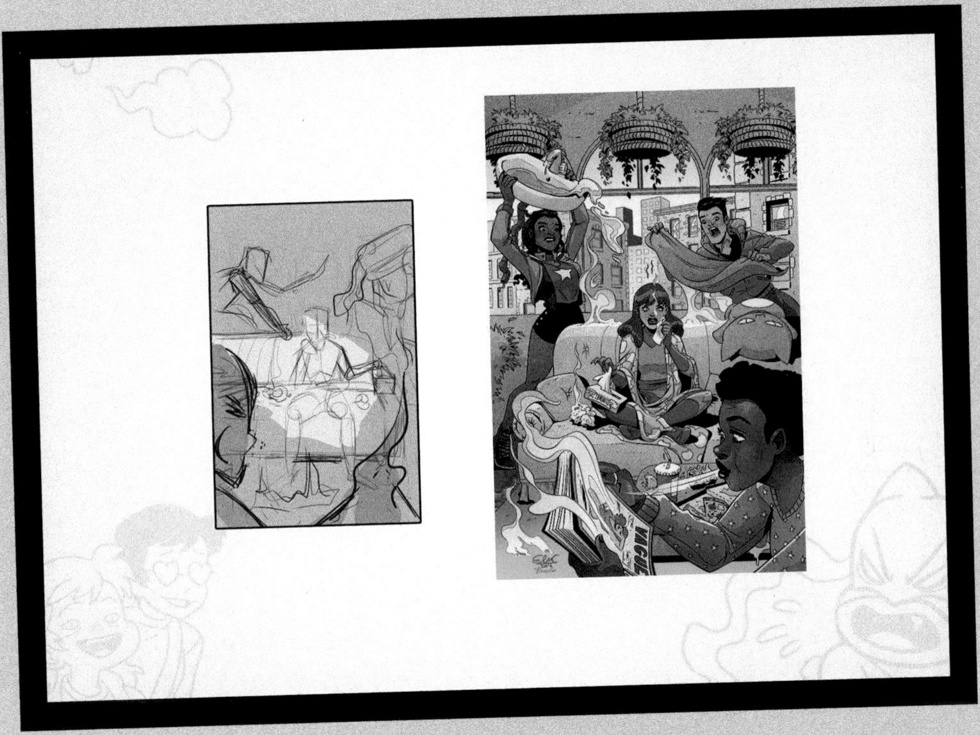

#15 SKETCH BY **Elsa Charretier**

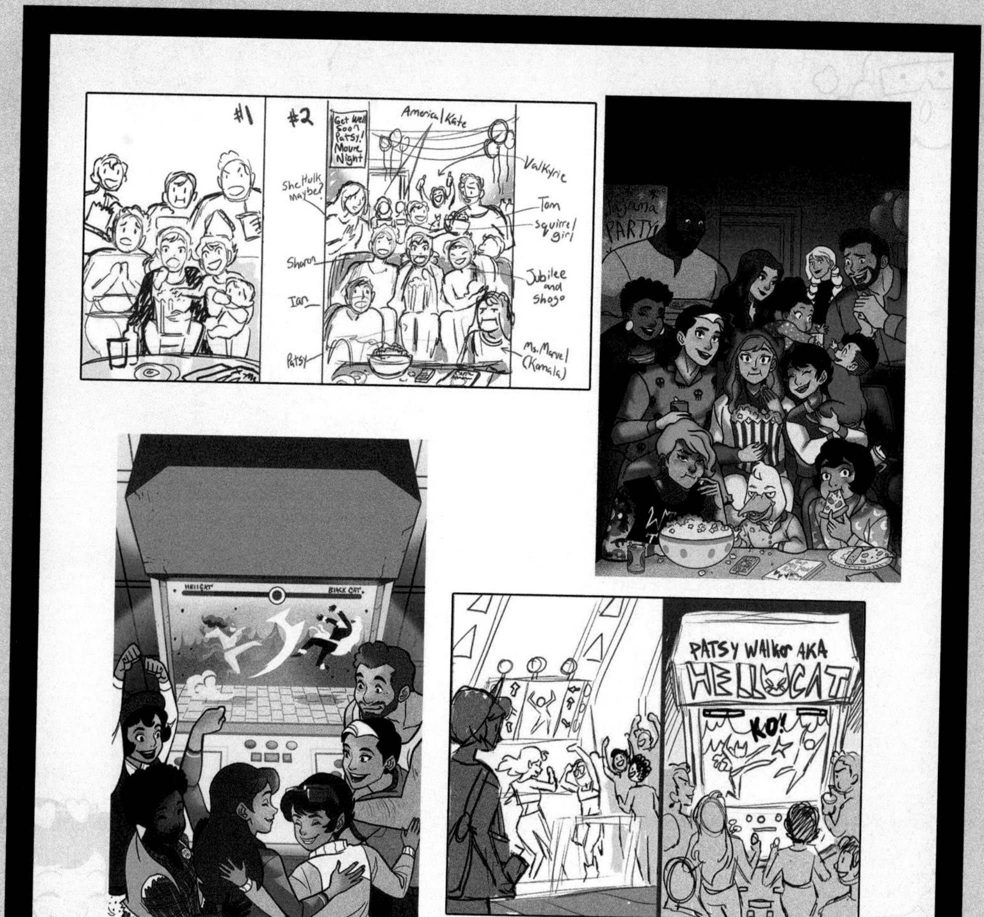
#1
#2
Get Well Soon Patsy! Movie Night
America/Kate
Valkyrie
She Hulk maybe?
Tom
squirrel girl
Sharon
Jubilee and Shogo
Ian
Patsy
Ms. Marvel (Kamala)
HELLCAT
BLACK CAT
PATSY WALKER AKA
HELLCAT
KO!

#16 & 17 SKETCHES BY **Brittney L. Williams**